which?
essential guides

D0545546

DIVORCE
& SPLITTING UP

About the author
Claire Colbert qualified as a solicitor in 2001 and went on to work in the area of family law. She is a Resolution accredited specialist and a member of the Law Society's Family Law Panel. Claire is married with two children.

DIVORCE
& SPLITTING UP

Claire Colbert

Which? Books are commissioned and published by Which? Ltd,
2 Marylebone Road, London NW1 4DF
Email: books@which.co.uk

Distributed by Littlehampton Book Services Ltd,
Faraday Close, Durrington, Worthing, West Sussex BN13 3RB

British Library Cataloguing in Publication Data
A catalogue record for this book is available from the British Library

ISBN 978 1 84490 107 4

1 3 5 7 9 10 8 6 4 2

Publisher's acknowledgements
This book incorporates material from *Divorce and Splitting Up*, published by Which? Books in 2009.
The publisher would like to thank Simon Crawford of Peden & Reid Solicitors, Belfast for his comments on the law in Northern Ireland, and Scott Cochrane of Brodies LLP, Edinburgh for his comments on the law in Scotland.

Senior Editor: Katy Denny
Project Manager: Kate Haxell
Indexer: Marie Dickens
Printed and bound by Charterhouse, Hatfield

Paper: Essential Velvet is an elemental chlorine free paper produced at Condát in Perigord, France, using timber from sustainably managed forests. The mill is ISO14001 and EMAS certified.

For a full list of Which? Books, please call 01992 822800, access our website at www.which.co.uk, or write to Littlehampton Book Services.

For other enquiries call 0800 252 100.

Contents

reason, the court process for the different aspects of divorce/dissolution is also explained.

There are some situations where emergency legal steps must be taken, such as when domestic violence has taken place or when you need to protect assets that are about to be misused.

LEGAL ADVICE

The law in England and Wales is significantly different to the law in Scotland and Northern Ireland and these differences are highlighted in Chapter 11.

This book is not designed to replace the legal advice than can be obtained from a good solicitor, but it aims to make the process (including the way you get that advice) feel less daunting and more clear. I hope that the information given will help you deal with some difficult decisions you will need to make and provide you with the basic knowledge and confidence to understand the steps ahead and make the right choices for you.

It is important – as changes can take place – that you check court fees and form numbers before making any application to the court.

Legal terminology is explained throughout the book and there is a glossary on pages 249–251 to help ensure that you are aware of what exactly is meant by the words used.

Jargon buster

Spouse A husband or wife in a married male-female couple.

Civil partner A partner in a same-sex civil partnership.

Partner A cohabiting partner (in a same-sex or male-female couple).

Cohabitant One of a cohabiting couple (both same-sex and male-female).

Ex A former spouse or partner or civil partner.

cp A civil partner or a civil partnership – depending on context.

Divorce The ending of a marriage or civil partnership. Although the legislation uses the word dissolution for the ending of a cp, divorce is the normal way of talking about it.

Introduction

When a long-term relationship breaks up you can easily feel as though there is no light at the end of the tunnel. This book aims to help you through what can be a difficult time, and will help you prepare and organise yourself for the future.

Dealing with the breakdown of a relationship is never easy for anyone. It is often made more difficult and stressful because of concerns about the legal and practical issues that need to be resolved when you split up with a partner. The law can appear a minefield when it is not something you are used to dealing with, or when you are facing court proceedings you never imagined you would be involved in or would need to know about. The language can seem complicated and difficult to understand and this can make the process feel intimidating to the most confident or educated person.

This book is designed to help you through the legal process of divorce and separation, as well as helping you to work through the financial consequences that follow. Some issues will be quite short-term, but other things you will need to decide will be more fundamental and will affect your financial position in the longer term.

Depending on your personal situation, the options and remedies open to you will vary: the law for civil partners or spouses differs greatly to that for couples who live together and have not married or formed a civil partnership. Some sections of this book relate to specific circumstances such as divorce, but the initial chapters apply to all couples who are splitting up, whatever their legal status.

CHILDREN

Securing time with your children is often the most pressing and emotional matter to be resolved. The way arrangements for children are considered and decided upon by the court, when parents cannot agree what is best, is dealt with in Chapter 5.

FINANCE

The financial consequences of the breakdown of a relationship can also be very difficult to resolve. This book aims to help you consider the options and alternatives and to work out what is best in your personal situation.

It is not always necessary to end up in a court battle to resolve issues and the alternatives to court litigation are described to enable you to choose the right method to sort everything out for you. Trying to resolve issues amicably and in a civilised way is always going to be the best option, but if this is not possible, for whatever

Legal costs

Getting legal advice on the issues surrounding the breakdown of your relationship is very important, but the potential costs of this advice do need to be thought about. Often legal costs can build up during a dispute and once the issues have been resolved there may be less money available for you to move on with your life than you had hoped, as these legal costs have to be paid.

PART 1

Costs in family proceedings

The issue of costs can create particularly severe problems when one of you is determined to mount an expensive legal campaign against the other. Whenever you use the law to fight over the children, or over maintenance or property, both of you will generally have to instruct solicitors (and perhaps barristers, too). As a result, you will have two bills to pay at the end of the case.

When you are embroiled in a court battle with your ex about any aspect of your separation, it can be easy to lose sight of the effect that battle could have on costs.

The arguments are often of such personal importance that one party can believe that they have to fight to get the 'right' outcome, or see that 'justice' is done. In this instance it is unlikely that the law will produce the outcome you are seeking, and it may be an expensive lesson. Court battles can sometimes be hard to stop and you may find yourself in a lengthy, costly dispute over an issue that could have been resolved another way. There will also be the costs your ex incurs as they fight from their side, leading to two large bills to be paid.

Obviously, there are situations where there is no choice but to involve the court. Be guided by your solicitor as to the battles that are worth fighting, and the costs you may incur compared to the benefit of what you are seeking. This is one of the reasons it is so important that you get the right solicitor for you and this is explained further in Chapter 3. Your

 This could be the most important chapter of the book for you: please do not be tempted to skip it.

solicitor can help you in reviewing options and working out which way to proceed to tackle your legal problems in the least costly, but most effective, way.

Good family lawyers are skilled in negotiating a sensible outcome for you without having to go to court. It is also possible to negotiate through mediation or reach an agreement with your ex directly. These options will significantly cut the legal costs you will both incur.

HOW SOLICITORS CHARGE

Solicitors charge according to the amount of time they spend on your case. A solicitor will log every single thing that he or she does on your file: receiving and sending letters and emails, making telephone calls, seeing you or witnesses, reading papers, drafting documents, going to court (which includes travelling, waiting and the actual hearing, as well as putting papers in order for trial).

Most solicitors charge on an hourly basis. They usually record the time spent on a case in 'units' of five or six minutes each.

Making a short telephone call or writing a letter might not take as long as this, but the practice is to record them as single units each. If any item of work takes longer than a single unit the time recorded will be rounded up to the nearest unit spent.

A further figure (generally worked out as a percentage of the bill) is sometimes added as a mark-up for 'care and attention'. This is an extra charge solicitors can make if your case has been complex or has had to be dealt with especially quickly, but they should make you aware of this before the work is started.

When you first instruct a solicitor, or are making enquiries about firms of solicitors, you should check the hourly rate of the person who will be acting for you. Make sure you ask whether the figure you are quoted includes VAT and if there is any discount for the first appointment, which may be lengthy. Solicitors' firms generally have staff who have different levels of legal education and/or experience. Naturally, the hourly charge of a senior solicitor or a partner in the law firm will be more than that of a trainee or a legal executive. It is important

"The more you spend on lawyers, the less you will have left for yourselves."

Jargon buster

Assessment Checking of the amount charged in a bill by the court or Legal Services Commission.
Attendances Face-to-face meetings.
Brief fee The amount paid to a barrister for an appearance in court. This can be increased by a fee for each additional day spent in court – a 'refresher'.
Bundles Putting papers in a specific order for court.
Conference A meeting with your solicitor and barrister.
Counsel A barrister.
Disbursements Payments made on your behalf, for things like expert reports, valuations.
LSC (Legal Services Commission) This body administers the legal aid Scheme.
Perusal Reading the papers on the file.
Refresher The additional amount on a brief fee for each day's work by the barrister in court.
Telephone attendances Phone calls (made or received).

 See Chapter 3 for information about solicitors. See Chapter 4 for a full explanation of what mediation is, how it works and where to find a mediator.

> **"Time is money when you are using a solicitor. Prepare what you need to say before you phone them or go to an appointment."**

Solicitor's fees

A solicitor's hourly charging rate can be anything from £120 upwards (plus VAT) in a firm outside London; in London it may range from £125 to £350 (plus VAT). Hourly rates of £400 (plus VAT) or more may be charged by senior solicitors at some upmarket London firms.

that you instruct someone of the right level of experience to avoid unnecessary costs. The solicitor should be able to tell you if they have the right experience (or if they are too senior) to deal with the issues you need help with.

Bills of costs in legal aid cases are constructed on a slightly different basis. Although, in legal aid cases, the time spent on any one piece of work is taken into account, there are usually pre-set hourly rates for some aspects of the work: travelling to court, for instance, is charged at a lower rate than actually appearing before a judge. Also certain

items, such as routine telephone calls, may be charged at flat rates.

HOW BARRISTERS CHARGE

If your solicitor thinks that your case needs the services of a barrister, either for specialist advice or to represent you in court, you will need to pay a further fee for this. Barristers generally charge on the basis of each piece of work they do: a set amount for a conference, or written advice, or an appearance at court.

Your solicitor negotiates the barrister's fee. Bear in mind that if your case gets to the stage of a court hearing and a barrister is instructed to appear for you, the 'brief fee' (the fee for the court appearance) will be charged even if the matter is settled by agreement shortly before the hearing and your barrister does not actually have to represent you at the hearing.

If this route is taken, the barrister's fee can subsequently be reduced by the court (or in legal aid cases, the Legal Services Commission) in a process known as assessment (see page 27).

PAYING COSTS YOURSELF

If you are paying privately, your solicitor will probably ask you for some money in advance 'on account of costs'. A sum of £500 would not be unusual; indeed, £1,000 is probably more realistic.

Your solicitor should send you a bill at regular intervals (you can ask for them

The Law Society is the professional body regulating solicitors in England and Wales. Its website has useful information about the rules under which solicitors operate and about their charges: www.lawsociety.org.uk/choosingandusing.law

Rules of engagement

If you do not pay your solicitor's bill, he or she is entitled to say that they will do no further work for you until the costs are settled. They can also retain your file of papers as security for payments.

If you are dissatisfied with the response you receive, you are entitled to have your bill assessed (see page 27). Normally, you should do this within one month of the date on the bill. Your solicitor should remind you about this in a form of standard wording on the bill. He or she can sue you if you do not pay.

to be sent every month) so that you keep abreast of the legal costs you are incurring as they arise. Many solicitors will be happy to let you pay by a regular monthly standing order to help spread the cost. This is a good way to avoid large bills.

Solicitors have clear professional rules about the information that they must give their clients about costs. At the beginning of your relationship you should be given a letter with full information about the way in which costs will be charged and about the firm's complaints procedure. You should be given regular (at least every six months) updates on your costs. You should also be told if the firm increases its hourly charge. If you have been given an estimate of the likely costs, you should be told if this is going to be exceeded.

When you get a bill from your solicitor you can ask for a breakdown showing all the items that have been charged for. If you feel that the charges are too high, you should discuss the issue with him or her – or with someone more senior in the firm – and you may be able to agree a reduction as soon as the issue arises.

CAN YOU AFFORD THE BILL?

You may not be eligible for legal aid but still find it hard to pay the solicitor's bill.

Some solicitors have arrangements with banks and credit-card companies and will let you pay using credit cards.

If you are certain that at the end of the case you will get a settlement out of which you can afford to pay your costs, you may be able to persuade your bank to lend you the money, or your solicitor may be prepared to enter into an agreement that he or she will be paid out of this money. This is not a 'contingency fee' agreement – your solicitor is not saying that he or she will be paid only if you win, or that you agree to pay a percentage of what you get. You will be liable for costs if you do not get what you expected, but they should be charged according to the solicitor's normal rates, as agreed at the beginning of the case.

If your solicitor proposes such an agreement to you, you should be given a draft of the terms and you should consult another independent solicitor before you enter into it. You will need to bear in mind the risks involved and be aware that costs can increase very rapidly, sometimes in ways you had not expected.

Legal aid

You need to consider whether you will be eligible for legal aid (public funding). This does not mean that you will get your solicitor for free (see page 19 regarding the Statutory Charge), but it will help you meet at least some of the costs. Legal aid is not available for all issues, so you should check this early on.

You can check your eligibility for legal aid on the Community Legal Service website. Both your capital and income are taken into account when your eligibility for legal aid is considered. However, capital that is in dispute between you and your ex is not included in the calculation. So if you are not working and have little or no income of your own, you may qualify for legal aid even if you have quite a lot of capital that you own as a couple. It can put you at an advantage if your ex has to pay privately for his/her solicitor.

Legal aid essentials

You may need the following for your first legal aid appointment:
- **Your National Insurance number.**
- **Your most recent wage slips.**
- **Proof of income support or income-based jobseeker's allowance if you are out of work and claiming benefits.**
- **Proof of a tax credit (for example working tax credit).**
- **Evidence of a partner's income if you live together.**

" You do not need to take evidence of your ex's income, as this is not counted if you are divorcing or separating. "

Not all solicitors offer legal aid. If you think you are eligible, check whether a firm offers legal aid when you first make an appointment. If the firm does offer legal aid and you are eligible, you will find that different levels of the funding apply to different stages of the legal process.

 Community Legal Service's national helpline is 0845 345 4 345. www.communitylegaladvice.org.uk and follow links to 'Can I get legal aid?' and to the eligibility calculator.

FIRST-STAGE LEGAL AID – LEGAL HELP

First-stage legal aid covers a session of initial advice and the work that the solicitor will do in an undefended divorce/dissolution. However, it covers only the divorce/dissolution itself, not the financial side of things or any dispute over children. For those there are other forms of legal aid.

When you see your solicitor at the first meeting, he or she will work out whether you qualify for Legal Help. They will fill in a form with details of your income and capital. Your disposable capital and disposable income must be under certain limits (which are reviewed annually in April by the LSC). Your solicitor will be able to tell you immediately whether you are eligible for Legal Help and you will be asked to sign the form with your details to confirm that they are true.

If you are eligible for Legal Help you will pay nothing to the solicitor. At the end of the case, your solicitor will send the bill to the LSC, which will pay him or her. If you need advice on another legal matter (for example, you might have to deal with a building society over debts and possession proceedings), a new Legal Help form can be completed.

If you are receiving Legal Help, you won't have to pay court fees for divorce proceedings, which is a considerable saving.

 If at the end of the case you get or keep assets, you will have to pay back to the LSC what it has paid to your solicitor. Known as the Statutory Charge, this does not apply to legal aid for mediation.

SECOND-STAGE LEGAL AID

As stated earlier, Legal Help does not help to arrange the financial aspects of your split, or any dispute over children, apart from your solicitor taking initial instructions from you to find out what the position is and opening negotiations.

Unless your financial circumstances are very straightforward, or you have sorted them all out before you see the solicitor, you will probably need some legal advice and help with negotiating a settlement. If the financial problems are more complicated, or you are on bad terms with your ex, you may need to go further and put the matter before the court. To cover the cost of this you can apply for second-stage public funding (formerly referred to as 'full legal aid'), which itself has two levels – Approved Family Help and/or Legal Representation.

 The LSC website publishes information leaflets on legal aid: www.legalservices.gov.uk/public/help/information_leaflets.asp. The leaflet 'A Step-by-Step Guide to Legal Aid, Help with Paying for Civil Cases' contains up-to-date financial limits.

MEDIATION AND PUBLIC FUNDING

You cannot make an application for second-stage public funding until you have first been put through a process to see whether your case would be suitable for mediation. Your solicitor will refer you to one of the locally approved mediation services. They will contact you and your ex to arrange an initial appointment. At the first appointment the mediator will explain to each of you how mediation works and explore with you whether you would want, or be able, to take it further.

The scheme recognises that there are some situations that are simply not going to be suitable for mediation: for example, cases where there has been domestic violence, or child-care cases where the local authority is involved. Also, even if you are prepared to use mediation, your ex may refuse, in which case mediation cannot take place. If your case is not suitable (see below), the mediator will refer you back to your solicitor so that you can apply for further funding.

This process of screening for mediation inevitably delays the grant of a full certificate of public funding, if that is what you are going to need. However, try to make the most of the opportunity. See Chapter 4 for further information on mediation and its advantages.

If mediation is suitable and you work out a settlement this way then you can have legal aid (called Family Mediation) to cover the mediator's costs. Your solicitor is paid for by legal aid called Help with Mediation. Your solicitor should advise you during the mediation and will in due course put your agreement into a legally binding form.

Uniquely, you do not have to pay the statutory charge (see page 22) for the work that the mediator and solicitor do and the amount that he or she is paid. This is an incentive for using the mediation route to settlement.

Help with Mediation is available only if you are taking part in family mediation or you have successfully reached an agreement and need legal advice or support from your solicitor. You can have help from a solicitor until the work that is done for you reaches a particular charging level.

If mediation is not suitable, then you need the other form of Approved Family Help legal aid: General Family Help. A General Family Help certificate will be limited to cover up to £1,500 of work.

If proceedings go as far as a contested hearing, then your solicitor must get the certificate extended to cover Legal Representation, which is the second level of the second stage of public funding. Legal Representation can be granted on an emergency basis; if you need to go straight to court, the certificate will immediately cover Legal Representation.

APPLYING FOR APPROVED FAMILY HELP AND/OR LEGAL REPRESENTATION

To apply for any form of Approved Family Help and/or Legal Representation, you have to fill in two long forms. One form deals with all your financial circumstances, in considerable detail; the other deals with the legal proceedings that you want to take. If you are in work you will be given a third form to take to your employer so that he or she can confirm your wages. Your solicitor will help you to fill in the forms and should check that everything is correctly completed. He or she should also explain to you about the statutory charge (see page 22) and give you a leaflet about it.

The financial limits for Legal Help (see page 15) are not the same as those for General Family Help/Legal Representation; it is possible to be eligible for General Family Help/Legal Representation even if you are not eligible for Legal Help. If you are receiving income support or income-based jobseeker's allowance, you will automatically be eligible for General Family Help/Legal Representation without any inquiry being made into your financial circumstances.

Your completed forms are sent off to the LSC, which works out whether you are entitled to Approved Family Help/Legal Representation. It also assesses, from the information you have given on the form, whether you have a worthwhile case: the 'merits test'. If you meet these two criteria then the forms are passed to the assessment office of the Benefits Agency to check your financial circumstances.

If you qualify for Approved Family Help/Legal Representation, you may be asked to pay nothing, or a contribution towards your legal costs. This may be a one-off payment out of capital or, more likely, a regular amount each month for as long as the case takes. If

Jargon buster

LSC Legal Services Commission, formerly known as the Legal Aid Board. They determine if you are eligible for legal aid and to what extent.

Public Funding Commonly known as legal aid.

Legal Help Initial legal aid to cover divorce/dissolution advice and only the taking of initial instructions on any other issues. This is not repayable under the LSC's statutory charge.

Family Mediation Legal aid limited to costs of a mediator helping you reach a settlement with your ex. Not repayable under the LSC's statutory charge.

Help with Mediation Legal aid for costs you will incur with your solicitor while going through mediation and for drawing up a mediated agreement into a legally binding document. Not repayable under the LSC's statutory charge.

Approved Family Help Legal aid for advice upon, negotiating and considering the financial aspects of your split, disputes concerning children and domestic violence. Payable back to the LSC under the statutory charge except in certain situations.

Legal Representation Legal aid for costs of a contested hearing. Recoverable by the LSC under the statutory charge except in certain situations.

Statutory charge The amount LSC can claim back from you for the legal costs they have funded, if you recover (or preserve) any capital or property.

you are asked to make a contribution, it is important that you ensure that you pay the amounts regularly. If you miss payments, your certificate will be taken away from you and you may have to pay all your costs yourself. The payments are made to the LSC, you do not pay your solicitor directly. In due course, as with Legal Help, your solicitor submits his or her bill to the LSC and is paid by it. As with Legal Help, if at the end of the divorce you get or keep assets, you will have to pay back to the LSC what it has paid to your solicitor. This clawback is called the statutory charge (see page 22).

If, when you receive the assessment from the LSC, you think that the contribution that you have been asked for is too high and a mistake has been made, you can ask for the amount to be reassessed. But this will take time and delay the granting of your certificate. It is often better to pay the first instalment you have been asked to pay and get the certificate issued before asking for the contribution to be reassessed.

It can take some weeks for the LSC to process your application. If you are eligible and you are not being asked to make a contribution, you and your solicitor will hear from the LSC with a copy of your certificate. If you are asked to make a contribution, you will not get the certificate until you have accepted the offer of funding and paid the first instalment. This can hold up your case because a certificate is not retrospective in effect; the LSC will not pay your solicitor for work done on financial matters before the granting of

Updating the LSC
You must tell the LSC if:
• **There is any change in your financial circumstances.**
• **You stop living with your spouse/partner.**
• **You start living with someone as a couple.**
• **You change your address.**

the certificate. If you have Legal Help, then your solicitor may be able to deal with some matters within its scope, but remember that the time the solicitor can charge under Legal Help is restricted and for marriages/cps is mostly used up in dealing with just the divorce/dissolution.

EMERGENCY APPLICATIONS

You can get Legal Representation on an emergency basis – mostly this will be used for domestic violence injunctions. Solicitors in firms that are contracted to do so by the LSC can grant an emergency certificate without applying to the LSC office beforehand. Otherwise the application can be made by post/fax and granted the next day. In extreme (and rare) cases, a certificate may be granted over the telephone. An emergency certificate will cover the first stages of the work that needs to be done.

When you make the application you have to promise to make a full application and complete all the forms. You also have to promise that, if it turns out that you are not financially eligible, or you do not accept the offer when it

Are you entitled to legal aid and would the statutory charge apply?

Legal help

Advice at the start of your case. Also covers undefended divorce/dissolution.

Approved family help

To get legal aid for further steps, you must first check out mediation and see if it is suitable for you.

Mediation is suitable

Not suitable

General family help

To cover negotiations and issuing court proceedings.

Family mediation

To cover the costs of mediation.

if matters go as far as a final contested hearing

and

Legal representation

To cover being represented at court.

Help with mediation

To cover the costs of the solicitor advising on the mediation and putting the agreement into a legally binding form.

Statutory charge

Applies to these forms of legal aid.

Statutory charge

DOES NOT apply to these forms of legal aid.

is made to you, you will be liable for the entire cost of the case.

Your contribution to your legal aid will be reassessed if your disposable income goes up or down, or if your disposable capital goes up. You should make your solicitor aware if your financial situation changes in any way. If your financial position has increased past the point where you would be eligible for funding, your certificate may be discharged (that is, stopped), so that you are then responsible for the costs of your case from that point onwards.

If the LSC decides that you have in some way misled it about your financial position, your certificate can be revoked. This means that it is treated as though it never existed. Your solicitor will then be entitled to seek to recover from you the full amount of

False declarations
If anybody intentionally fails to comply with legal aid regulations about information to be provided by him or her, or knowingly makes any false statement or false representation, he or she will be liable to a fine, or imprisonment for up to three months.

costs he or she would have charged on a private basis, rather than the reduced fees they would charge under the legal aid certificate.

If you don't answer letters from the LSC, or you do not make the monthly repayments, your certificate can be discharged. You would then have to raise the money to pay your solicitor privately.

Emergency funding

A solicitor is very unlikely to make an application for emergency funding unless he or she thinks that you will be financially eligible. It is therefore important to be very accurate about your financial circumstances when you tell the solicitor about them at the outset of your case. See Chapter 9 for Emergency Remedies.

FINANCIAL LIMITATIONS ON LEGAL AID

Just as there are limits on the amount of work your solicitor can do under Legal Help, there are ceilings on the costs for General Family Help and Legal Representation. For General Family Help your solicitor can do work until his or her costs reach £1,500. If it looks as though the costs will mount higher than this, he or she can apply to the LSC for an extension.

Paying Back the Legal Service Commission: The Statutory Charge from the LSC website: www.legalservices.gov.uk/public/help/leaflets.asp

He or she will have to justify why this is necessary.

A certificate for Legal Representation will also have a financial limit put on it. This will vary depending on what work it covers. The LSC can also put limitations on precisely what sort of legal actions your solicitor can take. Your solicitor should go through the certificate with you and explain any restrictions. Again, if more, or different, action is needed, your solicitor can justify this to the LSC and seek an extension to cover the further work.

Legal fees for someone on legal aid

If you have any form of legal aid, you stop being personally responsible for the costs of your case. Your solicitor cannot give you a bill for the work that he or she is doing for you under the certificate or ask you to pay disbursements (that is, costs and fees paid out by him or her on your behalf) for your case.

Solicitors are not paid by the LSC at the rates that they charge their private cases. Nor are they paid for all the work that they will do. This may mean that the solicitor will not be paid to attend court on your behalf if there is a barrister instructed for you, and so may send a clerk or a trainee instead. This may be worrying for you, but in practical terms the personal presence of your solicitor may make very little difference.

You cannot offer to pay an extra amount out of your own pocket for an extra service by your solicitor, as your solicitor is not allowed to be paid by you directly when you have legal aid.

❝ As you will not be paying your solicitor directly it is easy to forget that, as the case goes on, the costs will be mounting. ❞

Keeping track of costs

It is important to remember that you will have to face the costs when the statutory charge begins. Your solicitor should give you a regular (at least once every six months) update on the running total of your costs. This will have to be an estimate, because the bill will not be finalised until the end, when it is checked by the LSC or the court, but it should give you a realistic idea of how the costs are increasing.

It is worth remembering that costs do not tend to mount in a steady progression and can jump up suddenly; some procedures, like applications to court, are cost-intensive because they require a lot of time to be spent.

Your solicitor has a duty to keep an eye on costs for the LSC too – the LSC will not be prepared to fund litigation if it thinks that you are unreasonably escalating the costs. Your solicitor is expected to report to the LSC if he or she thinks that you are not acting reasonably. For example, if your ex makes an offer to settle the case, your solicitor, and your barrister if you have one, will advise you on whether you should take it or incur further costs trying to increase the settlement.

> **"Even if you get an award of costs from the court at the end of your case, this does not mean that your ex will be ordered to pay your entire bill. "**

If you refuse to take their advice to settle a case, they will have to consider whether to refer the matter to the LSC. This may seem very unfair, but if you were paying privately you would have to consider whether it was worth the risk of spending more of your money to achieve an outcome that might be uncertain.

THE STATUTORY CHARGE

When you sign the forms applying for public funding your solicitor should give you two leaflets: 'A Step-by-Step Guide to Legal Aid' and 'Paying for Your Legal Aid'. Your solicitor should also explain to you how the statutory charge works and answer any questions that you have.

The purpose of the statutory charge is to recoup some of the taxpayers' money that finances the legal aid fund. If you keep or are awarded (the legal term is 'recover or preserve') any money or property, at the end of the case you will have to pay the LSC back for the costs it has paid on your behalf. It does not matter whether you get the money or property as a result of a decision by a court or an agreement with your ex.

If you have already paid a contribution towards your certificate and it is more than the costs of the case, you will be entitled to a refund of the difference. However, in most cases the costs will be more than you have already paid. To recover the shortfall, the LSC is allowed first call on the money or property. Even if you get an award of costs from the court at the end of your case, this does not mean that your ex will be ordered to pay your entire bill.

The charge will cover all proceedings for which you had funding. So, if your legal aid covers an injunction, negotiations about the children and the financial issues, all the costs for these three things will be rolled up together, even if you recovered or preserved your property in only one aspect of the proceedings.

In practice, the only way of keeping any other property out of the scope of the statutory charge would be if you had reached a final agreement about it before the certificate was granted, or it was conceded that it was never a matter of dispute between you and your ex that you should have it. If this is the case, then it is sensible to tell the LSC about this at the time when you apply for a certificate, so that it knows you are not going to recover or preserve property as a result of the proceedings.

 Maintenance payments do not count as property but all lump sums do.

AT THE END OF YOUR CASE

Your solicitor is obliged to hold any money or property that you receive from your ex and pay it first to the LSC, so that it can take the statutory charge out of it before you receive it. If the sum that you have received from your ex is far more than the projected figure for costs, your solicitor may be permitted to release part of it to you, provided he or she retains enough to cover the bill.

The immediate payment of the statutory charge would obviously cause hardship if the property is the home in which you would otherwise be living, or a sum of money intended for the purchase of a home. If this is the case, the charge can be postponed. A charge like a mortgage is put on the house and the money and accrued interest on it is repaid only when the house is sold. Interest (currently at 8 per cent simple interest per year, but this rate may alter) is added to the original debt. If you do not agree to pay the interest, the LSC will not allow the charge to be postponed.

If the house is sold so that another home can be bought with the proceeds of sale, the LSC will generally agree that the charge can be put on the new home, provided the value of the new home is sufficient to cover the debt. If the charge is going to be postponed in this way, it is important that the court order or agreement records that the property is intended to be the home of the funded person, or the money is intended for the purchase of a home for the funded person.

The LSC sends annual statements to people who have charges on their homes to tell them the amount of interest that has accrued. This allows you to keep track of what you owe the LSC.

If you do not recover or preserve property at the end of your case, then the charge will not apply. This can happen in cases where there is no capital to be divided, or where there is no interest on which the LSC can take a charge. The most common example of this is where your home was rented. The settlement or court order may result in the transfer of the tenancy to one of you, but the tenancy is not something that can be charged with the debt.

Cost orders and assessment

The general principle in English law is that the loser pays the winner's costs. However, this is not consistently applied in family proceedings. The rules about costs depend on what type of proceedings you are involved in.

COSTS ORDERS AND ASSESSMENT

For a number of reasons it can be difficult to obtain costs orders in family proceedings. Primarily because it is hard to determine who has 'won' or 'lost'.

Family law does make provision for costs orders to be made, but the rules – and chances of success in obtaining an order requiring your ex to pay your costs – can vary greatly depending on the type of litigation and the reason you are suggesting your ex should be required to make a contribution to your costs, particularly when they have their own to pay as well. In this regard it is better to presume a costs order will not be made, rather than that it will.

DIVORCE/DISSOLUTION

Whoever starts the divorce proceedings (called the Petitioner) is able to make a claim for costs against their spouse/cp (the Respondent) within the petition. The spouse/cp is able to reply to confirm if they are happy to pay any of the other spouse's/cp's costs in the acknowledgement of service.

It is common for there to be an agreement to either make a fixed contribution or for each party to pay their own costs. It is unusual to make a claim for costs in a petition that is based on two years separation with consent.

The ability to apply for costs within a divorce is only available to the Petitioner; the Respondent will always pay their own costs. If the parties cannot agree how costs should be divided, if at all, the court will have a short costs hearing where both parties can express why they do or do not think a cost order should be made.

The costs that the Petitioner can recover are the court fees and solicitors costs they incur in issuing and finalising the divorce proceedings. The judge will decide what is an appropriate contribution, looking at the specific circumstances of the case. This is unlikely to be the full amount of the Petitioner's legal costs and the Petitioner will remain liable for any difference.

CHILDREN ACT APPLICATIONS

Although it is always possible to ask for a costs order against your ex within an application to the court about the issues or arrangements relating to children, it is rare for such orders to be made. Disputes that relate to children can often incur significant legal costs. However, it can be very difficult to determine who has 'won' or 'lost' a dispute over children, as both parents will feel they have been acting in what they believe is the best interests of their children. The court would not want to punish a parent who is acting reasonably in such circumstances.

It is possible to seek a costs order against a parent if he or she has been acting in a way that is unreasonable and has, for example, significantly delayed matters, caused unnecessary expense for the other parent, or if they have failed to recognise and comply with orders that the court has already made.

DOMESTIC VIOLENCE APPLICATIONS

Applications relating to domestic violence can be very expensive, as often court action is required urgently to protect you. The steps that will need to be taken can be costly and time consuming for solicitors.

In such circumstances it is possible to obtain an order that your ex should pay the costs that you have incurred in making the application. However, it is unlikely the costs order will be made at an emergency hearing, and more likely that the judge will deal with a costs claim at a later hearing when they give your ex an opportunity to state their side of things.

Jargon buster

Petitioner The person who asks the court for the divorce/dissolution, by filing a 'petition'.

Respondent The other spouse/cp, who responds to the petition.

Assessment Process where a bill/costs order is reviewed by the Court or LSC.

Taxation The old term for assessment of costs, which some solicitors still use.

Costs draftsman Specialist employed by solicitors to draft the bill for assessment in specially detailed form.

Statutory charge The amount that the LSC can claim back from you for the legal costs they have funded, if you recover (or preserve) any capital or property.

FINANCIAL DISPUTES IN DIVORCE/DISSOLUTION

If the financial consequences of the breakdown of your marriage/civil partnership are being dealt with through an application to the court, the general principle is that each spouse/cp will be responsible for their own legal costs. These legal costs are then factored into the overall needs that each person has when the court looks to divide the family assets.

This means that the legal costs you each have are likely to be seen as a debt to be paid from the overall pot of family assets, before it is divided. This approach should mean that a couple is discouraged from running up significant legal bills, as these will affect the amount that is available to meet each of their needs at the end of a case.

It is possible to obtain an order that your spouse/cp should pay a contribution towards your costs in some limited circumstances, which are when:

- They have failed to comply with something that has specifically been requested and ordered by the court.
- They have acted in an unreasonable way, which has increased your legal costs.
- They have rejected an offer that has been made that the judge considers was a reasonable offer and should have been accepted. If this is the judge's view, the costs you have incurred since the date you made that offer can be ordered to be paid by your spouse/cp, on the basis that those additional costs would have been avoided if they had accepted the offer instead of continuing to fight through the court proceedings.

If you are going to seek costs, you should make your spouse/cp aware of this as early as possible.

FINANCIAL DISPUTES BETWEEN COHABITANTS

The law that applies to cohabitants is different from the law for spouses/cps. The court are not looking at dividing family assets on the basis of who needs what, as they do within financial disputes in divorce/dissolution, and so the costs are not taken out of the combined assets before any division is made. Instead, the costs are treated on a winner/loser basis

and only the cohabitant who 'wins' the case will stand a chance of obtaining a costs order against the other.

Bad behaviour during the litigation (such as acting unreasonably or failing to comply with court orders) can lead to a costs order being made, as can the rejection of a reasonable offer to settle the matter.

COSTS ORDERS GENERALLY

If you do manage to obtain a costs order within any family proceedings, the order can be made on either a standard or indemnity basis. The costs order can be defined as being the costs of dealing with a certain application or issue, or it can be for the overall costs incurred throughout the whole of the proceedings to date.

If the costs order is on the standard basis, which is most common, this means that you are likely to recover the majority of your costs, but unlikely to recover all of them. A broad guide would be 60–80 per cent of the costs you have incurred for the specific issue that the court is deciding. Sometimes

&& If one person makes a reasonable offer to settle the case and the other refuses and continues to litigate, costs might be ordered against them. 99

the judge will order a fixed contribution towards costs, but more commonly it is left for the parties to agree the amount of the costs that should be paid.

An indemnity costs order is rare, but if obtained it means that the full costs of the person who has the benefit of the costs order should be paid by the other party. The costs are paid without reduction and if there is any dispute about costs that have been incurred, the court are more likely to order in favour of the person who has the benefit of the costs order.

AMOUNT TO BE PAID – ASSESSMENT PROCESS

The amount of costs to be paid following a costs order is initially dealt with by negotiation. However, if the amount to be paid cannot be agreed, a process called assessment takes places. This is the same process as someone who has legal aid has to complete at the end of a case, before the bill is paid by the LSC.

An application for a bill to be assessed must be sent to the court within three months of an order having been made by the court. This process requires a bill to be drafted in a specific format, outlining the costs that have been incurred chronologically with details of the work that has been done. The costs of drawing up this bill are added to the amount the claiming party is seeking from the other. This is then sent to the court (or to the LSC) for them to assess what costs should be paid as a result of the costs order that has been made.

As a result of this process there is a review of the costs that are being claimed. A decision is made by the court (or the LSC) as to whether the amount of costs being sought are fair and reasonable in the circumstances of the case. The judge will review each entry on the bill and can reduce any items they think were unnecessary or have been overcharged.

The bill is then sent back to the solicitor and whoever challenged the amount of the costs will be sent a copy. This is called a provisional assessment. Either the solicitor or the person against who the costs order has been made can reject the reductions or seek more reductions. This will require a costs hearing where the judge will go through the bill with everyone present and will make a final decision.

It is possible for the costs of this hearing to be ordered as part of the costs order as well, and so there is a financial incentive to all involved to try and reach an agreement without the need for a hearing.

Challenging the bill

There is a financial risk involved if you challenge your solicitor's bill, because unless you succeed in reducing the bill by at least 20 per cent, you run the risk of the costs of the assessment hearing being ordered against you.

COST ORDER CONSIDERATIONS

If one party is legally aided and a costs order is made against them (which is very unusual), their legal aid will not cover this: the costs will have to be paid by them directly. The court will decide what it is reasonable for them to pay and will only allow the order to be enforced with the court's specific permission. The costs can be limited to the amount of their legal aid contributions, and can also be ordered to be paid in instalments.

If a legally aided person obtains a costs order against their ex who is paying their own solicitor on a private basis, the costs that can be claimed are the costs on private pay rates, rather than limited to legal aid rates, which are much lower. This will have an impact on both parties if the litigation relates to financial issues in divorce/dissolution, as the costs claimed are taken out of the cumulate family finances and so will reduce the overall amount available for division.

Even if an order is made for your ex to pay some of your costs, it is important to bear in mind that:

- You remain liable for your solicitors' costs personally, and the costs order will be to reimburse you for those costs: it is up to you to pursue the costs against your ex. You are obliged to pay your solicitor when they send you their bill, even though you are to be reimbursed under the terms of the costs order, unless your solicitor is prepared to agree to wait until you have obtained the money from your ex.

- A cost order is only valuable if the person that is being ordered to pay the costs is able to be traced, and has the funds to pay the costs.
- If the order is made within financial matters in divorce/dissolution, generally the costs will be factored in as a need that will be taken into account when dividing the assets anyway, and therefore the costs order may not create any specific advantage.

LEGAL AID ASSESSMENT

The process of bill assessment outlined above takes place at the end of a case when one party has legal aid, even if no costs orders have been made. This may then form the calculation of the statutory charge, depending on the case and the circumstances.

The court (or the LSC) will review the bill in the same way and if you are the person who has the benefit of the legal aid, you are entitled to a copy of the bill and to make any representations to the court, or challenges to the bill, during the assessment process.

Again, if either the solicitor or the legally aided party is not satisfied with a provisional bill assessment made by the court, he or she can ask for a hearing and the judge will then go through the bill in the presence of everyone who has an interest in it.

Financial planning

As part of the process of splitting up it will be necessary for you to plan for the future. However, before you make any plans or decisions, it is important that you have a clear understanding of your finances and the options you have.

Your financial summary

Organising your finances will help you and make instructing your solicitor (if you use one) more efficient. As you start to prepare the financial summary, it is a good idea to keep the relevant documents and paperwork together in one file for quick reference.

You can use these guidelines to prepare a summary of information for your solicitor, who could then help to sort through it and assist you in planning for the future. You may not be able to work out all the figures – for example, your ex's position may be a blank – but you should still fill in as much of the picture as you can so that you are able to understand your situation as far as possible.

CAPITAL ASSETS
If you own your own home and any other houses

Current value (estimate).

How much did it originally cost?

Is the home in joint names and is it registered as joint tenants or tenants in common?

(You can get this information via the Land Registry website: www.landregisteronline.gov.uk or a solicitor can do it for you.)

How did you arrange your finances to pay for it? Who put down the deposit, and where did the money come from?

What are the estimated costs of sale or transfer?

If you own a leasehold property (that is, with a long lease, usually of 25 years or more):

What is the ground rent?

What is the service/maintenance charge (if there is one)?

How long is the lease?

If you have a mortgage:

Write down the details of the building society, bank or other lender:

Name and address.

Account/reference number.

How much is outstanding? When will it be paid off?

What are the monthly payments?

Are there any arrears?

Would there be any penalties to be paid if you change mortgage, and how much would these be?

Is it an interest only or repayment mortgage?

Would there be any Capital Gains Tax payable on a sale or transfer? (You may need to get specific advice on this point.)

If it's an endowment mortgage:

Who is the policy with and in whose name is it held?

When is the policy due to mature and for how much?

What is the current surrender/paid-up value of the policy?

Other assets

Any joint current accounts or savings accounts.

Your own savings in building society, bank or National Savings accounts.

Stocks, shares and unit trusts, with a current valuation of holdings.

Personal Equity Plans (PEPs), Tax-Exempt Special Savings Accounts (TESSAs), Individual Savings Accounts (ISAs) or other investments.

Endowment policies and/or life insurance policies: how much are they worth now? When do they mature?

(You could ask the insurance company/broker for current surrender values and check if any policy has been written in your ex's favour.)

Valuables (such as jewellery, antiques) with estimates of their value and brief details of how/by which of you they were acquired.

Do you and/or your spouse/cp come into an inheritance soon?

Does either of you have interests under a trust?

Details of future assets (such as demutualisation payments from a building society/insurance company or an insurance policy maturing).

Are you owed money by anybody?

Vehicles (such as cars, caravans, motorcycles).

Is there a family business and does it have any capital value?

Pensions

What pensions do you have? (Include details of any occupational pensions, superannuation schemes and personal plans – including, from April 2001, stakeholder schemes – to which you belong.)

Does the pension scheme or plan provide any benefits for a widower or widow or dependent cohabitant?

What is the value of the pension you expect to receive on retirement?

What is the Cash Equivalent Transfer Value (CETV) of your pension?

31

DEBTS

	My debt	Joint debt
In this section you can work out any large debts that you may owe on your own account or jointly with your ex.		
Loans secured on your home:		
Amount borrowed.		
Outstanding balance and date repayment should end.		
Other loans or hire purchase:		
Amount borrowed.		
Outstanding balance.		
Date repayment should end.		
Bank overdraft:		
Bank.		
Amount overdrawn.		
Credit cards:		
Card.		
Balance.		
Other debts, including tax arrears.		
Money owed to anyone else.		

INCOME AND OUTGOINGS

Here you can work out your monthly income from all sources.

Income

	Before tax/NI	Take home
From employment:		
Normal weekly or monthly earnings.		
Bonuses.		
Hours worked (full- or part-time).		

	Gross income	Net income
From self-employment:		
What do you normally earn?		
(You should get together your last three years' accounts and tax returns as proof of the figures.)		

Maintenance

How much maintenance (if any) do you get from a former partner for you or for children?

Do you get maintenance from anyone else? If so, how much?

Other unearned income

- Interest.
- Bonuses.
- Pensions.
- Other.

Your state benefits:

Child benefit, including lone parent benefit.

Jobseeker's allowance.

Income support.

Working tax credit.

Child tax credit.

State pension.

Incapacity benefit or other disability benefits.

Add up all the figures above so that you can work out how much you have to spend each month.

List of outgoings (monthly)

If you are working from weekly figures, do remember that there are 4.33 weeks in each month; if you simply multiply a weekly figure by four you will end up leaving four weeks out of your annual total.

Property costs:

Mortgage/rent.

Endowment policy linked to mortgage.

Council tax.

Water rates.

Electricity and gas.

Service charge.

Ground rent.

Fuel (oil/coal, etc).

Repairs/decoration/maintainance.

Household expenses:

Food/housekeeping.

House and contents insurance.

Repairs/service contracts.

TV licence.

Telephone/broadband charges.

Mobile telephone.

List of outgoings (monthly) contd.

Pet food/vet's bills.

Other property/second property/holiday home costs.

DIY/gardener/window cleaner/domestic help.

Loan repayments.

Life assurance.

Private medical insurance.

Pension contributions.

Vehicles (including company vehicles if applicable):

Insurance.

Road tax.

Maintenance/service/breakdown insurance.

Fuel.

Children:

Clothing and school uniform.

Books and toys.

Childminder/nursery/nanny/babysitter (gross cost).

Baby food/equipment/toiletries.

Doctor/dentist/optician/hairdresser.

School expenses:

Fees/private lessons/after school clubs (sports, music etc)/

pocket money.

Travel to school/school trips.

School dinners/drinks.

Personal expenses:

Clothes and shoes.

Entertainment/meals out/takeway/sports.

Travel to work.

Holidays (including the children)/weekends away.

Legal costs/legal aid contribution.

Doctor/dentist/optician.

Hairdresser/cosmetics/toiletries.

Prescription charges/medicine.

Professional memberships/subscriptions.

Laundry/dry cleaning.

Presents/gifts (Christmas/birthdays).

Books/magazines/newspapers.

Other items.

Total:

Financial checklist

Use this page to summarise all the financial information
that you have got together and give yourself an overview of
your present position.

	Mine	Joint
Assets:		
Home.		
Savings and investments.		
Vehicles.		
Other valuables.		
Debts:		
Secured on house.		
Unsecured.		
A Total of assets.		
B Total of debts.		
Net assets (Figure A minus Figure B):		
Pension (CETV).		
Net monthly income:		
Earned.		
Benefits.		
Unearned.		
C Total.		
D Monthly outgoings.		
Net shortfall/surplus:		
(Figure C minus figure D).		

Planning ahead

Once you have calculated your capital and income position, you can think about how you will manage once you separate. This may include moving and changing your short- and long-term needs to make ends meet. Your ex will need to do the same exercise, and it is helpful to have this information when you are considering options. It is important your plans are realistic to prevent longer-term issues following separation.

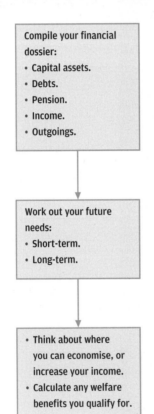

Compile your financial dossier:
• Capital assets.
• Debts.
• Pension.
• Income.
• Outgoings.

Work out your future needs:
• Short-term.
• Long-term.

• Think about where you can economise, or increase your income.
• Calculate any welfare benefits you qualify for.

Retirement plans
You are taking a big gamble with your retirement income if you take no steps to protect yourself against the effects of inflation. Options include saving in early retirement to top up your pension later on or choosing an annuity that increases each year.

ACCOMMODATION

Your housing needs are obviously your most important consideration, particularly if you have children. It is important that the options you are considering provide you with a safe, secure home that is affordable on the income you will have once separation has taken place. It is sometimes possible to stay at the home you shared with your ex, but this depends on the affordability of the property on your own, and your ex's housing needs, too. The key things you need to consider and research are:

Future plans
Making plans for the future always revolves primarily around accommodation and income.

- How much is your house worth, and if it were sold how much would be left after any mortgage was paid back and the costs of selling the property were met (including estate agents and solicitors fees and moving costs, which could be estimated at about 5 per cent of the value of the house)?
- Would there be any mortgage penalties for sale/transfer of the mortgage and are there any mortgage arrears that would need to be cleared?
- How much mortgage would you be able to raise on your own, and how much mortgage would your ex be able to raise?
- Would you be able to take over the existing mortgage and on what terms? Would you be able to raise any additional money against the house, so that this could be used to help your ex re-house, and how much would this cost you each month?
- How much would a house that would be suitable for you and your children cost? Which areas could you move to and what impact would this have on the children's schooling and your travel/work

commitments? What personal support would you have, or lose, if you moved (such as from family or friends, who may be vital now that you are going to be on your own).

- Even if you are not currently in rented accommodation, it may be worth investigating the rental market and council and housing association schemes to see if these would be options worth exploring further for you or your ex.
- What other assets do you have, and would using or selling these be an option? For example, are there any policies that could be cashed in or valuable things that could be sold. This should not be household items that will normally be needed after separation.

It may be that some of the options you investigate are not suitable for you, and this can be very disheartening. But without looking into all the alternatives, you will not be able to properly assess what is the best option for you.

Child maintenance

If you have dependent children, first work out how much child support might be payable under the formula laid down by the Child Support Acts. Turn to Chapter 6 to work out how much child support is likely to be payable.

 You could perhaps think of renting out a room to a lodger – under the 'rent a room scheme' you can receive up to £4,250 per year tax free (2010–2011 figures). Further information is on the HMRC website: www.hmrc.gov.uk

HOW MUCH WILL YOU HAVE TO LIVE ON?

Once you have calculated how much money you have coming in each month and how much you spend, it will be clear if there is going to be a shortfall.

There are going to be financial consequences to your separation that may mean your outgoings go up – such as more childcare costs if you are planning to increase your working hours – or down – such as council tax discounts for single occupancy. There may also be income changes that your new single status will bring, which could include entitlement to state benefits (see page 41), child maintenance being received or paid by you (see Chapter 6), and potential claims you can make against your spouse's/cp's income as a result of being married (see Chapter 9).

It is important that you notify your payroll department and the HMRC as soon as possible after you have separated. This will help ensure that any changes to your tax credits and benefit entitlements are dealt with quickly, and any new or increased entitlements you have are claimed at the earliest opportunity.

MAXIMISING YOUR INCOME

If you have not been working this may now need to be something you consider to help with any shortfall you have in your income each month. The impact of working, combined with any state benefits you would then be entitled to, may make a significant difference to the accommodation options that you have, and what is affordable for you.

This only applies to married/cp couples
A parent looking after children and therefore not working, or with limited income, may be able to claim maintenance to top up child support. A spouse/cp who does not work outside the home, or who is on a low income, may be entitled to spousal maintenance from the other spouse/cp if he or she earns enough. How much maintenance is not easy to quantify as the court will take a number of factors into account. If sufficient income is available a non-working spouse/cp can expect to receive not only enough to meet reasonable needs but also a proportion of the other's earnings. Depending on circumstances, the court will generally expect a spouse/cp who is not currently earning to make sensible attempts to be self-supporting in the future. There is no gender bias in the law, but women often earn less than their male counterparts and maintenance awards may compensate for this.

It is also worth considering renting out a room in your house, if this is practically possible. You should think about what financial impact this would have on your income and on your housing options.

NEEDS AND PRIORITIES

Once you have reviewed your income and outgoings (and your ex's), it may be that there is a significant shortfall and in this situation it is necessary to look at cost cutting and reassessing your needs.

The needs of children will take priority as far as income and capital division and accommodation requirements. Contents of the home will also normally follow the children to meet their needs. The other parent will need to buy or rent household equipment and these costs need to be factored into budgets.

Looking at your incomes, needs and available capital (if any), you will have to decide how things can be divided, being realistic about what is affordable and reasonable. You may have to accept that both of you are going to find things very different, and difficult, for a while. The lifestyle you had together is unlikely to still be possible after you separate.

WILLS

Although this may not seem a priority, it is important to make a will, or review an existing will, once you separate. If you do not have a will your assets on your death will pass under 'Intestacy Rules', which may mean that your estate is not divided as you would want it to be. If you are married, your spouse/cp is your next of kin, and unless you have a will stating otherwise, they would inherit from you if you were to die before the divorce/dissolution was finalised.

This is particularly important if you made mutual wills when you were a couple, which mean that if one of the

This only applies to married/cp couples
A will made by a spouse/cp is not automatically revoked on divorce/dissolution (or even an annulment of the marriage), but after the divorce will be interpreted as if the other spouse/cp had died on the date of the divorce/dissolution (or annulment). So, if the ex was named as an executor or guardian, that appointment will not take place unless there is any contrary intention expressed in the will. The gift in a will of any property to an ex will fail as well. If you wish your former spouse/cp to still receive gifts or be appointed as guardian/executor, you should draft a new will after the divorce/dissolution is finished.

Legal help making a will

You can ask for advice under the Legal Help scheme for preparing your will if you meet all the financial criteria listed in Chapter 1 and:
- are a single parent looking after a child and you want to appoint a guardian for the child to act after death, or
- are aged 70 or over, or
- are disabled, or
- have a child who is disabled.

couple dies before the wills are changed, the survivor is obliged to leave their assets as had been agreed at the time the wills were written. The survivor is not able to change their will after their ex's death, which may not be as they intended after the separation.

Mutual wills are quite uncommon and are not the same as mirror wills – where a couple simply agrees to make similar wills – as mirror wills can be changed at any time. If you think you may have a mutual will you should take steps to change it as soon as possible.

THE BENEFITS OF A WILL WHEN YOU HAVE CHILDREN

Clearly the ability to specify how you wish your assets to be divided after your death is very important. It is particularly so if you have children, as your will gives you an opportunity to make financial provision for them, as well as ensuring that after your death they are cared for as you would want.

If you and your ex have parental responsibility for your children (which is normally the case if you are married), on your death your ex will assume legal responsibility for the children. If you are the only person who has parental responsibility, when you die there will be no-one legally responsible for the children and the court will have to step in and appoint a guardian.

 This only applies to married/cp couples

Preventing disposal of assets
If you strongly suspect that your spouse/cp is intending to dispose of assets to try to escape financial obligations, do bear in mind that:

- You can ask the court to make an application under Section 37 of the Matrimonial Causes Act to prevent him or her from doing so.
- To do this, you will need to instruct a solicitor (see Chapter 7).
- This can be done as an emergency application if necessary.
- You should not delay if you think that you need to make such an application.

In this situation, you can say who you would wish that guardian to be in your will, so that the court is aware of this when they make a decision.

It is important to have considered who you would want to have care of your children if something were to happen to you, and who you would want to look after money you are leaving them if they were not be old enough to have this at the time of your death. The people you choose should be asked if they are happy to be nominated for such a role in your will, before your will is finalised.

 For more detailed information on wills see **Which? Essential Guide *Wills and Probate*.**

Financial help from the state

Financial help from the state may seem rather off-putting, especially if you once thought that you were not the sort of person who would have to turn to state help at any stage in your life. However, you should check your entitlement; such support could be vital and could make a significant difference to the options available to you after you split up.

The types of benefit that you may be eligible to apply for are:

Child Benefit A tax-free income benefit received for a parent of child under 16, or over 16 in eligible circumstances.

Income Support An income top-up for people working under 16 hours per week.

Support for Mortgage Interest (SMI) Assistance with paying mortgage interest.

Jobseeker's Allowance (JSA) An income top-up for those who are unemployed and seeking work (or working less than 16 hours per week and looking for work).

Working Tax Credit Income top-up paid to parents who qualify: if you work over 16 hours per week and have more than one child you are responsible for, or if you are not a parent, you work over 30 hours per week and qualify on other grounds.

Child Tax Credit Income top-up for parents who qualify (you do not need to be in work).

Housing Benefit Benefit to assist with rent.

Council Tax Benefit Assistance in certain circumstances with the payment of your council tax (if you are in rented or privately owned accommodation).

Loans from the social fund Interest-free capital loans to assist with budgeting for exceptional expenses, or crisis loans.

There may be other benefits you can apply for if your specific circumstances allow, such as if you are a carer or have a disability. This chapter does not cover such claims, but information can be sought from:

HMRC For Child Benefit/tax credit queries: www.hmrc.gov.uk/individuals 0845 3021444 (CB) /0845 3003900 (TC)

Jobcentre plus 0800 055 6688 or call in to your local job centre in person.

DWP/Public Services www.direct.gov.uk for general benefits advice and assistance.

Local Social Security Office Call in for advice and assistance on general benefits eligibility.

 Help and advice on benefits are available from your social security office and the Department for Work and Pensions (DWP) helplines. You can download information from the DWP website: www.dwp.gov.uk and the Directgov website: www.direct.gov.uk

If you receive Jobseeker's Allowance or Income Support, you will automatically be entitled to legal aid (see Chapter 1). Therefore it is helpful (though not always possible), to get your benefits position sorted out before you consult a solicitor.

INCOME SUPPORT

Income support is available to lone parents who are looking after children under 7 years old. You must be not working, or be working fewer than 16 hours per week. Income support has now changed for lone parents with children aged 7 years and over. From November 2008 most parents' entitlement to Income Support was stopped and instead the claim would be for Jobseeker's Allowance. This change is being phased in and will affect you if you make a new or repeat claim with:

- A youngest child aged 12 or over from 24 November 2008.
- A youngest child aged 10 or over from 26 October 2009.
- A youngest child aged 7 or over from 25 October 2010.

If you need to claim Income Support, you can visit, write to or phone your local Jobcentre Plus or social security office and you will be issued with a claim form. You can also start the process via the DWP website by downloading a claim form. You will be asked to attend an interview with a Personal Adviser. You are obliged to attend this interview if you want to claim benefit. Failure to do so may result in the loss of benefit, but you do not have to seek work as a result of the meeting. Information about these meetings is available from your local office, or you can download it from the DWP website.

The government has been running a New Deal scheme for lone parents that offers help and funding in getting lone parents back to work. Details can be obtained from the DWP or from your local Jobcentre.

To be eligible for Income Support, your capital must be worth less than £16,000 (but this does not include the value of your home). The amount that you get depends on your age and on the age of the children living with you, as well as any other income that you have coming into the house.

The first £6,000 of capital is ignored. If your capital is worth between £6,000.01 and £16,000 (inclusive), what you receive by way of Income Support will be affected by the assumption that you have a weekly income of £1 for every £250 (or part of £250) over £6,000.

From April 2010 any maintenance a lone parent receives does not effect their benefit entitlement.

HELP WITH THE MORTGAGE

If you pay a mortgage, you can have some help with the interest, but not the capital repayments. This is called Support for Mortgage Interest (SMI). Due to the economic downturn there were significant temporary changes made to SMI from 5 January 2009. It is not known how long those changes will remain in place.

The maximum mortgage loan taken into account was £100,000, but is currently, under the temporary changes to SMI, £200,000. Payments on a loan above that figure will not be met by the DWP.

This is only a brief summary of the rules, which are complicated. The DWP publishes helpful advice on their website, and the benefits office will give you precise advice about your own situation.

If your mortgage does not qualify for help, you may be covered by the terms of an insurance policy. You will need to check the terms of the policy carefully; most cover redundancy but not family breakdown. Moreover, most policies do not kick in immediately, and when they do they may run only for a fixed period, such as two years.

JOBSEEKER'S ALLOWANCE

Jobseeker's Allowance is another state benefit you may be eligible for. To qualify, you must be unemployed or working on average fewer than 16 hours per week.

To apply, get a claim pack from your local Jobcentre Plus or social security office. This has the claim form in it along with a Jobsearch Plan. You will have to attend an interview and take the forms with you. The interviewer draws up a Jobseeker's Agreement with you.

❝Income support claimants are entitled to help with rent or mortgage, but there are limits.❞

The rates at which the benefit is paid are the same as for Income Support, and you will qualify for Housing Benefit and Council Tax Benefit as well.

CHILD TAX CREDIT AND WORKING TAX CREDIT

These two tax credits support families with children and working people on low incomes. All families with children can claim. You can get a tax credit if your joint income is up to about £50,000, and rather more if you have a baby under 12 months old. You can check your eligibility on the HM Customs and Revenue (HMRC) website or by contacting the Tax Credit Helpline, 0845 300 3900.

You do not have to work to claim Child Tax Credit. If you are not in work, the Child Tax Credit is paid in addition to any Income Support or Jobseeker's Allowance that you are entitled to for yourself. Child tax credit is paid for children up to 16 years old and for 16–19-year-olds who are in full-time education or on an approved training course.

Only the family with the main responsibility for the children can

 Go to www.hmrc.gov.uk for general information on tax credits.

claim the credit, so if the children's time is divided fairly evenly between both parents, you will need to negotiate this. HMRC will decide who is entitled to the credit if there is a dispute. This benefit cannot be split by HMRC, in the same way as Child Benefit cannot be split.

In addition to Child Tax Credit you can claim Working Tax Credit if you are working 16 hours or more a week and have the responsibility for at least one child. You can claim an element of child-care costs if they are provided by a 'registered' or 'approved' scheme. If you don't have children and are 25 or over, you must work at least 30 hours a week.

Your capital is generally disregarded unless it produces an income for you. Income is generally taken into account only if it is taxable, so maintenance payments – whether voluntary or via the CSA – will not count. If you are entitled to these tax credits you can also claim a range of other fringe benefits, such as free dental care and prescriptions. The HMRC Leaflet WTC6 sets these out in full.

Applying for tax credits

You can apply by contacting your local HMRC office or Jobcentre Plus office for a form, or by making an online application on the HMRC website.

❝ If you have more money coming in than the allowances and premiums that you qualify for under DWP regulations, you will receive less Housing Benefit. ❞

HOUSING BENEFIT

Housing Benefit is available if you are living in rented accommodation. If you claim Income Support or Jobseeker's Allowance, you can claim Housing Benefit at the same time via the DWP. Otherwise, you make the claim to your local authority.

If your landlord is the local authority, the amount of rent will be reduced directly. If you pay to a private landlord, the benefit is paid to you by cheque or a direct payment into your bank or building society.

Housing Benefit is assessed for a period of up to 60 weeks at a time, but may be shorter if your tenancy ends during that period, or if the local authority has other arrangements. The maximum that you can get is 100 per cent of the 'eligible rent', which is not necessarily the amount that you pay to your landlord.

You will need to get detailed advice from your local benefit office or from the Citizens Advice Bureau about the calculation.

COUNCIL TAX BENEFIT

If you claim Income Support or Jobseeker's Allowance, you can claim Council Tax Benefit at the same time. The maximum that you can get is the whole of your council tax bill, subject to restrictions.

As for Housing Benefit, if you have more money coming in than the allowances and premiums that you qualify for under DWP regulations, you will receive less Council Tax Benefit.

LOANS FROM THE SOCIAL FUND

If you have been receiving Income Support or Jobseeker's Allowance for at least 26 weeks, you may be able to get payments from the social fund for items of capital expenditure that would be too large to meet out of your income.

There are different kinds of loan. To spread the payment for an exceptional expense you could get a 'budgeting loan'. This could be for rent in advance or for removal expenses to new, secure accommodation, or to assist with the costs of looking for or starting work – including childcare costs. Budgeting loans are for sums between £100 and £1,500. Any award is reduced by capital over £1,000. The loan is interest-free but is repayable, usually within 104 weeks (two years), with the repayments coming out of the Income Support or Jobseeker's Allowance paid to you.

You can also get a 'crisis loan' for emergencies or as a consequence of a disaster, if there is no other way of meeting the needs. The fund officer at the DWP will want to be satisfied that the loan is the only way of preventing serious damage or risk to the health or safety of you or your family. Social fund loans come out of a fixed budget; if the fund has reached its limit for the year, your application may be refused on these grounds alone.

THE IMPACT OF BENEFITS

Receipt of financial help from the state may make the income position more comfortable for you, and give you options to enable you to afford to stay in your home and meet your income needs.

It is important you remember that welfare benefits are always susceptible to review by the government and so any change in your circumstances (such as a new partner or change to your job), can have a significant impact on your eligibility to receive assistance. If you know there are about to be changes that would affect your benefit entitlement, ensure you make this clear in your application to avoid having benefits recouped from you at a later stage, which may have a dramatic impact on your income.

Once negotiations with your ex have concluded about capital/income payments that you will make to each other, you should also update your application as this could change the amount of benefits you are entitled to receive.

45

Managing debts

Getting into debt has become a common problem. For many families, the financial issues involved in a split are less about dividing up assets than about dealing with the heavy burden of debts and who will, or should, take them on. Often, the stresses caused by financial debts can themselves be the cause of the family break-up.

WHO IS RESPONSIBLE?

Broadly speaking, an ex will not be responsible for debts incurred by the other person alone. But there are exceptions: an ex will usually be responsible for the other's unpaid council tax bills and sometimes other outgoings on the home. You also share responsibility for joint debts, say from a joint account, or for joint mortgage repayments or rent. The debts of one party can also impact upon their needs within the divorce/dissolution proceedings, and so may affect any distribution of capital considered reasonable (see Chapter 9).

If your ex has left the home leaving behind high unpaid household bills, the date of separation is important. If he or she has failed to pay the council tax, you must inform the local authority of the date of separation and thus at least cut off your responsibility for paying your ex's share of the council tax debt accruing after that. Your council tax bill will also be reduced if there is now only one adult living in the home.

By advising the gas, electricity and telephone companies, you can also get the meters read as near to the separation date as possible and ask for a transfer of the accounts into your own name. This will, obviously, leave you with having to pay future bills and so may not be appropriate, but it can be one way of avoiding responsibility for some previously built-up debts.

If on the other hand you are paying maintenance to your ex, but he or she is not paying the bills, this leaves you in difficulty. As long as your name is on the account, the primary responsibility is yours. If the agreement is that your ex will pay the bills, make sure that

 For further advice about debts, try contacting the National Debtline: www. nationaldebtline.co.uk You can also find advice from the Office of Fair Trading: www.oft.gov.uk and the Council of Mortgage Lenders: www.cml.org.uk

the relevant accounts are transferred into his or her name.

WORKING OUT DEBT REPAYMENTS

The first step is to assess the priority of debts with the help of expert counselling. You will probably be advised not simply to pay off the creditor who shouts the loudest.

Don't avoid debt

Although it may be tempting to try to avoid your creditors, you may well find that by contacting them and showing that you are willing to try to repay them you can work out a realistic level of repayment.

Also, it will be less expensive for them to agree a repayment with you than to incur extra legal costs in having to take you to court.

If things go too far

If you find it impossible to pay off your debts or to repay a creditor to whom you owe over £750, you could ask the court to make a bankruptcy order. If you take this action yourself it will cost you a deposit of £360 plus court fees of £150.

There is an exemption from the court fee if you are on Income Support or income-based Jobseeker's Allowance, or are getting the maximum Working Families' Tax Credit. Check with the court for details. You will thus largely be relieved of the burden of your creditors.

However, once you are made bankrupt there are limitations: you cannot hold a bank account or obtain credit of over £500 without disclosing your bankruptcy, nor be a company director (or a solicitor, for example). Depending on the circumstances, most bankrupts are discharged after one year, when they have a clean sheet.

But even if you think this is the only way out of your debts, obtain legal advice before going ahead.

❝ Creditors will very often accept a reduced payment made regularly rather than nothing at all, and will feel happier knowing that you have not fled the country. ❞

 For further information on bankruptcy, see the helpful government website: www.insolvency.gov.uk

47

Joint accounts and credit cards

With a joint bank or building-society account on which either of you can draw, there is the risk that the account could be cleared out by one of you, or an overdraft used to its maximum, without the other knowing about it. To prevent this, you can ask the bank or building-society manager to change the arrangement so that cheques can be drawn only with both signatures. Alternatively, you could ask for the account to be frozen (although then neither of you would be able to draw out funds).

Similarly, where each of you has a credit card or cash-withdrawal card for drawing against one account, it is usually wiser, from the main cardholder's point of view, to put a stop on the cards.

You must tell the card company and send back the cards (including, if possible, your ex's card). A new card will then be issued to the main cardholder only.

Your rights and the family home

If you are considering a divorce/dissolution, you should think about whether, as a precautionary measure, you need to protect your interest in the family home. After all, it will almost certainly be your biggest asset. You also need to consider how the property is registered and whether to change this, if you are married or not.

 Home rights only apply to married/cp couples.

HOME RIGHTS

Home rights are in essence short-term rights which exist while the marriage/cp lasts (until the final decree of divorce/dissolution). The long-term decisions about the rights to live in the home, or to get a share of the proceeds if it is sold, will have to be made as part of the financial settlement.

If violence has been threatened or used against you, making it unsafe for you to live in the family home, you can apply to the court to protect yourself (as described in Chapter 7). You can sometimes gain an occupation order that can exclude your spouse/cp or allow you to re-enter the home. The court will also be able to make an occupation order overriding a person's home rights.

Home rights

The spouse/cp who does not legally own the family home – that is, whose name is not on the title deeds – has certain 'home rights':
- The right not to be evicted without a court order if he or she is in occupation.
- The right (if the court thinks fit) to return to the home if he or she has left it.
- The right (if the court thinks fit) to exclude the owner spouse/cp from occupying the home for a period (usually only when violence has occurred).

The same occupation rights apply if the home is rented. They can also apply to a property that the couple intended to use as their home, but which they never actually occupied.

REGISTERING HOME RIGHTS: OWNER-OCCUPIED HOMES

If you are a joint owner of the family home, you do not need to do anything to register your home rights separately. Third parties (for example, a potential buyer or mortgagee) will become aware of your interest when they carry out a search of the property title, so your spouse/cp cannot try to sell or mortgage the property without your consent.

However, if your spouse/cp, not you, is the sole owner of the family home, you must register your home rights to ensure that they are protected against third parties.

How you register your home rights depends on whether the title to the family home is 'registered' or 'unregistered'.

Jargon buster

'Registered' means registered at the Land Registry. Most homes will have titles registered at the Land Registry, as the whole of England and Wales is now subject to compulsory registration of title. However, if your home was until recently in an area of voluntary registration, and you bought it some time ago, the title to your home may not yet have been registered.

The Legal Help scheme

The Legal Help scheme allows for a solicitor to deal with registration of a land charge or a notice if you are financially eligible. All Citizens Advice Bureau (CAB) can help with filling in the forms to register home rights and some have a supply of the necessary forms.

If the title is registered

The district Land Registry for your area will advise you how to register your matrimonial home rights and should provide the various forms and tell you about the procedure.

The application is made on form HC1, which needs to be sent to the Land Registry office that deals with the area the property is in. If the application is in order a notice will be registered against the property and your spouse/cp will receive written notice that this has been done.

If the title is unregistered

You should apply to register an entry against your spouse/cp's name, called a Class F Land Charge. The form to be used, K2, is available from law stationers' shops and the fee for registration is £1 per name.

 The easiest way to check if the home is registered is to use the Land Registry website: www.landregisteronline.gov.uk

The information required includes the full name in which the property-owning spouse/cp bought or acquired the property. If you are unsure of the precise name shown on the documents, register the charge against all possible permutations; for example – John Smith, J Smith, John Peter Smith, J P Smith. The charge is ineffective unless it is in exactly the right name.

If you are in any doubt, or time is short, apply to register at both the Land Registry and the Land Charges Department until you have sorted out the position. If you find that the title is registered, you should cancel the charge at the Land Charges Department.

IF YOU REGISTER A CHARGE OR NOTICE

Anyone buying the property or granting a mortgage on it would, as a matter of routine, check the appropriate registry and discover your notice or charge protecting your rights. (Even if a buyer or mortgagee does not actually search the register or has no knowledge of the registration, the effect of registering a land charge or notice amounts in law to notice of a non-owning spouse's/cp's home rights.)

If the house is then bought or mortgaged, this is done subject to your home rights and the buyer or mortgagee

cannot turn you out unless you have agreed to give up your rights.

The effect of registration normally ceases once a decree of divorce is made final. If the question of the family home has not been settled by then, the non-owning spouse/cp should ask the court, before the decree is made final, for the registration of the Class F Land Charge or the notice to be renewed after the final decree. If this is granted, further forms need to be submitted to the Land Registry or at the Land Charges Department.

Alternatively, if you are making a claim for a share of a property, you should register a 'pending action' claim, which similarly puts third parties on notice of your interest.

FINDING OUT IF YOUR SPOUSE/CP OWNS A SECOND HOME

Sometimes there may be good reason to suspect that your spouse/cp has bought another home – say if he or she has moved in with a new partner in a newly bought home that he or she says belongs to the new partner. You can now easily check this on the Land Registry website, if you have the address of the property.

If your suspicions are confirmed and your spouse/cp is shown as a legal

 'Protecting Home Rights under the Family Law Act 1996 (Public Guide 4)' from HM Land Registry: www.landregistry.gov.uk This gives detailed information and instructions about protecting your home rights.

owner, once you have made financial claims in the divorce proceedings you may also be able to register a 'pending action' claim on the title of the second property if you think that your spouse/cp may try to sell it to avoid paying money.

> **!** This section applies to all couples who are joint owners of a property; you do not need to be married.

MOVING OUT

If you hope eventually to have the home to live in permanently, it is tactically best to try to stay there if possible. Even if you are not planning to remain in the long term but want to persuade your spouse/cp to make other financial provisions for you, staying put may help you in your negotiations.

However, the strategy of staying put can sometimes be counterproductive: remaining at close quarters with your spouse/cp once the decision to separate has been made can give rise to tensions that may undermine the prospect of successful negotiations. It may be helpful to discuss with your solicitor the pros and cons of moving out, whether on a temporary or a permanent basis.

It may be tempting, if the situation between you and your spouse/cp has become very volatile, to lock him/her out of the home while he or she is away. However, remember that your spouse/cp has home rights, that is, a right to occupy the home, at least while the marriage is in being. They can apply to the court for an order restoring to him or her the right to occupy the home.

SEVERING A JOINT TENANCY

If you own your home (or any other land or buildings) jointly, you need to check whether the property is held under a 'joint tenancy' or a 'tenancy in common'. If you have a mortgage, ask your lender. If you do not, you will need to look at the title deeds or the Land Certificate. Ask a solicitor to check the point for you.

Some solicitors advise separating couples to end a joint tenancy and,

Jargon buster

Joint tenancy Under a joint tenancy, each person's interest in the property is not quantified: you own the whole of the house (or flat) jointly. When one of you dies, the whole property automatically passes to the survivor, irrespective of any provision the former may have made in a will.

Tenancy in common Under a tenancy in common, on the other hand, the interests of each person are fixed (usually on a 50:50 basis, but it can be in any proportion) and separate, so that each person can separately dispose of his or her share by will.

pending a financial settlement or a court order, divide your respective interests in the property by becoming tenants in common. This will not affect your day-to-day status as co-owners, but if one of you dies the deceased's share of the property would be part of his/her estate, distributed under the terms of his/her will or according to the rules of intestacy.

If you are married/cp, the intestacy rules make your spouse/cp your next of kin until the final decree of divorce. If you are not married your partner will never be treated as your next of kin.

However, there is also the risk that if your ex were to die in the meantime, you would lose the chance that you would have had of inheriting his/her share of the home when it was held under a joint tenancy.

You will have to weigh up the risks both for and against – there is no clear-cut right or wrong course of action applicable to all. Whether it would be in your interest to sever the joint tenancy is something you should first discuss with a solicitor. If you do decide to sever the tenancy either of you can do this by sending a 'notice of severance' to the other owner at any time. A notice of severance will convert your ownership from a joint tenancy into a tenancy in common.

A notice of severance

The notice can simply take the form of a letter stating: 'Please accept this letter as notice of my desire to sever as from this day the joint tenancy in our property known as [insert address of property] now held by us as joint tenants both at law and in equity so that henceforth the said property shall belong to us as tenants in common in equal shares.' You should sign and date the letter and send it to your spouse/cp/co-owner. You should keep a copy of the letter.

 If you sever a tenancy, you must make a will stating where you want your share of the property to go.

Sorting out finances

When divorce proceedings have been started there are lots of options and remedies available to a spouse/cp to deal with how assets will be divided, and any maintenance that should be paid (see Chapter 9). If there are no divorce proceedings underway, the options available range from informal agreements to the use of the court, but court powers are not on such an extensive scale as they are when divorce proceedings exist. If you are cohabiting the options are more limited, but do include a separation agreement and the court options outlined in Chapter 10.

The remedies that are available, if there are no divorce proceedings, are:

- A separation agreement, which can be informal or formal.
- If things cannot be agreed, an application can be made to the magistrates' court or the county court for maintenance for you, an application for children or/and any step-children, or a request to the CSA for a maintenance assessment, before divorce proceedings are issued.

Informal agreed arrangements

Many couples manage to separate successfully and agree who will pay for what, including the maintenance for any children. If you can successfully agree between you, you do not need to have a formal agreement or an order. However, you should be aware that there is no way of enforcing the agreement, which may cause problems if the payer is unreliable. Most of such arrangements are on a short-term basis only, and it may seem unduly complicated and costly (if lawyers are involved) to formalise the agreement in a written separation agreement.

However, if the separation is going to be long term – for instance, if you propose to separate for two years and then divorce on this basis – it is probably a good idea to draw up a formal separation agreement. A separation agreement not only makes the arrangement more certain, but if certain formalities are complied with you can refer to the agreement at court, which may be useful if your ex does not keep to the agreement.

Cohabitants can use separation agreements as well as married/ cp couples, but they tend to be less common. This is because there is no right to adult maintenance if you are unmarried and therefore a maintenance arrangement between an unmarried couple is quite rare.

Formal separation agreements

Separation agreements are sometimes referred to as 'deeds'. Technically, a legal document is a deed if it is made 'under seal'. There is no longer a requirement for traditional wax or round red stickers to be put on the document, but your signatures must be formally witnessed.

The document should generally be drawn up as a deed if 'real' property (houses and land) is being transferred between you, or if it contains a financial obligation that you might later want to enforce.

To ensure that a separation agreement does have effective legal force it should be made only once you are both sure that you know all about each other's financial position: what you earn, what you own and what you owe.

It would be sensible for you each to consult a solicitor for advice and ask a solicitor to draft the agreement. A mediation service can also help you to negotiate the terms of the agreement.

Separation agreements are usually fairly flexible in content and are designed to cover the particular things that you want to deal with. A typical deed will probably cover the following issues:

- That you have decided you want to live separately, and the date on which the separation started (this date is useful for tax purposes and also for later evidence to the court of the period of your separation).
- Agreements about where and with which parent the children will make their main home. You can also deal with contact arrangements if you want them fixed, or simply express a joint intention that contact will be frequent, and state whether or not the children will stay overnight.
- Who is going to live in the family home, or whether it is going to be sold and how the proceeds are going to be divided.
- Who is going to pay for what in the future.
- How any joint assets are going to be divided and if there are to be transfers of assets from one party to the other.
- Who is going to be responsible for any family debts that exist.
- Maintenance for the children.
- For married/cp couples, maintenance from one spouse/cp to the other.
- Division of the contents of the family home.
- Ownership of other assets, such as the car.

If you are married/cp the agreement can also contain an expression of your intention about whether there will eventually be divorce proceedings.

Although part of the reason for making a separation agreement is to avoid being unduly legalistic, you need to make sure that anything you agree to will not have unwanted long-term consequences. Transfers of property or large assets at this stage may have implications for Capital Gains Tax. All the financial arrangements may be considered by the court (in later divorce proceedings for instance). You need to take legal advice as to whether you are making a commitment that is sensible, and how the agreement would be treated by the court later.

Most people would like to think that the separation agreement would remove the possibility of any later legal argument in court. But, if you are married/cp the court will not let its powers to make orders be removed by private agreement, so you cannot make a binding promise that you will never invoke the power of the court at a later stage. However, the court will be inclined to uphold an agreement that both parties have made if they both had legal advice at the time that they made it, that the financial disclosure on both sides had been full and frank, and that it is a fair and reasonable agreement.

If one of you does not keep to the separation agreement, it is possible to go to the court to enforce the agreement. This does not happen very often, but it can be done in certain circumstances.

MAINTENANCE FOR A SPOUSE OR CIVIL PARTNER

If an agreement about maintenance is breached it may be easier to make a court application for maintenance, as outlined below. This, in itself, is probably enough sanction to encourage most people to keep to the arrangements that they have agreed together.

Magistrates' court – Family Proceedings Panel

You can apply to the magistrates' court for maintenance for yourself and a lump sum order up to £1,000. There is no limit on the amount of maintenance that the court can order. You can also apply more than once for a lump sum – there is no limit on the number of applications in the legislation. The court can also order a lump-sum payment of up to £1,000 for each child.

You can make this application yourself; you do not have to have a solicitor to help you. If you are eligible for Legal Help (see Chapter 1), your solicitor can assist you with this. You can go to the court to get the application form yourself and the court staff will help you to fill it in, but they cannot give you legal advice. No fee is charged for this.

There is a straightforward form on which you set out your financial position. In order to qualify for an order you have to establish that your spouse/cp:

- Has failed to provide reasonable maintenance for you or to make a proper contribution towards the children of the family (see below), or
- Has deserted you, or behaved in such a way that you cannot reasonably be expected to live with him or her (such behaviour could include adultery).

Once you have made your 'complaint', the court will fix a day for the hearing and issue a summons to your spouse/cp, who has to be given at least 21 days' notice of the hearing.

If you manage to agree a maintenance order before or at the hearing, the court will make an order in those terms, provided it seems to be appropriate. If the order is agreed, a capital sum can be ordered that is more than the £1,000 limit. If you cannot agree, the court will hear evidence from both of you about your financial positions and will then order what it thinks is a reasonable sum.

Normally you will have to wait between one and two months for the hearing to come to court. If you need an order more urgently than this, you should explain this to the court when you make the 'complaint' and the court can be asked to fix an expedited hearing, or to make an interim order to tide you over till a full hearing can be given. An interim order can last for a maximum of three months, which should give time for a full hearing to take place.

The county court

The alternative to the magistrates' court – and this traditionally makes orders which are rather on the low side – is to make an application to the county court under Section 27 of the Matrimonial Causes Act or Schedule 5 of the Civil Partnership Act 2004. The fee for this is £200. You have to satisfy the court that your spouse/cp has failed to provide reasonable maintenance for you (or a child of the family). The application must be accompanied by a sworn statement setting out your resources and needs.

In theory legal aid should be available for such an application, but the Legal Services Commission (LSC) will probably

Court orders

The factors the court must take into account in making an order:
- The welfare of any child of the family.
- Your incomes and earning capacities.
- Your needs, obligations and responsibilities
- Your ages.
- Any physical and mental disabilities.
- The duration of the marriage.
- The previous standard of living.
- The contribution that each of you has made to the family.
- If it would be inequitable to disregard it, the conduct of either party.

want you to use the magistrates' court if at all possible as the costs are lower, so your solicitor will have to justify why the county court would be preferable.

You, or your solicitor, will have to serve your spouse/cp with the application and your statement. He or she, in turn, should file a financial statement in reply within 14 days of receiving yours. The court will fix a hearing, which will be heard in private.

The court procedure described in Chapter 9 will apply to this type of application as well. This means that there will be a First Appointment and a Financial Dispute Resolution Appointment (see Chapter 9 for details) if the case proceeds.

Given the length of time that this application takes, and its cost, it is probably not a good idea to make it unless you know that you are not intending to get divorced or if a long-term separation is planned. Otherwise you are simply going to duplicate the proceedings and run up the costs you will incur, as these issues could all be resolved within divorce proceedings.

Child Support Agency

Once you have separated and your spouse/cp is not living in the same household as the children, the CSA has jurisdiction to assess the maintenance that should be paid for any children you have together. All the details are set out in Chapter 6.

Children Act application

You can apply under the Children Act 1989 for financial orders for the children of the family at any time. If you think that you are going to be filing divorce proceedings reasonably soon, maybe within a year, then it is probably not a good idea to start Children Act proceedings as they will simply duplicate the financial proceedings under the divorce and add to the costs.

Financial applications and domestic abuse

If you need to get an injunction to protect yourself from abuse it is possible to ask the court to make an order to cover payment of outgoings – like rent or mortgage payments – at the same time as it makes an occupation order (see Chapter 7). This short-circuits the previous necessity of having to make a separate application to the court for financial support to cover basic running costs for the home.

Getting legal advice

While a do-it-yourself divorce can be relatively straightforward if you and your spouse/cp can reach an amicable agreement, you will almost certainly need a solicitor's help if this is impossible. If nothing else, you should seek legal advice to prevent you giving up any rights that you have simply because you do not understand the law.

What a solicitor can do for you

If there are going to be questions about dividing property or sorting out arrangements for the children, it is a good idea to have at least one meeting with a solicitor so that you can get some early advice. This may prevent matters from becoming complicated, or one of you getting less than his or her entitlement, and can generally help to take the heat out of the situation as you will be aware of your rights and responsibilities.

If you can sort out your financial affairs between yourselves or with the help of a mediator (see Chapter 4), so much the better. However, it is still wise for you both to ask a solicitor whether the arrangements seem fair, and to ensure that they are framed in a watertight manner so as not to leave you open for future unexpected financial claims, and so that they do not result in any unnecessary payments of tax. This can ensure that what follows is as you both had intended.

If you are intending to use mediation as the primary means of sorting out your arrangements comprehensively, ask your solicitor about his or her attitude towards this. Some solicitors have been trained as mediators themselves, or are likely to have a constructive approach towards agreements worked out through mediation, as long as they do not work against your (and the family's) best interests.

However, there are a few, perhaps more old-fashioned, solicitors who may

Using a solicitor
If it is not possible for the two of you to achieve a fair agreement on your own or using a mediator, a solicitor can negotiate on your behalf. It is not possible for you and your spouse/partner to instruct the same solicitor, or firm of solicitors, as there is a potential conflict of interest between you. So you will both need to see independent solicitors.

be instinctively anti-mediation and they may not be helpful in advising you objectively if you do reach arrangements in this way.

DECIDE WHAT'S BEST
A solicitor can be of great help, but try to use his or her services efficiently

and economically. Ask yourself whether you want to obtain legal advice or want someone to 'fight' for you. Wanting a solicitor to act for you in a contentious way will involve you in expense that may be out of proportion to anything gained. It is also not at all cost-effective to use a solicitor as an emotional support, whatever the temptations, as this is not a good use of your money.

Time and money are invariably interlinked. The more you use a solicitor's services, the greater the hole that will be cut into your family finances. What a solicitor can effectively do for you is explained in detail in this chapter. It is of the utmost importance that you consider the question of costs before launching into a major battle. Spending an hour or so (at the very least) with an experienced and competent solicitor to get advice on your legal position is likely to be a worthwhile investment.

Of course, how much you want to (or are forced to) involve your solicitor may be constrained by how much you can afford to pay. Explanations and warnings about the problem of costs have already been given. If you have not already done so, read Chapter 1 now.

HANDLING YOUR DIVORCE

It is possible to handle an undefended divorce yourself without a solicitor, although it is probably fair to say that

❝ If your spouse/cp refuses to cooperate in any way, or you receive a divorce petition, obtaining a solicitor's advice would certainly be useful. ❞

it is at least as hard as doing your own conveyancing on your house (and the financial pitfalls can be worse if something goes wrong). Do-it-yourself divorce packs are widely available but the packs may contain out-of-date forms, so you should double-check these with the court. Be wary of taking important steps without legal advice: the packs can give you general but not individual advice, which can be provided only by solicitors or a Citizens Advice Bureau (CAB).

Be particularly wary of the common assumption that getting a divorce means an end to your financial obligations to your spouse/cp. Divorce and money matters are considered quite separately by the court, and getting a divorce does not mean an automatic end to your money concerns.

Do not be led by advice from friends who are not legally trained in this area, but who may feel that they are experts because they have gone through the process themselves. Remember that every case is different and advice that is specific to your particular situation can be very valuable.

 You can also download forms and information leaflets from: www.hmscourts-service. gov.uk Your local county court can also supply you with copies of these.

Sorting out problems over children

Protracted litigation over the children can be extremely expensive. Also, it is harmful both to the children and to you, and rarely produces a satisfactory result. If you cannot come to an agreement by yourselves or through mediation, see if you can arrange a meeting for both of you and your solicitors. A good solicitor will be able to give you sensible advice about the way in which you should deal with the arrangements for the children, and about the attitude that a court would take if you felt that you had to resolve a dispute by going to court.

Disputes over children cannot be 'won' or 'lost', and ultimately you are likely to prefer a solution that you reach yourselves, rather than have to accept one imposed upon you by a judge who, however wise and well meaning, does not – and cannot – know you or your children.

Getting a court order for maintenance and division of property

A solicitor will know the appropriate court for the particular order you need and the procedure for applying. He or she will be able to advise you on the attitude that the court will take and your prospects of success. This will help you to decide if a particular application is appropriate or worth spending money on.

Getting information about finances

You may find that you are faced with a long, uphill battle to get financial information out of your spouse/cp. However reasonable you want to be over things, and whatever you do, he or she may refuse to disclose assets.

Withholding information at the early stages of financial negotiations does nothing but run up costs and reduce the amount that there is to go around. If you go to see a solicitor, your spouse/cp may then do so, too, and may be persuaded to come clean about details of his or her financial situation. You will both need to disclose your finances fully to each other before a proper agreement can be reached.

Sorting out cohabitation problems

Although these fall generally within the scope of family law, not all solicitors have much experience or knowledge about the law as it relates to cohabiting couples. If you have an argument about the ownership or entitlement to the home, you need to find a solicitor who does know about this area of law and understands the specific trust and property law involved.

Getting an agreement about finances

Good solicitors will impress upon both of you the advantages of cooperation and will help you to negotiate an agreement about finances.

Other solicitor's services

A solicitor can also:

- Put an agreement into wording that is clear and will be acceptable to the court.
- Arrange maintenance and the division of property in a more tax-efficient way.
- Draw up a 'clean-break' settlement where appropriate (particularly where there are no young children).
- Point out things that you may not have thought of: for example, that one of you may be losing substantial widow(er)'s pension rights under the other's pension scheme.
- Explain how the pension law works.
- Take into account the effects of any proposed order on welfare benefits entitlements.

If your resources leave very limited room for manoeuvre, fighting it out in court may not be worthwhile. It is pointless getting your solicitor to try to push for more, or less, if the cost of getting it is going to be more than the amount you are asking for. If money disputes go on for months or years, the costs will run into thousands of pounds even where small amounts are in dispute. Even if you are in receipt of legal aid and do not initially have to pay your solicitor's charges as they arise, you have to do so ultimately under the statutory charge (see Chapter 1).

If you have reached an agreement with your ex and the issues seem fairly clear cut, it may still be worthwhile considering having one interview with a solicitor to check over the terms of that proposed agreement, particularly if you have reached agreement only about the broad outlines of how you are going to split your finances. Sadly, agreements, especially unwritten ones, have a habit of unravelling over time unless all their consequences are thought through and the agreements recorded officially to reflect what you agree.

A note of warning is relevant at this point. Sometimes couples go to their solicitors with an agreement that they have worked out and are disappointed when the solicitors – very properly – point out the pitfalls concealed within the agreement as it stands. They then blame the solicitors for 'messing things up'. This is to misunderstand the solicitor's role. Solicitors are trained, and paid, to look for the flaws in agreements and attempt to make them watertight. If you have worked out an agreement without first taking legal advice, you may find that you have not taken into account all the long-term legal and practical implications for the future. If your solicitor points them out, he or she is not being unreasonably perverse, but is doing a proper job and acting in your best interests to save you from issues or problems that could be very costly later on.

Formalizing an agreement need not jeopardise amicable relations with your spouse/partner: indeed, doing so could pave the way for a less painful split.

The right solicitor

Before you embark on the search for a solicitor, it is worth considering what he or she can and cannot do for you, and keeping in mind the criteria that you are going to use to help you make your choice. It may be easiest first to define what your solicitor should not be.

Not a hired gun

A solicitor is not (or should not be used as) a hired gun. He or she should be prepared to give you balanced, practical advice, not simply tell you what you want to hear. It is possible that in certain matters you are not right, and your solicitor should retain a degree of professional detachment in your relationship so that he or she can point your error out to you, fairly and sympathetically, so that you are armed with the right information to decide how you want to proceed.

Not a counsellor

A solicitor will give you advice, but he or she is not your counsellor, in the sense of being a therapist. Good solicitors will inevitably have acquired some counselling skills – or even have some counselling training – but that is not their primary function when they are dealing with your split.

If you need counselling or therapy, you should go to someone who is properly qualified to provide this for you in a therapeutic environment. Using your solicitor in this way will prove very expensive and will interfere with what he or she needs to do for you. Your solicitor may well suggest that counselling might help, and may even be able to recommend someone who is skilled in dealing with the area of family breakdown.

Not a friend

Your solicitor is not your friend, though a good solicitor will have a friendly manner and be kind and sympathetic. Resist the temptation to be too intimate in your relationship. There needs to be a certain amount of professional detachment between the two of you, for your good as much as for the solicitor's. Pushing the relationship to friendship will probably result in longer conversations – and greater expense for you.

If you have a friend who is a solicitor it may be possible to instruct him or her. However, you may find that such a friend would prefer not to act for you, even though he or she will offer you supportive general advice.

WHAT TO LOOK FOR IN A SOLICITOR

What people want in a solicitor varies tremendously – a solicitor who is perfect for one person may not be ideal for another. Before you start looking for one, it is worth thinking about the sort of person that you would like to act for you.

You may have certain personal preferences: would you, for example, feel more comfortable with a solicitor of the same gender as you? Would you like him or her to be older than you? Do you want to be steered by your solicitor or do you want to 'direct' him or her? Clearly, the qualities, both professional and personal, of the solicitor are crucial.

The following factors are indicators of a good solicitor:

- **Intelligence and thoughtfulness.** These are probably more crucial than experience. A good family solicitor will be inclined to approach your difficulties with your ex in a constructive way, exploring whether an amicable solution can be achieved. But this does not mean he or she should be a pushover – your solicitor should be prepared to be tough on your behalf if need be. However, be wary of any solicitor who talks in swaggering terms (for example, 'We'll take your husband for every penny he has'). However hell-bent you are on revenge, you must bear in mind that an overly aggressive approach is going to be enormously expensive and, very often, counterproductive.

- **Organization and efficiency.** Look at the way in which the solicitor's firm presents itself – is the phone answered promptly? Does the secretary seem sensible, and does he or she take down a proper message? Are your calls returned as promised? Do you know who will take a phone call if the solicitor is not in the office?

- **Their office environment.** Solicitors' offices are busy places to work, but if they are downright dirty and depressing and nobody has made any effort to make the waiting room a reasonable place to sit in, it can speak volumes about the firm's attitude to its clients.

- **Good communication.** Does the solicitor treat you like a human being, or as just a problem to be processed? Are you listened to politely and carefully? Does he or she behave in a professional manner? For example, other clients' paperwork should not be left out where you can see it.

If you are not happy with your solicitor it is probably best to change to another one early on in the case. Even if you are legally aided you can still change solicitors, but you would need to explain to the Legal Services Commission (LSC) why you were not happy and why you needed to change, and get the transfer of the certificate agreed.

"It helps if your solicitor is experienced in family law, but this is not crucial in a team or department setting where there are experienced staff to turn to if the need arises. "

Unprofessional behaviour
You should not have to put up with unprofessional behaviour from your solicitor. When you are feeling unhappy because of your family situation, it is easy to feel that you just have to take what you find, particularly if you are legally aided. However, this is absolutely not the case and you should not have to accept unprofessional conduct of any kind.

FINDING A SOLICITOR

It may be that a solicitor you have used in the past for some other matter (for example, buying a house) does family work or has a colleague who does. It might be worth asking and having a preliminary discussion on the telephone. However, if he or she has previously acted for both you and your ex,

professional rules say that he or she may not be able to act for you (or your ex) because of the potential for 'conflict of interest'.

Ask acquaintances who have been through a family split whom they used, although you should be wary of recommendations in cases which are very different from your own. It is also worthwhile making enquiries at your local CAB or advice centre, or even your local county court (each court keeps a list of solicitors who appear before the court). The Law Society's Regional Directories of solicitors practising in the area and showing the categories of the work they undertake are available at the CAB, public libraries and court offices throughout the UK. The Directories and CAB should also be able to point you in the direction of lawyers who have LSC contracts if you are seeking legal aid.

Resolution (which used to be called the Solicitors Family Law Association) is a very good source for tracking down a specialist family lawyer. It is an association of over 5,500 matrimonial lawyers in England and Wales who must subscribe to a code of practice (which you can read on their website) designed to encourage and assist parties to reach acceptable arrangements for the future in a positive and conciliatory – rather than in an aggressive and litigious – way. This does not mean that a Resolution solicitor

Finding a solicitor: Community Legal Service: 0845 345 4345: www. communitylegaladvice.org.uk Law Society: 020 7242 1222: www.lawsociety.org.uk Resolution: 01689 820272: www.resolution.org.uk

will be 'soft'. His or her advice to you and manner of dealing with the various issues that arise will be positive.

Resolution can provide a list of the solicitor members in your region, or you can search the Resolution directory on its website. If there are no Resolution solicitors practising in your area, you can use the website or telephone the Records Section of the Law Society of England and Wales.

The task of finding a solicitor through the Yellow Pages and its electronic version, www.yell.co.uk, is relatively easy because in most directories there are special sections for solicitors who are members of Resolution, identified by its logo, as well as for solicitors who offer legal aid. Look under the heading 'Solicitors' (usually there is very little listed under 'Divorce').

When you first contact a firm of solicitors asking for an appointment, say that you wish to be advised in connection with your matrimonial difficulties and ask whether the firm has a solicitor who specialises in family matters, preferably one who is a member of Resolution. If you have been cohabiting, you should check the solicitor's experience in this field.

Accreditation schemes

Both the Law Society and Resolution have accreditation schemes for family lawyers. To be a member of the Resolution scheme a person has to:

- Have been a solicitor for at least five years (or a Fellow of the Institute of Legal Executives).

- Pass a special examination.
- Have worked at least half of his or her working hours over the past three years as a family lawyer.
- Subscribe to the code of practice.

The Law Society's Family Law Accreditation Scheme has different standards: solicitors or legal executives have to have been qualified for three years and should have worked as family lawyers for a set number of hours during the past three years.

Lawyers who are not solicitors

There are many experienced matrimonial lawyers employed by solicitors' firms who are not qualified solicitors. Previously called 'managing clerks', they are now known as 'legal executives'. Many are Fellows of the Institute of Legal Executives or are working towards qualification as Fellows. (Traditionally they came into the profession straight from school and learnt on the job. Increasingly these days they have degree-level education.) They are likely to be just as competent as the solicitors whom they work with, and the same considerations apply to them as to solicitors when you are finding someone suitable to act for you.

Jargon buster

Resolution Family lawyers association offering advice and assistance about finding a lawyer who can help you. Offers accreditation and membership to specialist family lawyers. Formerly called the Solicitors Family Law Association (SFLA).

Lawyer Someone trained in the law. Does not specifically confirm their qualification or experience.

Partner Solicitor who owns a share of the law firm. Usually senior and experienced and so likely to have a higher hourly charge.

Associate Mid-level solicitor within a law firm, who has been promoted due to their expertise or experience.

Solicitor Someone qualified to provide legal advice in England and Wales.

Legal Executive Lawyer able to provide assistance and advice, likely to be just as competent as a solicitor. The difference is the route they have taken to get to the job.

Paralegal Assistant with no specific legal qualification or experience.

Trainee Solicitor Person who has completed education but is completing their obligatory training at a law firm (usually two years in duration). Their work will be supervised by a senior member of the law firm.

Low-priced interviews

Many solicitors offer a free first interview, or one for a fixed price. Advertisements in Yellow Pages will often have this information. You can also ask your local branch of the Law Society if it knows of solicitors in your area who offer a similar service, or just ask the solicitor's office when you first call them.

Fee-earner Term used within law firms for anyone that does work that can be charged to a client.

Barrister (Counsel) Advocate instructed by a solicitor to represent you at a court hearing or give specific detailed/technical advice on any complex issues.

Mediator Impartial third party assisting in reaching a resolution without court involvement (see Chapter 4).

Collaborative Lawyer Lawyer trained to deal with matters under a specific alternative dispute resolution method (see Chapter 4).

McKenzie friend A helper (not necessarily a lawyer) who can accompany a person in a court room, but cannot address the court or examine witnesses.

 The Bar Council's Pro-Bono Unit is a scheme whereby barristers (or counsel) offer free legal advice to deserving cases: 020 7611 9500: www.barprobono.org.uk Email: enquiries@barprobono.org.uk

Getting the best out of your solicitor

Try to use your solicitor's time as efficiently as possible. A succinct letter to him or her setting out what you want to do (your 'instructions') may well be more cost-effective than a long, rambling telephone conversation.

If you can go prepared for your first interview, so much the better. Some solicitors send a questionnaire to their clients to be completed and returned before the first interview, which can save you time and money.

Documents to take with you to your first solicitor's appointment

- Your marriage/cp certificate (if you are married).
- Any correspondence or assessments from the Child Support Agency.
- Copies of any court orders made about your marriage – or about your children.
- Typed or neatly written notes setting out:
    - your name in full, and those of your spouse/partner and children
    - dates of birth of yourself, your spouse/partner and children
    - details of any children in the household who are not children of you both
    - your address and (if different) that of your spouse/partner
    - your home and work telephone numbers (and your email address if you have one)
    - your occupation and that of your spouse/partner
    - your National Insurance number (for legal aid applications)
    - names and addresses of the children's schools
    - dates of any previous marriage of yourself and/or your spouse/partner and dates of any final decrees
    - if you have already separated, the date and circumstances of the separation.
- A summary of your financial position (see Chapter 2).
- Any correspondence that you might have received from your spouse/partner's solicitor.
- Photographic identification and a utility bill confirming your address for identification purposes.

It may help to go prepared with notes of what you want to ask and then to take notes of the advice given. Indeed, this is a sensible precaution as otherwise it is all too easy to forget everything your solicitor has told you.

Remember that you can accept or reject advice as you wish. But before you reject advice, make sure that you understand the reason you have been given this advice.

Using your solicitor's time wisely and cost-effectively means not leaving it to your solicitor to do everything. Because of the time basis you will be charged on, the more time he or she spends on the case, the higher the bill will be. Quite a lot can be done by you yourself that will save costs, but you need to tell your solicitor first what you plan to do.

Open your own file at home and be organised about keeping correspondence and any relevant documents safe, and keep copies of letters that you send to your solicitor and receive from them.

You are entitled to be told at any stage how the case is progressing and how much it is costing. Your solicitor should send you a client care letter (see below) at the outset. Remember that you can ask him or her for interim statements of how costs are building up if they are not supplied automatically.

❝To use your solicitor to the best advantage, do not hesitate at any time to ask him or her to explain and discuss any points about which you are not clear.❞

Don't ignore costs
Although it can be tempting to forget about the question of costs, this is an area which you ignore at your peril. Running up hefty legal bills, whether you are paying privately or have public funding, will severely damage the ability of both you and your ex to begin your lives afresh. Costs are dealt with at length in Chapter 1.

Client care code

All solicitors must comply with a client care code, which sets out how clients should be kept informed and advised on who will be handling their case and about costs.

What this means in practice is that at the outset of your case – once you have

Family Law Protocol: www.lawsociety.org.uk and search for 'family law protocol' to download it from the Law Society's website, or buy it from the Law Society: NB currently out of print, a new edition hoped to be published soon.

seen and informed a solicitor that you want him or her to take on your case – you should receive a fairly detailed letter (sometimes called a 'client care' letter) that complies with the code. This might tell you, for example, the name of the person dealing with your case, the name of the head of the department and information about costs. It should also identify the person to complain to in the firm if you think you have got poor service.

If your solicitor does not send out such a letter, it may be an indication that he or she is not really on the ball – so you may get better service elsewhere.

The Family Law Protocol

Family law solicitors should all conform to the guidelines of good practice set out in the Family Law Protocol, which is a code published by the Law Society and devised by it in conjunction with Resolution, the Legal Services Commission and with the Lord Chancellor's Department.

The conduct it sets out is not mandatory but advisory. However, if a solicitor does not observe the rules of practice that it sets out, he or she could run the risk of costs orders being made against him or her.

COMPLAINTS ABOUT SOLICITORS

Occasionally the relationship between a client and a solicitor can break down. If you have a grievance against your solicitor (for example, if he or she persistently fails to return your telephone calls or respond to your letters), it may be worthwhile having a word with the person identified in the client care letter as the one to complain to. You could also try talking to the head of the family law department or otherwise the senior partner of the firm.

Switching to another solicitor can be an expensive process, as the new person will have to read through all the paperwork that has already been produced: this can itself cause extra delay. So, if a sincere personal intervention can restore a good working relationship with your solicitor, this is often the best action to take.

However, if the situation fails to improve, you may wish to complain formally about your solicitor. Complaints are handled by the Consumer Complaints Service of the Law Society.

Law Society Consumer Complaints Service: Victoria Court, 8 Dormer Place, Leamington Spa, CV32 5AE: 0845 608 6565. General enquiries: 01926 820082: www.legalcomplaints.org.uk

COMPLAINTS ABOUT BARRISTERS

Another possibility is that you may have a complaint against your barrister (known as 'counsel') if one is instructed by your solicitor to act on your behalf – for example, at a court hearing. Complaints about barristers can be hard to succeed with, but it is a good idea to check with your solicitor first to see if your grounds for grievance are well founded. Complaints about barristers should be made to the Bar Council.

TAKING A COMPLAINT FURTHER

Once your complaint against a solicitor or a barrister has been investigated, the next stage, if you are still unhappy, is to write to the Legal Services Ombudsman. They oversee the handling of complaints against solicitors, barristers and licensed conveyancers.

OTHER SOURCES OF ADVICE AND HELP

Anyone in difficulties over finance, tax, housing, the children, or rights generally, can go for advice to a Citizens Advice Bureau (CAB). The CAB have numerous leaflets and information about local sources of help and services. Their services differ across the UK, but many can provide you with everything from an impartial listener to representation at social security appeal tribunals or advice about money and county court representation. The CAB are especially good at providing debt-counselling services. You can find the address of your local branch in the telephone directory.

 The Bar Council: 289-293 High Holborn, London WC1V 7HZ: 020 7242 0082: www.barcouncil.org.uk Office of the Legal Services Ombudsman: Third Floor, Sunlight House, Quay Street, Manchester M3 3JZ: 0845 601 0794: www.olso.org

Using the internet

As the many 'go further' boxes throughout the text indicate, the internet is now an easy source of information. Family law is no exception. But you should bear in mind that the information on the internet is not monitored for accuracy: you must be sure only to rely on information from reliable, official sites. Even then, it is important to check the date when information was posted, to make sure that it is up to date. You should also check with a solicitor that the information relates to your specific circumstances.

USING THE INTERNET TO FIND A SOLICITOR

Given the increasing use of the internet as a source of information, you may wish to find a solicitor this way. The usefulness of the internet in this area is still somewhat limited, but improving all the time. Family lawyers are increasingly using the internet as a means of contacting potential clients by creating their own websites, but there are some exceptions.

Your chances of success in finding a local solicitor on the internet are closely linked to where you are – London and other major cities are generally better served. The easiest way is to go via the websites listed at the bottom of page 66. You can use search engines and use particular keywords – 'divorce', 'family lawyer', 'family mediation' – ensuring that your search is limited to the UK. You could also type in your locality (for example, Oxford) and see what comes up.

Many legal websites are somewhat 'boring' but at least they should give you an idea of what is on offer at a firm.

> **❝ It's always worth looking at a number of websites and comparing information so that you get a broad view of your position. ❞**

 Resolution have set up a website to provide general advice on splitting up, parenting after separation, money, child maintenance and domestic violence: www.resolution.org.uk/advice_centre

Other sites will include full explanations of their services and fees, pictures of solicitors (so you can see what they look like) and sometimes 'update' pages that you can visit to get free information.

ONLINE LEGAL ADVICE

It is important to weigh up the likely bias of any website that you go to, as this may distort the information that it supplies.

Websites tend to fall into one of three categories:

- Government or government-funded sites: these will be dedicated to providing quality impartial advice. Generally they will be kept up-to-date.
- Reputable charities and advice organisations: these also tend to be a good source of accurate information. The larger and more well-established the organisation, the better the advice is likely to be. Some will have a particular bias in terms of their focus: advice for gay and lesbian couples, or for lone parents, for instance.
- Pressure and special interest groups and private websites: you may have to be more careful with these. They may have sprung from particular grievances or problems with the legal system. The legal advice that they offer may be distorted by this and, because they may not be very well funded, they may not have the resources to keep the information on the site up to date.

❝ You should know that getting your divorce via the internet will not make it any quicker than it would otherwise be, and the court fee will not be cheaper. The court procedure remains the same. ❞

Online divorces

There are internet services that offer you a divorce package. They will supply you with divorce forms (for a fee) and (for a further fee) help you to fill them in. However, if you do want to do your own divorce, you can get the forms and guidance free from the Courts Service website www.hmscourts-service.gov.uk and complete them yourself. It is probably not a very good idea to do this unless your marriage has been fairly short, you have no children and you are entirely amicable about how you are going to divide up the family assets. Also bear in mind that the financial issues will need to be approved by the court, even if you have agreed them between you, and this will be an additional cost/service, separate from the divorce itself.

Mediation and collaborative law

There are a variety of ways for couples to resolve the issues that they face following the breakdown of their relationship. This chapter deals with mediation and collaborative law and how these options can assist in resolving conflicts over division of money, housing, pensions and the arrangements for children. A benefit of such alternative dispute resolution is that legal costs can be kept down.

4

Family mediation

Family mediation was a concept started in the USA in the 1960s, and which is now used throughout the UK to assist couples in reaching agreement, through a voluntary process, on the problems that follow separation.

WHAT IS MEDIATION?

Mediation can be defined in a number of ways as there are a variety of situations where the skills of a mediator can assist in bringing resolution to a dispute. Mediation is a form of Alternative Dispute Resolution (ADR), which enables parties to try to negotiate and reach an agreement without going through the standard adversarial court process. One definition of mediation, which explains it clearly, is that it is an attempt to bring about a peaceful settlement or compromise between people in dispute, with the objective intervention of a neutral third party (known as the mediator).

Some courts suggest mediation to the parties for certain legal issues to prevent further legal costs being incurred. When one party is in receipt of legal aid they are required to explore mediation as an option (see Chapter 1).

Mediation is now very popular, and in 2006 the government launched a Family Mediation Helpline (see box below) which was part of an initiative designed to

Definition of mediation

Mediation defined in The Code of Practice for Family Mediators produced by National Family Mediation (NFM) and the Family Mediators Association (FMA):

'...a process in which an impartial third person assists those involved in family breakdown, and in particular separating or divorcing couples, to communicate better with one another and to reach their own agreed and informed decisions about some or all of the issues relating to, or arising from, the separation, divorce, children, finance or property'.

encourage couples to consider alternative ways of resolving family despites.

The process of mediation can be used for cohabiting couples, separating couples or divorcing couples for any issue surrounding the breakdown of their relationship. Mediators are trained to

 Family Mediation Helpline: 0845 60 26 627: www.familymediationhelpline.co.uk
The Advice Now website has useful information on mediation and leaflets that you can download: www.advicenow.org.uk/family-mediation/

determine situations where mediation is not appropriate, which can include cases where the conflict is extreme, there are child protection or safety issues, where there is an imbalance of power between the parties for any reason (which could be where one party is suffering from a mental or physical illness), or if for some reason the parties are not capable of negotiating.

Even in situations where there are a number of complex issues, mediation can still be used, as mediators are trained to use their skills and specialist techniques to help parties reach an agreement. The mediation process is explained further in the next section of this book.

The basic requirements of a successful mediation are:

- **Voluntary participation.** Mediation can only work if it is embarked upon voluntarily by both parties: there is little point having someone at mediation who feels forced to be there. This makes the compulsion for legal aid applicants seem unreasonable, but mediators can assess which cases are suitable in the circumstances.
- **A neutral and impartial mediator.** To be an objective intervener, the mediator must stay neutral and impartial though the mediation process. Without this you may feel as if your views are not being heard and so there would be no trust in the mediator's attempts to help reach a compromise between you both. The role of the mediator is to reduce hostility and misunderstanding, improve communication and focus on

---

Definition of mediation

Mediation defined in Resolution's Family Mediation Code of Practice:

1.1 a couple or any family members
1.2 whether or not they are legally represented
1.3 and at any time, whether or not there have been legal proceedings
1.4 agree to the appointment of a neutral third party (the mediator)
1.5 who is impartial
1.6 who has no authority to make any decisions with regard to their issues
1.7 which may relate to separation, divorce, children's issues, property and financial questions or any other issues that may raise
1.8 but who helps them reach their own informed decisions
1.9 by negotiated agreement
1.10 without adjudication.

---

reaching an agreement that will be long lasting (focusing on the children where relevant). The mediator should seek to assist the parties in reaching a solution which works for everyone, where neither party feels as if they are a winner or loser.

- **Access to legal advice throughout the process.** Court proceedings do not need to have been started, or threatened, to start mediation. However, it is vitally important that you are aware of your legal rights during the process and that both parties are able to seek independent legal advice at any stage to ensure the agreement they are negotiating is within the range of what would be considered fair and reasonable.

- **Full and open disclosure.** Documentation provided during mediation needs to be on an 'open' basis, which means that this can be used later and relied upon if there is a future court case about such issues. The reason for this is that those embarking on mediation must be able to rely on what they are being told as truthful, full and frank disclosure and without this there would not be enough trust to start negotiations.
- **Legal privilege.** Although the financial disclosure that you exchange through mediation is open, the negotiations that you have at mediation are privileged. This means that those discussions and negotiations cannot be referred to or used if there are any court proceedings in the future.
- **Confidential information.** It is still possible to keep some information confidential; such as one party's address if they do not wish to release it, or information that does not affect the issues the parties are trying to resolve.

There are two exceptions to the principles of confidentiality and privilege in mediation, which are when there is a risk of significant harm to someone (especially a child), or when there is a disclosure made during mediation that revealed that you had finances that were acquired as a result of some criminal activity (which includes benefit or tax fraud). In either of these situations the mediator would have to end the mediation and either take steps to protect the person at risk of harm, or make a report to the relevant authority, as they are obliged to do by law.

Jargon buster

Conciliation This means the same as mediation, though is sometimes used to indicate that it is taking place in court, rather than entirely voluntarily. Not to be confused with reconciliation.

AIM or 'all issues mediation' Mediation over finances and issues about children.

Child only mediation Mediation only concerned with issues about the children, such as residence and contact.

Lawyer mediator A mediator who is also a qualified lawyer, but who will not take a lawyer's role in the mediation.

Family mediator A mediator who is not a lawyer but will have come from some other background, often social work, teaching or counselling.

Family mediators

These have historically been cheaper than lawyer mediators (for more details on how much mediation costs, see the end of this chapter). Some family mediation services charge fees based on a couple's income or even offer free sessions.

TYPES OF MEDIATION

Who you use to mediate can change the type and method of mediation you participate in. You can go to a family mediator, who will have a therapeutic/ counselling background and may have worked in social work or mental health. The alternative is to use a lawyer mediator, who has a legal background and is experienced in family law and how the court would approach the issues you are facing. It is possible to have a combination of types, which is called co-mediation and would involve a family mediator and lawyer mediator working together.

Whichever route you choose, you should check the experience of the mediator you are going to see before using them. Also consider the costs that you are likely to incur, as lawyer mediators usually charge more than family mediators, subject to any discounted rates they may offer in certain circumstances.

The advantage of lawyer mediators is that they can give you general guidance about the law during the mediation process. They are not able to specifically advise you or your ex and you will need individual advice from your own solicitor about the specific facts of your case. However, although the lawyer mediator is not advising you, their guidance is on the basis of what is fair under legal principles. Their role is to ascertain the necessary information and disclosure, and then using their background knowledge help you work out solutions that are sensible and realistic, while also being

Benefits of mediation
Each spouse should still get independent legal advice, but because a couple may well reach an agreement more quickly through a mediator than through separate solicitors, cost savings can be achieved.

Co-mediation

The type of mediation service where a pair of mediators - a family mediator and a lawyer mediator - work together, known as co-mediation, was pioneered by the FMA, and is now used in many NFM services as well.

legally acceptable. The information they can provide can include up-to-date information about the law, maintenance and benefits, which will help you feel that the choices you are making are on a fully informed basis.

It is still best to get independent legal advice – during and after the mediation process – to ensure that the agreement reached is fair and reasonable to you in your specific situation. The mediation process actually requires legal advice from your own solicitor once an agreement has been reached. If you have been fully informed and legally advised throughout the process it can mean the agreement is more likely to be within the realms of what the court will find acceptable.

The mediation process

Most mediation services start by offering you each a short, individual meeting so that they can explain to you how the mediation process works and check whether mediation would be suitable for you.

THE FIRST SESSION

Mediation can take place at any time, even before legal proceedings have started. If you qualify for legal aid this is worked out and you complete the forms at this first meeting. This is sometimes called an 'intake meeting'. Some services offer joint intake meetings that you both attend, others generally see you each separately. These meetings give you each the chance to decide whether you want to go ahead.

If you both want to go ahead, and the mediator thinks it will be suitable for you both, then you will be invited to the first mediation session. This will probably last for one to two hours. Most services will arrange this so that you are both in the same room with the mediator, but sometimes it may be better for you to be in separate rooms and for the

mediator to go between you. This is called 'shuttle mediation'.

For mediation to work, both of you need to attend. It can be a daunting prospect to face your ex in the same room to discuss what future arrangements should be made, but a skilled mediator, who will always be impartial, will help by managing the process so that both parties can make their views clear.

It is the mediator's responsibility to be even-handed, to create a balance between the parties so that they can both negotiate properly over conflicts. Even where you feel very much in conflict with one another, addressing conflict is common in mediation and the right solutions can often be found. Mediation is very often the most appropriate forum for conflicts to be resolved.

A POSITIVE APPROACH

A mediator will not impose his or her own views, but will try to help you find common ground so that together you can come to arrangements that will work for each of you individually and for the family as a whole. Sometimes this process can mean that a mediator

" If you are afraid of your partner, or do not want to see him or her, tell the mediation service. They should be able to make sure that you feel safe and offer separate waiting and meeting rooms. "

will encourage the more passive partner to put his or her own views forward and ensure that the more dominant partner stays quieter.

The agreement to mediate forms the basis of the terms on which a mediator will act in a mediation, and will therefore set out what you agree to in the mediation.

❝ At the first session the mediator will explain what the process of mediation is all about and the terms of the mediation agreement. ❞

HOW IT WORKS

Mediation works by setting agendas covering the issues each of you wants to discuss – it is up to you both to decide what you need to talk about. The agenda for the first session could cover, for example, the decision to separate, arrangements for the time being over the children and payment of bills. The process of mediation can take about five to six sessions, although more or less may be necessary depending on the issues involved. Mediations are usually relatively informal, with first names being used if you wish.

As part of the agreement, in all-issues mediation you must both consent to

❝ The mediator will establish ground rules to create a more positive framework for working things out. ❞

give full disclosure of your finances. Each of you may be expected to fill out a comprehensive form giving details of your financial circumstances including:

- Savings and assets.
- Debts.
- Pensions.
- The home.
- Any business interests.
- Income you receive.

You will have to supply supporting documents where possible. The forms are then sent to the mediator (usually by at least the third session), with a copy for the other party. If you have already compiled the financial dossier in Chapter 2 you will find that this is an easier task.

To ensure that both of you are fully aware of the whole picture of the family's finances, the mediator will often put up the figures on a flipchart. Getting things up on a chart in this way helps identify any areas where more information is needed, and clarify which money matters are issues between you. The lengthy (and costly) process of 'disclosure' in court cases is short-circuited by this method, because one of you can often quickly identify if the other is holding back information and ensure that the figures are corrected.

81

Often, various alternative arrangements or options are written up on the flipchart. Each of you can put forward your own options. If either of you gets stuck, the mediator can help out, so more creative solutions to difficult problems can be worked through and tested as to how well they will work for you in reality.

MEMORANDUM OF UNDERSTANDING

As and when an agreement is reached, the mediator will prepare a summary of the agreement for each of you and your solicitors. This is generally called a 'Memorandum of Understanding'. The mediator will also prepare an 'open' summary of information about money matters, but any agreement reached is 'without prejudice' – that is, it cannot be made known to the court at a full hearing if the agreement subsequently breaks down. The agreement can then be translated by

❝If you reach a financial agreement this must be put into a court order or a legally binding form such as a 'deed' setting out the agreement. You will generally need a solicitor to do this for you to ensure that it reflects your agreement and that you understand it fully.❞

the solicitors into court documents – for example, a consent order.

Having your own solicitor also means you have legal back-up in case any urgent legal action needs to be taken – for example, to prevent your spouse/cp from disposing of assets – or if the mediation does not result in an agreement (in which

Are solicitors still necessary?

Even if you have gone in for mediation, it is still a good idea for you individually to get legal advice about what rights and responsibilities you have (so that you can negotiate on an informed basis) and also to double-check the terms of any agreement made during mediation. You can check whether the agreement will be watertight, whether anything has been missed out and whether you are giving away something you should not.

 Family Mediators Association: 0117 946 7062: www.fma.co.uk
Family Mediation Helpline: 0845 60 26 627 or see their website: www.familymediationhelpline. co.uk Or you can use Resolution: www.resolution.org.uk

case you will probably still have to go to court or your solicitors may be able to negotiate on your behalf).

Legal advice is complementary to the mediation process, but by using a skilled and knowledgeable mediator you could save thousands of pounds in legal fees by avoiding a full-blown legal battle, as the negotiations and disclosure will be done through mediation rather than solicitors.

MEDIATION AND THE CHILDREN

Mediation takes a family-based approach, rather than the adversarial approach adopted in the family court (where parents have to be on opposite sides, which can make things even more difficult when it comes to dealing with the children). You need to try to work together to sort out how the children will be looked after when the family separates, and the family-based approach of mediation can often help you cooperate as parents in planning for your children's and your own futures.

If problems over arrangements for the children are just a part of broader difficulties over finance generally, mediation involving a lawyer mediator would be a better option for you. Try to ensure that, if possible, comprehensive, or 'all-issues', mediation is available.

The emphasis in mediation is on enabling you to create solutions that

❝ If the dispute is only over the children, mediation by a family mediator may well be the best option. ❞

allow you both to remain parents in as full a sense as possible. By meeting in a neutral environment in the presence of a non-partisan, experienced professional (or sometimes two professionals) trained in assisting couples to come to realistic agreements, you both may find that you can at least (and perhaps at last) communicate directly rather than talking at each other or entirely missing each other's points. With your agreement, the children themselves may occasionally be invited to the mediation, but they should only attend if being there would help them and would be in their best interest.

 The UK College of Family Mediators: www.ukcfm.co.uk or look in Yellow Pages under 'Mediation' (www.yell.com)
Relate : 0300 100 1234: www.relate.org.uk

Is mediation appropriate for you?

The potential benefits of mediation are numerous, but it doesn't necessarily suit every couple or every family situation.

You need to decide whether you feel that, with expert help, you would be able to negotiate with your spouse/partner with respect to each other. If you feel you would give in too easily, or try to dominate the process and refuse to listen, then mediation may not be right for you.

FREE MEDIATION WITH LEGAL AID

If you qualify for legal aid for Help with Mediation, you will get funding for your mediation and subsequent advice from a solicitor without making a financial contribution and without incurring the statutory charge (see Chapter 1).

What does mediation cost?

Three to six mediation sessions are typical where there are a number of issues to resolve; fewer sessions if the dispute involves a single issue. It is impossible to give detailed guidelines on fees as these will vary from service to service. Fees will generally be charged by the hour and many services will have a sliding scale of contribution based on your income. Each of you will be separately assessed and charged. Expect to pay for each session as it takes place.

Advantages of mediation

- **Control over the outcome.** You create tailor-made solutions to problems involved in the family split – arrangements not imposed on you by the court. Solutions worked out in mediation can cover aspects where the court would have no power to make court orders.
- **Speed and cost-effectiveness.** The process is speedier and more cost-effective. Costs are likely to be measured in at most hundreds, not thousands, of pounds.
- **Respect for the family.** Mediation can help improve communication between you both and aid cooperation over the children. The process of splitting up can be made more dignified.
- **Confidentiality.** The whole discussion in mediation is private and confidential. If you want to ensure privacy over how you work things out, mediation may be right for you.

Collaborative law

Collaborative law is a hybrid between lawyer mediation and solicitor negotiation, which may be another Alternative Dispute Resolution method that you could consider.

This is a process that started in the USA and has become increasing popular in this country. Many solicitors are now being trained as collaborative lawyers, so that they have the skills and techniques to offer this as an alternative form of dispute resolution to their clients.

Collaborative law is not the same as mediation, but is another way of reaching agreement on the issues surrounding family breakdown, without going to court.

The incentive to reach a resolution is that you and your ex have to agree at the outset that you will not go to court, which enables you to embark on this process without the threat or fear of court proceedings hanging over you. Should either of you decide to go to court instead, the collaborative process would come to an immediate end and you would both need to instruct new solicitors, which could lead to significant legal cost and delay.

In the collaborative process you both:
- Have lawyers.
- Enter into a binding agreement that you will not go to court.
- Have a duty to give full and frank disclosure of all your financial circumstances.

> **" Either of you can choose, at a later stage, to opt out of the process and go to court instead, but you will need a new lawyer to take the case on. "**

The process involves a number of meetings at which both clients and lawyers are present, and everyone tries to work towards an agreement. Unlike mediation, during which the mediator can give information but not advice, the lawyers advise their clients during the process. Some of the advice may be given by a lawyer to his or her own client, but advice can also be given and discussed openly in the meetings. This can avoid some of the frustrating delays in mediation that occur when people need to consult their lawyers about what they have negotiated.

A number of techniques that are used in mediation are also used in the collaborative law process. Rather than the traditional approach of dealing though your respective solicitors, you and your ex will work with both of your solicitors to reach the best solutions for you and your family. The process is very open and avoids correspondence. You will set the agenda and the pace at which issues will be considered, as there is no court deadline to work to. One of the advantages to the collaborative law process is that – as in mediation – you and your ex will be making the decisions about your future together, rather than having such decisions imposed on you by someone else. At the conclusion of the process the lawyers will draw up the agreement into a consent order or deed so that agreement is legally binding where possible.

Collaborative law
Collaborative law is not necessarily cheaper, and legal aid is currently not specifically available to cover the collaborative process, so ask for an estimate of costs when you are considering this option.

❝ Your lawyers may also make sure there is a team of other people available, such as financial advisers and counsellors, so that you can have the benefit of these skills as well. ❞

How much does it cost?

Lawyers will charge their normal hourly rates and the work that they will do is very labour intensive because of the number of meetings that occur. A case may well resolve in a shorter length of time because the delays that correspondence causes will be reduced, and this may save costs. However, the actual time spent dealing with your case will not always be less. What should save costs is your decision not to go to court. It is hoped that in the future legal aid will be available for collaborative law, but this is yet to happen.

How do I find a collaborative lawyer?

The number of trained collaborative lawyers are growing rapidly as training programmes spread the practice. Those who practice it in England at the moment are members of the Collaborative Family Law Organization, which is under the umbrella of Resolution. There is a directory of members on their website.

Not all solicitors are collaborative lawyers and both you and your ex will need to instruct independent collaborative lawyers for this option to be successful.

Collaborative Family Law Organization (Resolution):
www.resolution.org.uk-alternatives to court
Resolution, PO Box 302, Orpington, Kent BR6 8QX: 08457 585671.

Children

If you, as an individual or as a couple, are thinking about splitting up and you have children, you need to think carefully about how you tell them and what plans you make for their future. This chapter offers some general pointers about sensible ways of handling the situation. It also explains the legal side of things, and what happens if you can't agree.

Preparing the children

Separating from your partner or spouse is not only going to be emotionally difficult for you, but also for your children.

The anxiety, unhappiness and stress you are going though will be felt by your children. Undoubtedly you will be worried about how good a parent you are able to be in such difficult circumstances, particularly if as a result of the separation you will not be seeing your children on a daily basis any more. However, you must remember that:

- Whatever happens you will both stay parents to your children, for the rest of your lives.
- You need to take care of each other as a family through this stressful time.
- No matter how bad things feel right now, they should get better and as time passes the way you and the children feel about the split should improve.
- The way you deal with this situation, and the communication and relationship that follows with your ex, will be vitally important in being able to cope with each other at events and occasions in

the future, which will be crucial to your relationship with your children.

Although you will be focused on the situation you are currently going through, it is important that you sit down as parents and think about the longer-term issues and plans regarding the children, as well as the short-term ones. Cafcass (see page 100) has produced some helpful leaflets for parents and children which can be downloaded from their website (see box opposite below). They offer advice and guidance about how to approach the issues surrounding your separation and how best to put the needs of your children first.

TELLING THE CHILDREN

If at all possible, it is best for both parents to be present when the children are told about the plan to separate or divorce. This is not always possible, but if it is, it can help the children accept what is happening. It is also important to think about what you are going to say beforehand so that you are able to tell the children what the plans are and avoid any uncertainty for them, which can cause significant worry for children of any age. If you are able to tell the children together, and explain the separation and future plans, they are more likely to be trusting of what they are told.

&& However much your relationship with your ex has changed, remember that you are both going to go on being parents for the rest of your lives. 99

Tips to making the process as bearable as possible for them include:

- Let them ask questions and talk about how they feel.
- Give them time to adjust and accept the changes and effect of separation.
- Do not tell them just before bedtime, when they may then feel very isolated and worried.
- Provide hugs, love and unlimited reassurance.
- Tell (or discuss with them, if they are old enough) the contact plans you have made.
- Play fair and do not apportion any blame for the relationship breakdown in front of the children. Also try not to cloud their views of the other parent, however tempting this may be.
- Appreciate and allow for their individual maturity and understanding.
- Avoid exposing the children to rows and arguments over contact or any continuing conflict.
- Seek help and advice early on from friends, family and professionals.
- Tell the children's carers and teachers so that they are aware of what is going on and can keep an eye out for any changes in behaviour or concerns.

How the children may feel

Regardless of their age children are likely to go through a process of shock (although you believe they knew the split was coming), disbelief and denial. They may also feel they need to keep you together, even if they are aware of how unhappy you have been: they will want to try and stop any changes to their world as they know it, which is what makes them feel safe and secure.

It is common for children to blame themselves for the relationship breakdown, perhaps linking it to their 'naughty' behaviour or not being good enough. These emotions highlight the need for both parents to explain that the decision is an adult one, and not linked to the child's behaviour or the love you have for them in any way. It may be these reassurances needed to be repeated during and after the separation process.

The age of the child/children at the time of separation can mean a different approach is required, which should be tailored to each child.

Young children

It is important, even if the children are young when you split up, that you are honest with them about the break-up. Do not give them any false hope or expectation about reconciliation or that this is a temporary situation if you know that it is not.

Family leaflets for adults and children:
www.cafcass.gov.uk/publications.aspx

Their age and maturity may require you to use simple terminology and terms, and avoid words such as 'law' and 'court', which can frighten them as they link such words to criminal law and prison.

Allow them to be upset and express their emotions. Repeated reassurance and confirmation of how much they are loved by you will be crucial to assist them through the process. Keeping their normal routine, as much as possible will help them feel safe and secure. However, you should be prepared for signs of anxiety from the child about being separated from you, even for short periods of time. You may also see changes in behaviour and a regression in development, such as bedwetting or angry outbursts.

Older children

Although they may go through many of the same emotions and reactions as younger children, there is likely to be more expression of anger, blame and more questions asked of you by older children.

You will need to make it clear that they are not being asked to choose between their parents and that they should not blame one parent, which may be their initial reaction.

If you are close to the child it could be easy to allow a blurring of the support aspects of your relationship, which can be very dangerous. Despite the temptation to let them become a friend/confidante during a difficult time for you, the child needs the support from you to allow them not to feel any such burden and to keep the adult/child boundary clear.

Adult children

Even children who are in their late teens or 'grown up' need to be told about a break-up in the same way, with explanations and reassurance, as they can be as badly affected by the separation of their parents as a younger child.

If they are living away, or at college/university at the time of your separation, avoid telling them when they are about to spend a period of time away from you, such as at the start of a new term. Appreciate and recognise the distress they may feel by the loss of the security they have grown up with, which they may now feel is gone.

WHAT YOU CAN DO TO HELP
Tips from parents who have been through it:

❝Tell the schools as soon as you have told the children, or even beforehand. It is bound to affect their school work or behaviour to some extent. If the school knows, staff will be sympathetic and do what they can to help.❞

❝Try to stick to old domestic routines, and stay the same about discipline and behaviour. It would have been very easy to spoil them to make up for hurting them so much. They needed the old routines so they didn't feel the whole world had come smashing down around them.❞

❝You need to talk to the kids a lot, but you have to try not to confide in them in the way that you would in an adult friend. There were times when it was very tempting, but I didn't want to burden them with my side of the story.❞

❝Take advantage of any offer of adult help that you can get. If friends offer to take the children out to let you have a rest, accept gratefully. Life as a single parent is very hard work. It is not an admission of failure to accept help.❞

❝Widen the family circle. It is easy to retreat into your small family world when a divorce hits you. But it can be very claustrophobic and make you more miserable. Instead, try to invite the children's friends home, and get other adults to come round. If you can make your home into an open, friendly place, the children will find it easier to adjust to the new situation.❞

❝Children can be helped by adult friends of their own. And many find it easier to talk with uncles, aunts, godparents or family friends, so try and encourage this.❞

The legal position

The law concerning children is largely outlined in the Children Act 1989, which introduced the concepts of parental responsibility, residence and contact. There are no assumptions that one parent will be better at looking after children than another and there are no legal guidelines about the 'right' amount of contact as this varies for each child. The Act puts the needs and welfare of the child as the priority of the court when making any decision.

PARENTAL RESPONSIBILITY

The Children Act defines Parental Responsibility as 'all the rights, duties, powers, responsibilities and authority which by law a parent of a child has in relation to the child and his property'. In practice, this means the responsibility and the right to make choices over the issues involved in bringing up a child, like:

- Where the child will live.
- Where the child will go to school.
- What religious upbringing the child will have.
- What medical treatment the child will have.

If you have Parental Responsibility, you can also apply for a passport for the child.

See the chart opposite for how Parental Responsibility (PR) is obtained. Both parents also get Parental Responsibility

if they adopt a child. Anyone who gets a Residence Order (see page 97) gets Parental Responsibility with it. Parents continue to share this after divorce until the children are 18, whether the children live with them or not.

If you are living together as parents, the law assumes that you will make joint decisions and exercise your parental responsibility together. Once you are separated you can both legally exercise that responsibility without consulting the other, but it obviously makes sense to continue to discuss matters, such as those listed above, and to try to reach joint decisions. Sometimes in an emergency, like a medical crisis, you will have to act alone, and the law allows you to do so.

The presumption of the Children Act is that, for the most part, parents are capable of deciding matters for their

 To get a Parental Responsibility Agreement form and instructions about how to complete it go to the Courts Service website: www.hmcourts-service.gov.uk In the 'forms and guidance' section get form C (PRA1) Parental Responsibility Agreement.

This chart illustrates how PR can be obtained

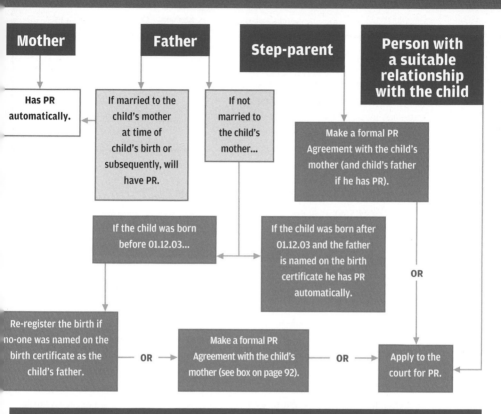

Same-sex couples and PR

Significant law changes have happened in the last two years leading to a change in the acquisition of PR for couples of the same sex in a relationship who have a child who lives with them and who is biologically linked to one of them. The law now states that:

For a child's parent who is a non-biological female partner, PR is obtained if:

- She is registered on the birth certificate.
- She enters into a PR agreement with the birth mother.
- The court make an order for PR.
- She is the civil partner of the birth mother at the time of the birth, or subsequently.

For a child's parent who is a non-biological male partner, PR is obtained if:

- He is registered in the birth certificate.
- He enters into a PR agreement with the birth mother.
- The court make an order for PR.

The law relating to adopted children remains the same: both adoptive parents have PR.

children without the intervention of the court. Before this Act, in every divorce where there were children orders were made for 'custody', 'care and control' and 'access'. This no longer happens, and the old terms have been abolished (even though they are still used by the media). If parents can agree arrangements about where the children will live ('residence') and how and when they will see the parent with whom they do not live ('contact'), the court will not make any orders. Orders are only ever made if there is a dispute between the parents and they cannot agree. In that situation the judge may decide that it is best for there to be an order to prevent further disputes.

RESIDENCE

You will need to decide where the children are going to make their main home. This is often fairly obvious, with most children staying in the original family home. But other arrangements can be made. If you are going to move them out of their family home, do remember that they will need their own things with them.

Some families feel that the children can have two 'main' homes and divide their time equally between their parents. If this is your feeling, you need to be absolutely sure that you are doing this because you think it is best for the children and for no other reason or motivation. The needs of the children must be put as your priority and you need to be sure that whatever arrangement you put in place is not upsetting or unsettling for them, even if you feel that it is 'fair' for you.

Children's possessions
Children have close and intense relationships with their own possessions. Make sure that they are allowed to take with them whatever they feel they need, even if you think that it is unnecessary.

CONTACT

If the child is living with one parent, the arrangements for when they see the other parent also need to be decided.

Contact

The term 'contact', as used in the Children Act, can mean anything from long overnight visits to telephone calls and letters. There is no single pattern of contact that is laid down as the 'right' contact pattern or approved in any official way. Each family must make its own arrangements. Whatever you can agree can later be altered to suit changes in, for example, the children's interests or domestic arrangements.

Contact centres

Contact centres offer a safe space in which parents can have contact with their children in a supervised environment. They are sometimes run by Cafcass (see page 100) and sometimes by local charities and volunteers. Couples can choose to

Contact dos and don'ts

- DO keep the arrangements regular, but flexible if need be. It's important that children have a framework and a routine that they can rely on. Don't change arrangements arbitrarily and if you do need to make changes, ensure you give the other parent sufficient notice.

- DO plan the contact times ahead together. Keep a large calendar for the children to put stickers on the contact days, which will help them to keep track of their weeks.

- DO remember that in the early days following a split, any contact is better than none. It may not be possible to sort out a regular pattern of contact after you first separate; both your lives may be in too much upheaval. It may be tempting to say that there will not be any contact for a while because you fear that it might disrupt the children too much, but this is normally not best for the children.

- DO keep time. If you agree to collect or return children at particular times, you should stick to them. Similarly, if the children are being collected from you, you should have them ready at the correct time. If something unexpected causes a delay, call and inform the other parent.

- DO NOT use your children against the other parent. Children will know if they are being used as spies, and it is unfair to pull their loyalties in two ways.

- DO NOT behave as though the child's time is a possession you are entitled to. According to the law, contact is the child's right to see the parent and not the other way about.

- DO use telephone calls as a way of keeping in touch. If you are the one phoning the child, try to agree with your ex about when would be a convenient time.

- DO NOT turn every contact visit into a wild outing somewhere. Low-key activities may be just as pleasurable and valuable for your children. What they want is your time and attention; spending money on them does not compensate for a lack of time or love.

- DO NOT assume that if the children come back from a contact visit cross, fractious or hyped-up, the visit is causing them harm. Children are often like this at the end of any hectic day so don't blame your ex or the visit. The children may be a little more upset because the hand-over from one parent to another reminds them of what they have lost, but this does not mean that contact is something traumatic that should be avoided.

- DO use all means to stay in touch: if you are the non-resident parent, it is easy to feel that you have lost, or are losing, your relationship with your children. Children are capable of sustaining close and intimate relationships with people that they do not see everyday and using the telephone, email, letters, picture postcards, text messages and internet instant messaging can all help.

- DO stay positive about contact and encourage the children to participate, even if you do not feel this way. Children will pick up on your negativity and this may cause them unnecessary worry and upset.

- DO make sure that the children are sent to contact with the clothing and footwear they need. Also ensure that you return such items with the children.

use them, or a court may stipulate that contact takes place there, for example, if a parent has threatened to take a child away from the parent that he or she lives with and there are worries that the threat might be carried out. Sometimes they can be used in less upsetting cases, where there has not been any contact for a long period of time and the absent parent needs to rebuild a relationship with the child.

Using such centres is rarely seen as a permanent arrangement. The hope is that a relationship can be rebuilt and that both parents can come to trust each other and the children can feel comfortable with seeing the parent whom they do not live with. In any case, some centres, owing to a shortage of space, can offer the service only on a short-term basis.

Court powers

Make use of mediation, if you can, to resolve disputes. If all else fails, you may have to use the court, but the court will also try to resolve issues by mediation.

The Children and Adoption Act 2006 changed the powers of the court to try and empower them with options to enforce and promote contact. This includes the power to make a contact activity direction, which can include requiring one parent to attend classes, obtain medical or psychiatric treatment, counselling or guidance sessions that may assist in establishing, maintaining or improving contact with a child. This power can extend to making a requirement for a parent to attend violent behaviour programmes and sessions of mediation as a condition to contact with the child continuing. These conditions are not suitable for every case and will need to be appropriate in your specific circumstances.

The Act also provided the court with extended powers for breach of contact orders, including the power to impose an unpaid work requirement on a parent for breach of an order, or to order one parent to pay compensation to the other for financial loss incurred as a result of their breach of the order. Such provisions being appropriate in your situation will depend on the specific circumstances of your case, and you should seek specialist legal advice to clarify what would be appropriate.

Extra activities

As children get older they may have very full social calendars of their own. They may be involved in after-school and weekend activities. Somehow, you need to balance all these and accept that if you have contact visits at the weekend, you will need to take the children to their activities. Remember that it is the children's right to time with you, not your right to time with them.

 Cafcass produce some useful leaflets for any parents dealing with the effects of separation: www.cafcass.gov.uk/publications

When you can't agree

If you and your ex cannot decide what arrangements should be put in place for your children, you should seek legal advice. Bear in mind that any applications to the court about your children can be expensive, both financially and emotionally, and the court will look at what is best for the child, rather than what seems fair to you.

It is always best to try and reach an agreement with your ex about the arrangements for the children. You can do this by direct discussions, through mediation or with the assistance of solicitors. Court battles about children can be very upsetting for everyone involved, and will often require you to provide personal details about your family life and relationships that will then be open to the scrutiny of those involved in your case to determine if an application should be allowed.

You may find yourself having to suggest that the other parent should not have residence/contact for personal reasons, to try and prove that what you want is best for the children. This may lead to a complete breakdown of communication between you and affect your parenting relationship in the future.

ORDERS THE COURT CAN MAKE

The following orders are made under section 8 of the Children Act 1989, so they are called 'section 8 orders'. They all restrict in some way the exercising of parental responsibility (see page 92).

Residence order

This type of order confirms with whom a child will live, and where. In most cases it will be with one parent, but a residence order can allow for shared parenting, so the children divide their time between their parents' homes. A shared-residence order does not require time to be split equally. It can also be applied for by two people together; for example, a parent and a step-parent.

Contact order

This is an order that confirms when the parent with whom the children do not live will see them. Contact orders require the person with whom the child lives to allow contact with the applicant and the person looking after the child is responsible for making the order work. Contact orders can be for visits or staying overnight,

❝ In all cases, consider carefully whether, from the child's viewpoint, it is best for you to go ahead with an application to the court. ❞

telephone calls or letters, or all or any combination of these.

In some circumstances there may be conditions attached to an order. These could state that contact has to take place in a certain location or that another adult should be present during the contact visit.

Specific issue order

This decides a specific question connected with parental responsibility: for example, which school the child should go to.

Prohibited steps order

This has the effect of restraining in some way the actions of a person in relation to the child. No step stated in the order can be taken without the consent of the court. This could be used, for example, to stop one parent from changing a child's surname, or from taking the child out of the country without the other parent's or the court's consent.

Prohibited steps orders can be applied for in an emergency without the other party having to be notified of the hearing in advance. (Lawyers sometimes call this 'ex parte'.)

WHO CAN APPLY FOR SECTION 8 ORDERS?

Either parent can apply for an order, if necessary, even before you have separated or started other legal proceedings. The court orders can be used flexibly, and indeed other people, such as relatives or even the child him- or herself, may also be able to apply where appropriate.

The court can make a section 8 order in any family proceedings, thus widening

its own powers. It is not supposed to use section 8 orders without proper consideration: court orders, as mentioned earlier, should be made only if it is best for the children for there to be an order.

If the parents can decide between themselves who should look after the children and when the other parent sees them, it is likely that no formal court order will be made and the situation will continue fluidly, with both parents having parental responsibility and thus both deciding together how the children will be brought up. In the vast majority of families, the end result is precisely that – both parents with parental responsibility and no court order.

THE PROCEDURE

An application for a residence or contact order (or other section 8 order) starts when you apply to the court, stating what order you are seeking. The application fee is currently £175 (if you get certain benefits or legal aid, you may not have to pay the fee).

The application form (C100) asks for all the details of the child or children and asks you to say what sort of order you want made. There is a small section for you to say why you want the order made. This is deliberate; at this stage the court does not want long, detailed evidence filed. If the case cannot be resolved early on, you will have the opportunity to set out your reasons in greater detail via a formal statement, if the judge thinks this would be helpful in assisting them in making their decision.

This chart explains the procedure if an application is made under Section 8 of the Children Act

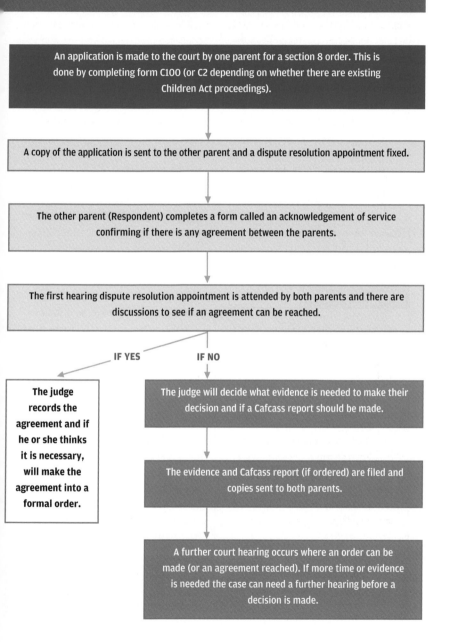

An application is made to the court by one parent for a section 8 order. This is done by completing form C100 (or C2 depending on whether there are existing Children Act proceedings).

A copy of the application is sent to the other parent and a dispute resolution appointment fixed.

The other parent (Respondent) completes a form called an acknowledgement of service confirming if there is any agreement between the parents.

The first hearing dispute resolution appointment is attended by both parents and there are discussions to see if an agreement can be reached.

IF YES

IF NO

The judge records the agreement and if he or she thinks it is necessary, will make the agreement into a formal order.

The judge will decide what evidence is needed to make their decision and if a Cafcass report should be made.

The evidence and Cafcass report (if ordered) are filed and copies sent to both parents.

A further court hearing occurs where an order can be made (or an agreement reached). If more time or evidence is needed the case can need a further hearing before a decision is made.

The form also asks you whether you have had a copy of the 'Parenting Plan: Putting Your Children First' booklet, which you can obtain free of charge from the court or online. (You can download a copy from www.tsashop.co.uk.) The form also asks if you have tried mediation and if not, why not. If you did, it asks the outcome.

The proceedings are designed to be accessible to people who are not used to the law. You should fill in the form carefully to ensure that all the facts are correct, but if you ask for the wrong order the court has the power to correct an application, or even to make an order that it has not been asked for.

Jargon buster

Cafcass The Children and Family Courts Advisory and Support Service: www. cafcass.gov.uk. Officers from Cafcass are sometimes referred to as court welfare officers (their old title). In most family cases they are formally titled Children and Family Reporters.
Private Law Proceedings Applications relating to disputes between parents.
Public Law Proceedings Proceedings where social services/the local authority are involved; for example, care and adoption.

STARTING OFF

The first stage will be that the court will fix a 'first hearing dispute resolution appointment'. You and your ex, and your solicitors (if you have them), will be asked to attend an appointment before the judge. There will also be a Cafcass officer, who is someone who is trained and experienced in dealing with children's legal issues. Some courts also invite a mediator to this meeting to see if an agreement can be negotiated.

In most courts you will be asked to go with your ex to talk to the Cafcass officer privately. Legal advisers are generally left out of the meeting. The Cafcass officer will try to explore with you what the issues and difficulties are. He or she will try to see whether an agreement can be reached.

This is really a compressed form of mediation, and there will be quite a lot of pressure on you both to try to reach an agreement. For this reason alone, it would be sensible to try to use mediation first, before you get to the stage of filing an application.

Next steps

If you can reach an agreement, then the judge will be told what you have agreed. You may feel at this stage that you want to agree only to a short-term arrangement, to try it out. Most judges will understand and think this sensible. You could, for instance, agree to a

---

 Check court fees and get copies of all the forms and information leaflets from the Courts Service website: www.hmcourts-service.gov.uk

Privacy

Since April 2009 the media have had the right to attend any family proceedings unless there is good reason why they should not be allowed in. They are not able to see documents and there are restrictions on what they are able to report on.

Giving clear evidence
If you are ordered to file a statement, try to confine yourself to setting out the facts. 'The facts' can extend to hearsay evidence (information you learned secondhand), but the court is far more influenced by clear, concise, factual and accurate information than they are by things you have heard from someone else.

pattern of contact visits for the next three months. The judge can then fix another appointment for the end of that period, which is then there if you need things reviewed or further assistance.

The judge, together with you and your legal advisers, has to decide whether it would be better to make no order (simply recording what has been agreed in a note on the file) or whether you need an order. The bias is always towards making no order, but if you have had a very difficult time in the past, and one or other of you has not been reliable at keeping agreements, the judge may feel that an order would help you both to know where you stand, which would then be best for the children, too.

Final decisions

If the conciliation process has not been successful, the judge will decide whether any short-term orders or arrangements should be made pending a final decision of the court. He or she will make an order about who is to file evidence and by when, including a statement by you and your ex if he or she thinks this would be

helpful. The judge may also order that a 'children and family reporter' (a Cafcass officer) should prepare a report about the children if there are issues about their welfare that the judge would like the officer to review.

Time limits will be set which must be strictly complied with; the Children Act specifically recognises that delay may be harmfully prejudicial in a children application. In practice, you may find that, owing to the workload of Cafcass, the welfare report may take several weeks/ months to be filed. You should also be

Cafcass report

A copy of the Cafcass report will be sent to you directly or through your solicitors (if appointed). It must not be shown to any third parties without the prior permission of the court.

Interim hearing

Before a final hearing the court may set a date for an interim hearing to try to resolve which issues are in dispute. Again, at this stage, the date for a final hearing will be fixed.

told the 'return date' – in other words, the date when the case will next come to court.

The Cafcass officer will usually interview each of you and the children. The older the children are, the more weight their views will carry. The Cafcass officer may also make enquiries of the children's schools and other relevant parties – for example, a child's grandmother, if it is proposed that she will be looking after the child while her son or daughter (the child's parent) is at work. The Cafcass officer will prepare a report which sets out the facts and circumstances and his or her impressions, and normally a recommendation to which the court will pay great attention (but will not necessarily follow).

THE COURT'S CRITERIA

The overriding principle of the Children Act is that 'the child's welfare shall be the court's paramount consideration'. In applying this welfare principle, the court has a checklist of matters it must look at in particular (see right). The checklist is neither exhaustive nor exclusive, but one that lays out simply what the court must consider.

The court may also consider other factors to be important in an individual case. For example, the parents' wishes and feelings, although not listed, may often have an important bearing on the eventual outcome of a case.

The wishes of the child

The fact that the child's wishes and feelings have been placed at the top of the checklist highlights the child-centred

66 Children's wishes and feelings will be explored by the Cafcass officer when preparing the report. 99

Children Act checklist

- The ascertainable wishes and feelings of the child (in the light of the child's age and understanding).
- The child's physical, emotional and educational needs.
- The likely effect on the child of any change in circumstances.
- The child's age, gender and background, and any characteristics the court considers relevant.
- Any harm the child has suffered or is at risk of suffering.
- The ability of each of the child's parents, and of any other person in relation to whom the court considers the question to be relevant, to meet the child's needs.
- The range of powers available to the court.

" Ultimately, and especially for younger children, it is up to adults to make final decisions. "

approach of the Children Act: children should, wherever possible, be put first.

The older the child, the more persuasive will be his or her views. Teenage children in any event often 'vote with their feet' over where they want to live, whereas younger children may find it very difficult to put what they want into words. In practice, the child's wishes are extremely influential. The views of mature, articulate children who have sound reasons for choosing a particular outcome, will often be the decisive factor. But, if the court suspects that children have been coached by one or other parent, 'their' opinions will carry little weight.

Although children's views will be respected, they should not be forced to choose unwillingly between two people, both of whom they love.

The judge's role

At a hearing the judge may very occasionally ask to see the children in private in chambers, without parents or legal advisers present, to talk to them and ask them what they want. If so, the court will ask the parents to bring the children along to court (usually this applies only to children aged 10 years or older).

The effect of change

The court has long recognised that changing the status quo can compound the difficulties of a child adjusting to the parents' separation. So a parent who is already looking after the children usually has a much stronger claim. However, this, does not apply if the children have been snatched from their usual home environment: the court can act quickly to return children to the parent best able to care for them. Likewise, splitting the family is almost always regarded as undesirable, so that wherever possible siblings (sometimes even half-brothers and -sisters) should be kept together.

The child's needs

If the child is very young, sickly or otherwise needs constant care, a residence order is more likely to be made in favour of the mother. Case law has also confirmed the presumption that a baby would stay with his or her mother. It is important to understand that there is nothing in the Children Act that contains a gender bias. It is not unusual, for example, for a court order to provide for older children to live with their fathers. The court will always look at each individual family: whichever parent has primarily looked after the children and with whom the children have the closer bond is likely to have a residence order made in his or her favour. This is where the status quo can be very important in determining the future arrangements.

❝ A parent offering a stable home life can be at an advantage when applying for a residence order. ❞

The child's age, gender and background

These factors help to show that the judge has to look at each family's own specific circumstances and so every application is dealt with on its own merits.

Harm or risk of harm

Alcoholism, drug abuse or violence (towards an adult or children) will prejudice a parent's case. A contact order may be given, but only if it is in the child's best interests (for example, if there were a strong bond between parent and child, if the parent were seeking treatment and if the contact were supervised properly).

Recent cases show that the parent's sexuality is immaterial in the eyes of the court. The most important considerations are whether the parent's relationship with the child is loving, caring and considerate. It is still sensible for a gay or lesbian parent to seek advice from a solicitor experienced in this area. There are several organisations focused on helping with issues surrounding lesbian and gay parenting.

Risk of abuse

If there is a real and significant risk of harm – such as sexual abuse – the local authority's social services department may become involved and may apply for an order that the children be taken into care. Such a case would become a 'public law' case (where the local authority, gets involved) instead of a 'private law' case (between individuals), and is likely to be heard in a different court. It is important to appoint a solicitor experienced in public law cases and who is (ideally) on the Law Society's Children Panel (whose members have been trained to deal with such cases).

ABILITY OF THE PARENTS

This ranges from practicalities such as whether a parent works outside the home or is able to respond to the child's needs. Overall, it is a matter of assessing which parent can best look after the children during the week (contact orders may be made for the children to see the other parent during the week, at weekends and/ or holidays). Sometimes the claims of both parents will be equal. A person's behaviour as a parent will be looked at, but their conduct as a partner will often be ignored (unless it has directly affected the children).

A parent offering a stable home life (especially if remarrying) usually has a stronger claim than an unreliable parent. A parent who abandons the children is likely

For solicitors who have experience in gay or lesbian issues try Stonewall: Tower Building, York Road, London SE1 7NX: 0800 0502020: www.stonewall.org.uk
Pink Parents: www.pinkparents.org.uk for all lesbian or gay family issues.

Domestic violence

The court also has powers to make court orders excluding suspected abusers from a child's home – where the local authority wants to take emergency protective action to protect the children. Interim care orders and emergency protection orders are also now available and if domestic violence occurs, children as well as adults can be protected by court orders (see Chapter 7).

to be at a disadvantage when applying for a residence order. Where relatives or other people (like childminders or full-time nannies) are involved, their capabilities may also be explored.

A child's right to contact

An important principle in the legislation is that it is the right of every child to have contact with both parents and the advantages of regularly doing so are indisputable. A parent looking after children and seeking to deny contact to the other parent faces an uphill battle.

In rare cases, where the parent looking after the children can show an 'exceptional and cogent reason' why the other should be denied contact, the court may accept that, for the time being, contact should not be ordered.

The court must ask whether the fundamental need of every child to have an enduring emotional relationship with both parents is outweighed by the depth of harm that the child would be at risk of suffering by virtue of a contact order.

Factors such as actual or potential abuse of a child counteract the presumption towards contact. Where a father has, say, a history of violence or abuse he may be denied contact in any form. In exceptional cases a mother's (or even a stepfather's) hostility to a father having contact has been enough to stop him from doing so, but the court has often insisted that he should have contact via letters or telephone calls. There have also been cases where one parent has been so difficult over contact that the children have been moved to live with the other parent, on the basis that this was more in their interests. However, if a parent is extremely violent or abusive, abuses drugs and/ or alcohol, or in other ways will have a harmful effect on the children, the negative effects are likely to outweigh the in-built balance towards contact.

Enforcement of a contact order

If you obtain a contact order and the other parent does not make the child available, you can take steps to enforce the order. The court's enforcement powers include ordering community service against the defaulting parent, cost sanctions, penal notices (potential prison stays) and committal orders. In extreme cases the court can transfer the residence to the other parent.

Other issues that can be brought to the court

The court can also deal with other specific issues of childcare between parents and other family members. This section will explain how they deal with such applications.

CHANGING A CHILD'S SURNAME

If a child is to be brought up in a new family, a parent (usually the mother) may want to change the child's surname to that of her new partner. Whether there is anything in the law preventing her from doing so depends on the existence of a residence order.

If such an order is in force, there will automatically be a provision stating that the child's surname cannot be changed without the consent of the other parent or the court. But if no such order exists, the mother can in theory change the child's surname, as she has parental responsibility that she can exercise independently. However, in practice, where two parents both have parental responsibility, the parent who wants a name change should first try to obtain the other parent's consent. He or she can then apply to the court for permission if the other parent objects. A parent who objects can in any event apply to the court for a specific issue order to stop the name change. The court application will be decided by

the principles that the child's welfare is of paramount consideration and that no court order will be made unless this is better for the child.

The court has tended to disapprove of changes of name, taking the view that the link between a child and his or her natural parent is symbolised by the surname and should not be broken, so changes of surname have usually been refused.

However, a mature child him- or herself may apply for a change of surname by way of a specific issue order. If the child has strong feelings about wanting to be included in the new family and sound reasons for making the application, the court may be persuaded to make an order for a change, given that the child's wishes and feelings rank number one on the welfare checklist.

Activity directions

Since December 2008 the court has been able to specify contact activity directions, which can include a requirement for one parent to attend classes, counselling, etc, and can make this a condition of contact.

CHANGING THE LOCATION OF A CHILD'S HOME

A residence order does not state where a child must live, and if one parent wishes to move (either to another part of England and Wales, or elsewhere) and the other parent does not agree, an application can be made and the court will make the decision by deciding what is in the best interests of the child.

In reviewing the application the court will consider the reasons for the move, the benefit to the child of the move and the effect this will have on the child's contact with the other parent. This can be a difficult decision for the judge, as they have to balance the parent's right to move against the effect that the move will have on the other parent's contact.

If you find yourself making this application, or defending it, you should take specialist legal advice to ensure the court has all of the information necessary within the evidence you will be obliged to file to enable all of your issues/concerns to be presented to the court.

TAKING A CHILD ABROAD FOR A HOLIDAY

If there is a residence order, the usual rule is that a parent who wants to take a child outside of England or Wales should obtain the other parent's written consent first. This is because it is a criminal offence to remove a child from the country without the written consent of both parents or the consent of the court.

Where a parent wants to take the child on holiday and has a residence order in his or her favour, he or she can take the child abroad for a period of up to a month. A contact order does not come with this permission and so a non-resident parent must seek the consent of the parent with a residence order. In either situation, if the other parent objects an application can be made to the court for its permission by way of a section 8 order. (See also Chapter 7 on child abduction.)

If there is no residence order, the civil law says nothing either to permit

DNA

If there is concern about who is the biological father of a child, the court has the power to order DNA testing under the Family Law Act of 1969. They will only order this if they consider that such a test is in the best interests of the child.

or prevent a parent from taking a child abroad. Again, if the parents are in dispute, one or other should apply for a section 8 order. But whether or not a residence order exists, the criminal law still applies.

In considering an application the court will use the same Children Act checklist (see page 102) to decide if the request or opposition is reasonable or justified in the circumstances.

APPLICATIONS BY GRANDPARENTS AND OTHERS

When a family splits up, sometimes the contact between the children and one set of the grandparents ends, as families divide into opposing camps. This is rarely good for the children: often they can be helped to cope with their distress by grandparents (or other close relatives or friends, say, perhaps a godparent), who can give a helping hand to guide the children through the sad and difficult times. Grandparents (or for that matter any other interested relative or family friend) can apply to the court for a contact order or other section 8 order. They do not have to wait until divorce or other proceedings have been started.

Before such an application can proceed, they may have to obtain the court's permission. The Children Act gives some categories of people the automatic right to make an application, see box above right.

Contact rights

You have an automatic right to make an application under the Children Act for contact or another section 8 order if:

- You have had the child living with you for three years or more in the last five years (and within the last three months), or,
- You have the consent of the person with a residence order in his or her favour, or,
- You have the consent of everyone with parental responsibility (or that of the local authority if the child is in care).

Otherwise, the court's permission must be obtained before the application will be given the go-ahead.

If applicants, such as grandparents, have lost contact with the children over many years and formerly had a bad influence on them, it is possible that their application for permission to apply to the court will fail. The legal test is whether a grandparent can show that he or she has a 'good arguable case' and that there is a serious issue to try. Usually the court will grant permission to apply and leave a full investigation to a proper court hearing involving all sides.

Applications for contact by grandparents are likely to be granted, unless there is deep bitterness between the families that would be exacerbated by making a contact

---

 For help and support for grandparents, contact the Grandparents' Association: advice line 0845 4349585: www.grandparents-association.org.uk

order. Contact orders can be in the form of letters, cards and telephone calls, so the court may make an order for contact in stages, building up contact from letters and telephone calls before a face-to-face meeting, especially if the grandparents have not met their grandchildren for a long time.

Applications for residence orders by grandparents are unlikely to succeed, unless the natural parents (or the local authority if the child is in care) are fully in support and the child has established a pattern of living with a grandparent.

LEGAL REPRESENTATION FOR CHILDREN

Applications to the court may not be the best way of sorting out children's problems. It is important to consider mediation or a form of therapeutic help.

A child can be separately represented in court. This generally happens where parents have different views of what a child thinks, and/or their views are firmly opposed.

A child's interests can be represented by a 'children's guardian', a person skilled and experienced in dealing with children, who will put the arguments for what is in the child's best interests. This often happens where the local authority is involved, and sometimes in private cases. The court can also (though rarely) appoint the Official Solicitor to act for the child.

APPLICATIONS BY A CHILD

If a child is old enough and sensible enough, he or she can make their own application to the court under the Children Act. Legal aid can be granted to the child.

Children have brought cases to ask the court for a residence order that they live somewhere else, or for a contact order that the parent who has left the home be made to see them (sometimes against their parent's will). The court needs to be convinced that the child making the application is mature and has sound reasons for asking the court for help, and is not making the application on impulse because of a row with a parent.

APPEALS

Successful appeals against decisions made by the trial judge (the one who originally heard the case) are extremely rare. The judge has a wide discretion, and appeals will be allowed only if the first decision can be shown to be 'plainly wrong'. This is so even if the appeal court feels it would have come to another decision itself. If further important evidence comes to light, then an appeal might work. If you do go to the Court of Appeal, you may be offered a mediation session to see whether the problem can be resolved out of court.

For children's representation contact Resolution: www.resolution.org.uk or the Children's Legal Centre: 01206 877963 or 0808 802 0008. Young people call free on 0800 783 2187: www.childrenslegalcentre.com

An appeal against a decision of either the county court (for family cases this is called a Family Hearing Centre), or the Family Proceedings Panel within a magistrates' court will go straight to the High Court. From the High Court an appeal will go to the Court of Appeal.

OUTDATED LEGAL TERMS

Before the implementation of the Children Act, there were three different legal concepts applicable to children: custody, care and control, and access. The legal usage of some of the words was (and is) different from ordinary English usage. Because these terms are still popularly used even though they no longer apply, it is useful to be aware of what they mean.

Custody

This meant the bundle of responsibilities that parents have towards their children, for example, the right and duty to make major decisions concerning their upbringing, their religion and education.
Sole custody (for one parent).
Joint custody (for both).

Joint custody was the court order that resembled most closely the pre-divorce role towards the children. In a sense, the effect of a joint custody order was primarily psychological, because it confirmed, for the parent who did not look after them, the fact that he or she had a recognised role to play towards his or her children. ('Parental responsibility' now fulfils this function.)

Care and control

This meant the actual physical 'possession' of the child. Orders were made only for the sole care and control: an order for care and control could not be split (unlike the new residence orders).

An order for care and control was granted to the parent with whom the children were living on a regular basis. Even in the unusual cases where children divided their time equally between their parents, only one parent used to have an order for care and control.

Access

This meant the actual visiting periods for the parent who did not have care and control.
Staying access: the child stayed with the non-custodial parent.
Visiting access: the non-custodial parent simply visited or took the child out for the day.
Reasonable access: the parents would agree this between themselves. Where the parents could not agree, the court may have made an order for **Defined access**, determining when the child would visit the non-custodial parent, sometimes specifying even the times when the child should be collected and brought home again.

Child maintenance

If you cannot agree the amount of maintenance that should be paid for your children, you will probably need to contact the Child Support Agency. This applies to parents in married and unmarried situations, although there are some exceptions where the court retains the power to make decisions about maintenance for children.

The Child Support Agency

The Child Support Agency is the government's child maintenance service, which, since legislation in 2008, is provided by the Child Maintenance and Enforcement Commission (CMEC). New rules came into force in March 2003 and again in 2008. At the time of writing it is anticipated that the new formula and calculations will be implemented by 2011, although this is always subject to change and review.

THE CHILD SUPPORT AGENCY

Legislation in 1991 introduced the first formula for the Child Support Agency (CSA) to calculate child maintenance. This was based upon the respective incomes and allowable outgoings of both parents and a formula was then applied that calculated the amount of maintenance to be paid for a child. This was replaced by a new formula in 2000, which calculated the maintenance payable as a strict percentage of the net income of the non-resident parent (NRP).

Legislation in 2008 amended the formula again, introducing a maintenance calculation to be based on a percentage of the NRP's gross income. There is at present no date confirmed for when the new formula will apply but it is anticipated this will be during 2011.

This means that until then, the CSA will continue to calculate maintenance under the current formulas.

It is intended that by 2014 there will be a single system of child maintenance in place, but how maintenance calculations will be dealt with during the integration of the two schemes has yet to be confirmed.

The 2008 legislation also created CMEC – the Child Maintenance and Enforcement Commission ('The Commission'), which, since November 2008, has been responsible for the CSA with the aim of making it more efficient and successful in calculating, collecting and enforcing child maintenance. CMEC also has specific functions in assisting parents to reach agreement without a formal maintenance assesment.

 The Child Support Agency (CSA) website is very clear and informative: www.csa.gov.uk: national helpline: 08457 133 133.

GETTING ADVICE ABOUT THE CSA

Solicitors, the Citizens Advice Bureau and some law centres may be able to advise you about the child support you could seek through the CSA. The calculations can appear complicated, and these advisors often have computer programmes which will work out how much maintenance you could be entitled to under the CSA formula.

Such advice can be offered under the Legal Help scheme (see Chapter 1), but this is extremely limited in amount and you cannot be assisted in completing forms, only in legal points or issues. It is possible to use a solicitor as a 'McKenzie friend' (see opposite) at a CSA tribunal hearing under the Legal Help scheme.

You cannot seek legal aid for challenging a CSA decision or asking for a review, unless your case is successfully appealed to the CSA appeals tribunal, or to the Child Support Commissioner, and a point of law requires you to apply for funding to take the matter to court. Legal aid is available if there is a paternity dispute.

Jargon buster

Terminology and jurisdiction used by the CSA.

Parent Parent of a child by blood or adoption. Step-parents are not liable for maintenance under the CSA, though they may be through divorce proceedings.

The non-resident parent (formerly called the 'absent parent') The non-resident parent (NRP) is defined as a parent who no longer lives in the same household as the child for whom the maintenance is applied.

The parent/person with care (PWC) The parent/person with care is the person whom the child lives with and who has the usual day-to-day care of the child.

The qualifying child The child must be under 16, or under 19 but still in full-time, non-advanced education.

Habitual residence The child and both the parents must be habitually resident in the UK. Habitual residence means usual residence with a settled intention to remain. If the non-resident parent is abroad, the CSA cannot deal with maintenance (unless the NRP is employed by a UK company), and the court will have to deal with it instead.

McKenzie friend A helper (does not have to be a lawyer) who can accompany a litigator in person in the court room, even in a closed hearing, but who cannot address the court or examine witnesses.

> **"** Step-parents are not responsible for the maintenance of their step-children under the CSA, although they may be in divorce proceedings if the children are 'children of the family'. **"**

POWERS OF THE CSA

The CSA has the power to calculate maintenance and enforce payment if the following conditions are met:

- There is a qualifying child or children.
- One parent (by blood or adoption) no longer lives in the same household as the child(ren).
- Both parents are habitually resident in the UK.

The CSA calculates the maintenance due to be paid according to the formula laid down in the 1991 Act and in subsequent legislation. It should trace the non-resident parent and pursue them for maintenance.

It has powers to investigate a parent's income and capital. If the non-resident parent does not pay, it has powers to compel payment, the most effective of which is by direct deduction from wages.

MAINTENANCE: WHAT ARE YOUR OPTIONS?

Before October 2008, if you were in receipt of benefits you had to use the CSA to deal with maintenance assessments. This has now been abolished and so everyone has the choice of either using the CSA or making an agreement with the child's other parent about the maintenance that should be paid.

A free advice and support service (Child Maintenance Options) has been created by CMEC to help you decide what child maintenance option is best for you. This service can provide information and support and can be used anonymously. There are also some limited situations where you can ask the court to assist with child maintenance.

PRIVATE AGREEMENTS

You can try and reach an agreement directly with your ex about the maintenance that will be paid for the child/children, which means you will not need to involve the CSA at all. This is obviously the most amicable solution, but whether this is achievable depends on your situation.

To have a private agreement, you and your ex will need to reach agreement about what is a fair amount of child maintenance to be paid. To assist with your discussion and

For further information on the services provided by Child Maintenance Options:
0800 988 0988: www.cmoptions.org

negotiations, you can seek advice from Child Maintenance Options about what would be payable if you were to approach the CSA. For guidance there are also maintenance calculators to assist you on the CSA website.

You need to ensure that whatever figure you agree provides you with enough money to cover your expenses. The website offers agreements that can be downloaded and completed by you to document your agreement. However, these are not enforceable and so any private arrangements entered into between parents must be done in the knowledge that either parent could change their mind about the agreement at any time and apply to CSA.

If you are divorcing, you can ask the court to make a consent order within the ancillary relief proceedings, confirming the maintenance figure you have agreed. This consent order would then be enforceable for a period of 12 months. If you wanted to vary the amount you would need to give your spouse/cp two months notice at the end of the 12 month period, after which time either you

(Either parent can apply for a maintenance assessment, though normally it is the parent with care.))

or your spouse/cp could apply to the CSA to vary the amount of child maintenance agreed.

CSA ASSESSMENT

If you meet the CSA conditions outlined on page 114, you can apply to them to calculate and pursue child maintenance for you. This avoids the need for any direct contact between you and your ex.

The CSA can help trace your ex or obtain financial information from them that they were otherwise unwilling to provide. It is a criminal offence to not give information requested by the CSA, or to give false information. There is no charge for the CSA's services and a CSA arrangement is legally binding.

Who can apply, when and how?

You can make an application as soon as you separate from your ex. You can get an application form by writing to or telephoning your CSA branch office. You can also download it from the CSA website.

Once the application has been made, the non-resident parent will get an equally long form to complete and send back. If they delay for more than 28 days, the CSA can levy an interim assessment,

Maintenance and benefits

Since April 2010, if you are receiving income-related benefits, you can keep all of the maintenance paid by your ex without it affecting your benefit payments. Child maintenance has no impact on your entitlement to council tax benefit and housing benefit.

115

at default rates: £30 per week for one qualifying child, £40 for two, £50 for three or more.

How are payments made?

Both parents will be asked whether their preference is to receive weekly or monthly payments, but the CSA will make the final decision.

When the assessment is made, the non-resident parent can either make the payments directly to the parent with care, or to the CSA by direct debit or standing order. The CSA will then ensure that the payments are passed on to the parent with care.

When do payments start?

Maintenance liability usually starts as soon as the non-resident parent is notified of the application. However, at this stage liability will not have been worked out and, as it may be some weeks before it is, the liability will build up from that date.

Voluntary payments can either be payments directly to the parent with care, or payments for regular household outgoings, like utility bills, or rent or mortgage. You should document these so that the evidence can be produced to the CSA.

> ❝ Both parents will be asked if they prefer weekly or monthly payments, but the CSA will make the final decision. ❞

School fees (see also page 119)

The CSA does not have power to order that a NRP should pay school fees. This must instead form part of an application to the court and subsequent court order, if appropriate. School fees payments are specifically for children in private education and do not cover after-school activities or day trips for children in state education. Such costs are deemed as covered by the CSA formula or spousal/cp maintenance if orders are made within ancillary relief proceedings during a divorce.

The amount of the voluntary payments should then be set off against the arrears. All voluntary payments can be made straight to the parent with care or they can be made through the CSA.

The CSA aim to set up a child maintenance arrangement within 12 weeks of an application being made, but there has been a lot of publicity about the delays that occur in this process.

Not just a simple percentage of income...

Along with the percentage calculations that are applied to the NRP's income, there are also deductions made for overnights stays that the NRP has with the child (which are calculated as a 1/7 reduction of maintenance for each night per week, on average through the year, that parent has the child for) If the NRP has other children living at his home on a permanent basis, such as step-children, the income is also reduced before the calculation is made. A percentage deduction is made for these children before the CSA calculate what income they should apply their formula to. See Appendices A1 and A2 for more detail.

> **“** To prevent the build-up of arrears, it is a good idea to start making voluntary payments to the parent with care as soon as possible. **”**

The CSA have a variety of enforcement options to recover maintenance payments from the NRP, including obtaining liability orders that can result in disqualification from driving, curfews, removal of the NRP's passport, civil debt recovery through the county court (such as. bailiff's warrants and charging orders), regular payment

What happens if the non-resident parent does not pay?

If the payments are being made directly to the parent with care, they will need to tell the CSA if these are being made late, or not at all. If the payments are being made to the CSA, it is supposed to chase them if they are more than two days late. It can charge a penalty for each week of late or non-payment and can also take enforcement proceedings to recover payments.

Variation and review

There is currently a review built into every assessment on a two-year cycle: this leads to a re-assessment taking place. You can also request a review if the NRP's circumstances change by more than 5 per cent. Maintenance awards made under the new proposals/formula will be fixed for 12 months, unless there is an income change of more than 25 per cent.

 One Parent Families/Gingerbread provides a fact sheet, 'Making arrangements for child maintenance', about using the CSA. Visit www.gingerbread.org.uk to access the fact sheet.

> **"The court has power to commit a non-resident parent to prison, or remove his driving licence as a sanction, if he refuses to pay."**

APPLYING THE FORMULA
Go to Appendices A1 and A2 on pages 241 and 244 to see how the current and proposed CSA formulas are applied.

 If you are on a low income you may be able to ask someone from your local Welfare Rights Advice Agency to come with you to an appeal tribunal and help you prepare your case.

deduction orders, lump-sum deduction orders and deduction from earning orders. There are also plans to enable the CSA/CMEC to be able to take money directly from bank accounts to cover maintenance and arrears.

CHALLENGING A CSA ASSESSMENT

If you feel that your assessment is wrong, you can seek to challenge it. The first stage in this process is an internal review, which will be carried out by a different Child Support Officer from the one who dealt with your case. If you are still dissatisfied, you can appeal to a Child Support Appeal Tribunal, and thereafter to a Child Support Commissioner. If you feel the decision was still wrong in law, you can appeal further to the Court of Appeal. All this will cost time and probably money – legal aid is not available until an appeal has been made to the Court of Appeal.

Financial applications to the court for children

If the CSA does not apply to you and your children, you will have to look at other ways of making an application for maintenance for the children. This section outlines some of the options.

As well as reforming the legal framework of the relationships between parents and children, the Children Act 1989 codified the law about financial applications for children. It also enables children over 18 to apply for periodical payments or a lump sum.

APPLICATIONS ON BEHALF OF CHILDREN

The court retains powers to make orders for step-children and other children for whom the CSA cannot act. This includes children whose non-resident parent works – and so habitually resides – abroad (where he is not employed by a UK-based company). Even where the CSA has jurisdiction over maintenance you can still apply to the court:

- For an order for school fees.
- For the particular needs of a disabled child.
- For a 'top-up' order if the non-resident parent's net weekly income is more than £2,000 (or more than £3,000 gross per week under the new formula).

The orders the court can make for children

- Periodical payments (maintenance). (Periodical payments can be secured, which means that they are guaranteed by a deposit of capital money, but this is very seldom done.)
- A lump sum.
- A settlement of property.
- A transfer of property to the applicant for the benefit of the child or directly to the child (a transfer of property could cover a transfer of a tenancy as well).

- To vary an existing court maintenance order
- For a capital sum or a property order. If you are in the process of a divorce and your children have been treated as children of the family by your spouse/cp, who is their step-parent, you can apply to the court in those proceedings. If there are no divorce proceedings then you make the application under the scope of the Children Act 1989.

119

Applications outside divorce proceedings can be made to either a magistrates' court (Family Proceedings Panel), the county court (Family Hearing Centre), or the High Court, although the magistrates' court has power to order only periodical payments or a lump sum.

The court must look at all the circumstances, including the income and the earning capacity of the parties (and the financial position of the child), their needs and obligations, any physical or mental disability of the child, and the way in which the child was (or expects to be) educated or trained; this approach is often summed up as 'needs and resources'.

If you are applying for support from a step-parent then the court must also take into account the level of support the child has had from the step-parent in the past, whether there is anyone else who is liable to support the child, and whether the step-parent has known that the child is not his/hers.

APPLICATIONS BY CHILDREN OVER 18

Children over 18 can apply for periodical payments (such as weekly or monthly payments), or a lump sum if he or she is in full-time education or training (although this would also cover situations where the son or daughter was working in the evenings to supplement his or her income while in continuing education). The court will take the same approach as outlined above.

Restrictions on applications

Applications by children over 18 can be made only if the parents (whether married or not) are no longer living together in the same household and there was no previous maintenance order in existence before the child's 16th birthday. In other words, this provision is intended primarily for children who plan to go on to further education and whose parents have comparatively recently split up. Instead of the parent being forced to go to court to chase up maintenance payments, the son or daughter can make his or her own application. Such children can also apply if they are not covered by the CSA, that is, they are 19 or over.

Emergencies

This chapter deals with situations in which you might need the law to protect you or your children. It covers domestic violence and abuse and child abduction. The law for married and unmarried couples is virtually the same in these cases. It also covers the steps you can take to prevent assets from being disposed of if you are married.

Protecting yourself from domestic abuse

This section will give you clear and practical advice if you have been, or are, a victim of domestic abuse. It covers aspects of the law, as well as places to get advice and sanctuary.

Domestic abuse (which ranges from physical violence to psychological cruelty) most commonly occurs within the confines of the home, behind closed doors, with no outsider witnessing the event. Domestic abuse cuts across all classes of society. Statistics estimate that one in four women will experience some form of abuse. Two women a week are killed by their partners. Men are also (though less frequently) victims of domestic abuse.

Increasingly 'domestic abuse' has replaced the term 'domestic violence', recognising that there is a wide spectrum of frightening behaviour that ranges from outright physical violence to psychological abuse. It is possible to be badly harmed without being physically assaulted. Children who are not being directly abused will suffer from seeing a parent being abused.

The problem of domestic abuse has received much greater recognition in recent years and there are government initiatives to try to tackle the problem, including 'Sanctuary schemes', to give women safe places in their own homes. The police, who at one time would refuse to get involved with a 'domestic', now have proper procedures and officers specifically trained to deal with domestic abuse, and their powers of intervention have been strengthened.

If you are the subject of abuse, you need to take steps quickly to protect yourself, and any children who live with you. Deal with the practical issues of safety first and then take legal steps to protect your rights.

If you are behaving abusively towards your partner, you too need to take fast preventive action, for example by leaving the home or seeking help to stop the abusive behaviour. There are perpetrator programmes to help people who abuse their partners to

 Freephone 24 hour National Domestic Violence Helpline runs in partnership between Women's Aid and Refuge: 0161 636 7525.

change their behaviour. Respect is the UK membership association for domestic abuse perpetrator programmes (see below).

MAKING SURE THAT YOU ARE SAFE

In principle, and generally, it is tactically better to remain in the family home until either an agreement is reached or court proceedings have been finalised. But in an emergency you may have no choice except to leave home for the time being so as to be safe from harm.

Leaving your home

If possible, take the children with you. It may be unsafe to leave them behind. If you can't take them, you need to take urgent legal advice about getting back to them. You won't lose your rights as a parent if you have to leave them. However, if the children remain with your ex for a reasonably long period of time, the court might take the view that it would be unduly unsettling for them to move home.

Finding somewhere to stay

If you leave your home because of abuse, there are generally two ways in which you can get emergency shelter, if you cannot stay with family or friends: you apply to your local authority, or you can look for a place in a refuge.

Aid agencies

Women's Aid: www.womensaid.org.uk
Refuge: www.refuge.org.uk
0800 200 0247
Wales Domestic Abuse Helpline:
0808 80 10 800
Pathway Project: www.pathway-project.co.uk
01543 676800
Southall Black Sisters: www.southallblacksisters.org.uk
020 8571 9595
Rights of Women: Confidential legal advice line for women, run by women. www.rightsofwomen.org.uk
020 7251 6577
NSPCC: www.nspcc.org.uk
0808 800 500
Advice for male victims of abuse: www.mensadviceline.org.uk
Male Helpline – 0808 801 0327
Alcoholics Anonymous:
www.alcoholics-anonymous.org.uk
0845 769 7555
Information on substance abuse:
www.drugsline.org
0808 160 6606
For lesbian/gay/bisexual: www.broken-rainbow.org.uk

Respect: 020 7022 1801 for information: www.respect.uk.net or you can email info@respectphoneline.org.uk.
Everyman Project: www.everymanproject.co.uk

Essentials to take with you

If you can get away from the home with a bit of planning beforehand, think about taking the essentials that you will need until you can return. Obviously you will need clothes and toiletries, but you might also require the following documents:

- Your National Insurance number.
- Your bank details and savings books.
- Your benefit books or details.
- Your passport and any children's passports.
- Any other personal identification of the sort that you need to open a bank account.
- Your children's health record books.
- A recent photograph of your ex – in case you need to have court papers served on him/her.

Contact numbers
The contact numbers for refuges are closely guarded, in order to ensure that victims of abuse in refuges and their families are not harassed further by their violent partners or ex-partners.

- There are a number of women's refuges across England and Wales that provide a temporary home for female victims of domestic abuse and their children. Refuge and Women's Aid can advise you about where to go.

If you have sufficient funds you can go into private rented accommodation. However, this is only an option if you have time to plan for your departure, and the resources to pay the rent.

- Your local authority is under an obligation to provide accommodation for you if you have priority needs (for example, you have young children living with you), and have nowhere else to stay. You will not count as being 'intentionally homeless' (which would allow them to refuse to house you) if you have left as a result of abuse and you are taking steps to return. Contact – by telephone, or in person if you can – the housing department of your local authority or the social services department. The accommodation they are most likely to offer will be a basic bed and breakfast hostel.

❝ If you are a man without children and you have left home because of abuse, your chances of being re-housed are slim. You may have to depend on your own resources or on the kindness of family and friends. ❞

MONEY TO LIVE ON

If you can make a planned escape, you should make sure you have some money put away or saved up that you can get hold of once you have left the home.

If you have joint bank accounts, think about taking steps to prevent your ex drawing out all the funds once you have left. You can arrange with the bank or building society that the account is frozen or changed so that you both have to agree before money can be withdrawn. As this might be a problem for you in the future, if you want to take money out, make sure that you have withdrawn enough money for your own needs first.

IF YOU HAVE BEEN INJURED

If you have been physically hurt, even if the injury is not serious, go and see your doctor or the casualty department of the local hospital as soon as possible. Make sure that a physical examination is carried out and the injuries are noted on your medical records.

Such records can provide useful evidence in court proceedings. Your solicitor may ask the doctor concerned to prepare a report. If you have visible injuries try to get someone to photograph them. Some solicitors keep a digital camera for this purpose. The photographs can be used in evidence also.

CONTACTING THE POLICE

Police forces have Domestic Violence Units, with staff specially trained to help and protect people experiencing domestic abuse. If you call the police for advice,

the DVU will probably contact you and explain what can be done to protect you.

If you call the police in the middle of, or just after, an incident of abuse they will take steps to protect you and any children as soon as possible. This may involve arresting your ex. The police can also impose conditions on police bail that are designed to keep you safe.

If you call the police during a violent incident (dial 999) it is vital that you give your whereabouts, particularly if you are using a mobile phone.

> ❝ The police, who at one time would refuse to get involved with a 'domestic', now have proper procedures and officers specifically trained to deal with domestic abuse. ❞

If your ex has been violent or acted in a way that is criminal, then the police can bring a criminal prosecution. The decision about this is made by the police and the Crown Prosecution Service. They act for the state, not for you, so the prosecution is not your choice. They will obviously need your help in any investigation. If you decide that you do not want to make what is called a 'complaint', the matter may stop there. But if there are other witnesses to the crime, a prosecution might be brought without your consent.

GETTING LEGAL ADVICE

See Chapter 3 for how to find a solicitor. Some solicitors in different areas have joined together to run a domestic abuse circle to ensure that a victim can get immediate access to a solicitor who specialises in dealing with these cases. If one firm cannot take on your case, they will pass you on to another. The police or your local Citizens Advice Bureau should be also be able to give you the names of local firms who can help you. Legal aid is available for domestic abuse applications if you meet the financial criteria (see Chapter 1 and page 128).

The Family Law Act 1996

Part IV of the Family Law Act 1996 How can it help me?
Get this leaflet from your local County court or download from the Courts Service website: www.hmscourts-service.gov.uk

---

CHANGING THE LOCKS

If you have got to the point where you feel you wish to, or need to, change the locks on the family home, preventing your ex from entering, or if you have been locked out yourself or are in danger of being locked out, see the chart below for your rights and those of your ex.

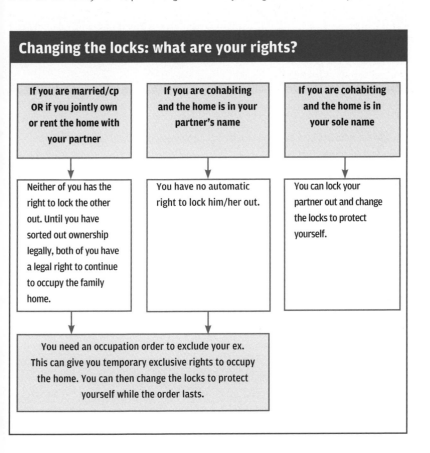

Changing the locks: what are your rights?

If you are married/cp OR if you jointly own or rent the home with your partner	If you are cohabiting and the home is in your partner's name	If you are cohabiting and the home is in your sole name
Neither of you has the right to lock the other out. Until you have sorted out ownership legally, both of you have a legal right to continue to occupy the family home.	You have no automatic right to lock him/her out.	You can lock your partner out and change the locks to protect yourself.

You need an occupation order to exclude your ex. This can give you temporary exclusive rights to occupy the home. You can then change the locks to protect yourself while the order lasts.

See Which? Essential Guide *Renting and Letting* for more details on tenancy law and rights.

Legal steps to protect yourself from abuse

Practical steps to avoid domestic abuse generally also need some legal protection. This can range from a stern solicitor's letter to a court order with a power of arrest.

If you find yourself in a position where you need to protect yourself or your children from abuse from an ex or family member, you need to obtain urgent legal advice. Advice for these applications can be funded under the Legal Help scheme or legal aid if you are financially eligible (see Chapter 1). If you or your children are at imminent danger of significant harm, it may also be possible to obtain emergency legal aid, which will cover the costs of an urgent application to the court if this is necessary to protect you. Funding applications of this type from your own capital can be very expensive, and often run into significant sums.

Your solicitor will be able to give you details and information about local housing and support, while also providing you with legal advice about the options you have. Initially, if it is appropriate, they may suggest sending a letter to your ex outlining your legal rights and warning them what action you will be forced to take if their behaviour continues. It may also be sensible for you to contact the police and commence criminal proceedings, to prevent further abuse

towards you. If you are applying for legal aid, the application will ask if these options have been investigated, and if not, why they are not appropriate in your particular circumstances.

Even after taking these steps, there are still some situations where a court application is required to prevent your ex from continuing to be abusive towards you or to have them removed from your home to protect you/your children. Acting speedily can have a significant effect on the chances of your application being successful.

If you are not eligible for legal aid, and cannot afford to pay a solicitor from your income/capital, you can act in person. The forms to make the applications can be obtained from your local county court, along with information and guidance about the process.

DOMESTIC ABUSE AND INJUNCTIONS

The Family Law Act, 1996, Part IV, covers all applications in all courts for domestic abuse injunctions. Under this law, married and cp couples, cohabitants and ex-cohabitants, other family members and people who have lived in the same household can seek the court's protection.

Which court?

All levels of court can make the orders, it will be up to you and your solicitor to decide which to use. If you have already started off divorce proceedings, it is likely to be the court that is dealing with your divorce case that you will apply to – otherwise it will be the local county court or possibly the family proceedings court (magistrates). Most injunctions are at present dealt with the in county court.

Obtaining an injunction to protect the children

In the rarer cases where it is only the children, rather than an adult, who are at risk, the court can make an order stopping contact between the violent (or abusive) adult and the children. Social services departments can also take action under an emergency protection order or an interim care order, and can seek an occupation order to remove an abuser (say a step-parent) from the family home.

The two main court orders available

A non-molestation order	Orders your ex not to assault, molest or otherwise interfere with you (or your children). 'Molestation' includes repeated telephone calls, as well as other forms of harassment.
An occupation order	Can order an abusing ex to leave the home and/or not come within a specified area around it (for example, 100 yards around the home). An occupation order can also allow an ex back into the home if she/he has left it out of fear of violence and can order the abusing ex to let her/him back in (and possibly require him/her to leave, too). Occasionally, the court may make an order confining a person to a defined part of the home, but this is rarely practicable.

Applying for an injunction

There are various documents that must be filed at court to start off the application for either a non-molestation order or an occupation order. This section will help you through the process and procedures.

To make an application for a non-molestation order or occupation order you will need to complete the following forms:

- An application form (FL401), which can be obtained from the court office or website (www.hmcourts-service.gov.uk). This will need to be completed and filed with the court in triplicate. A further copy may be required if you are seeking an occupation order, as a copy will need to be served on the landlord/mortgage company of your home.

- A sworn statement (or Form N285) that outlines the reasons for the application and why you need the order, to enable the court to decide what order is appropriate. Explain the effect the order will have on your health, safety and wellbeing (and for your children) and what the impact of the order would be on your ex. If you are not married the court will need to be sure you are entitled to make the application, so you need to include details of how long you have been in a relationship and how long you have been separated, if you have children or step-children and if there are any other court proceedings happening with regard to your family. If you are applying for an occupation order

Service of court documents

Your solicitor (or you if you are acting for yourself) has to make sure that your ex gets the court papers. This is normally done by arranging to hand them to him/her personally. This is so the court can be satisfied they have been properly delivered. Often a solicitor will get a 'process server' or a court bailiff to do this. It is helpful if you can give your solicitor a photograph of your ex and as much information as possible about where he/she works and spends leisure time.

you also need to give details of your housing needs and your ex's (along with the needs of any children) and your respective financial circumstances, including available income and capital. A fee, currently £60, needs to be paid when the application is sent to the court. Depending on your financial circumstances you may be exempt from this, and if so another form needs to be given to the court at the same time to enable it to issue the application without the fee.

WHAT HAPPENS NEXT?

Once you have sent your application to the court they will set a time and date for you and your ex to attend a hearing. Your application and sworn statement will be served on your ex (known as the Respondent from then on), with notification of when the hearing date has been set (see box opposite). There needs to be at least two clear working days between the day the Respondent is given the documentation, and the hearing date. The Respondent has an opportunity to respond to your application and statement, with his/her own statement and comments on what alternative housing options/alternatives are available and if they think the application is justified.

There is an exception when your application is made on an emergency basis. In this situation the Respondent is not given notice of your application before the hearing, which will be scheduled at the court urgently (usually the same day or with a few days), and he/she will not have a chance to respond to what you have said until a later date, after the court have considered your application at an emergency ('without notice') hearing. It can be difficult to get an emergency occupation order, as the judge will want to be sure of all of the facts before removing the Respondent from your home, unless there are extenuating circumstances.

In deciding if your application should be granted, the judge will review the evidence and if there are any alternatives to making an order. If you have applied for a non-molestation order, they will consider if there has been harm to you/any child as a result of the Respondent's conduct and the effect that making or refusing the order would have on the health safety and wellbeing of you, the children or the Respondent. In deciding if an occupation order should be made, the judge will consider:

- The housing/financial needs and resources you both have.
- The effect that making or refusing the order would have on the health, safety and wellbeing of you, the children or the Respondent.
- The conduct of you and the Respondent in relation to each other.
- A balancing exercise considering harm that will be suffered by you and any children, and the Respondent, if an order is made.
- What options and alternatives there are to resolve the problem, such as an undertakings, and if an order is necessary now if other proceedings are underway, such as financial applications following divorce proceedings.

To have an occupation order made, it is common for the court to require evidence of intolerable abuse or physical violence, as the order is a serious one that a judge will not make lightly. This type of application should not be seen as a way of 'getting the house', as an occupation order is normally only a temporary measure (for a specified time period) to protect you until the longer-term housing issues are resolved. If you reconcile and choose to resume cohabitation with the Respondent following an order having been made, the order will lapse and no longer have an effect.

POWER OF ARREST

The judge can decide that a power of arrest should be attached to an occupation order if violence has been used or threatened by the Respondent. A power of arrest means that the Respondent is able to be arrested from the moment the order has been served.

A power of arrest used to be able to be attached to non-molestation orders, but this is no longer possible or necessary, as breach of a non-molestation order is a now a criminal offence in itself.

If a power of arrest is made, the order must be personally served on the Respondent as soon as possible and a copy provided to the local police station. A power of arrest normally lasts for a fixed period of time and can be a useful incentive to stop the Respondent from breaching an occupation order.

UNDERTAKINGS

The Respondent can offer to make a promise to the court not to do certain things such as entering the home, or threatening you. Breach of an undertaking does not provide the potential criminal sanction protection that breach of a non-molestation order or power of arrest would have. The judge will not accept an undertaking if they think you need more protection than an undertaking gives. You should think carefully before you accept an undertaking as the protection offered is not the same as you would have if an order was made by the judge on your behalf.

IF YOU ARE A RESPONDENT

If your ex makes an application for an occupation order or non-molestation order against you, you should seek urgent legal advice to review your position. You may be eligible for Legal Help depending upon your financial circumstances. Your solicitor will prepare a statement in response to the application that has been made and review the options and alternatives. Legal aid is rarely granted unless you have good grounds to defend or contest the application that has been made. Defending the application on a private paying basis can be very expensive and reaching a compromise or alternative solution may be the best way forward.

If you know that you are at risk of being violent, or have been violent in the past you should do whatever you can to reduce the risk of that happening, even if that means leaving the property for a cooling off period. Be aware that things that judge believes have happened – such as violent behaviour – can be called a finding of fact that can be referred to in other proceedings you may be part of (such as contact/residence applications) and can be very damaging to your case.

Child abduction

Home office research has shown that approximately one quarter of child abductions are committed by a parent of the child, and over the last five years the number of such abductions has increased year on year. Abductions are statistically still very rare, but cause significant worry and upset for a family.

Taking a child out of the country without the prior written consent of the other parent, or the permission of the court, can be treated as a criminal offence under the Child Abduction Act 1984, which makes kidnapping a child a crime. There are also civil laws dealing with child abduction.

When the Children Act 1989 came into force, it provided a clear framework of when a child could be removed from England and Wales once a residence order had been made. When a residence order is in place, the parent who has residence can take the children out of the country for periods of up to a month, but not for longer than this. In other situations the consent of the other parent should be obtained before the child is taken abroad.

WHAT TO DO IF YOU ARE CONCERNED ABOUT RISKS OF ABDUCTION

If you believe that your child is at risk of abduction there are steps you can take if you can show your fear of abduction is genuine – such as if the child's other parent is a foreign national and you believe they may try to take the children back with them, or that they have threatened abduction.

In such circumstances, you can apply to the court for an order preventing the other parent from taking the child abroad without your permission (or the permission of the court), which is called a prohibited steps order. Alternatively you can apply for a residence order that will automatically restrict travel abroad for the non-resident parent. In the situation where you have concerns about abduction, seeking advice from a solicitor with experience in such applications would be best.

 Reunite (network for parents of abducted children): 0116 2556 234: www.reunite.org
International Child Abduction and Contact Unit: 020 7911 7045/7047:
www.officialsolicitor.gov.uk/os/icacu.htm

WHAT TO DO IF YOUR CHILD IS ABOUT TO BE ABDUCTED/HAS BEEN ABDUCTED

If your child has not been returned to you as you expected, or you believe that they have been abducted, you must act quickly. Any delay can limit your options and leaving things can mean that having your child returned could be harder to achieve and take a longer time.

This is a very specialist area of the law and there are a number of emergency steps that need to be taken to prevent the child from being taken out of the country, so urgent legal advice is recommended. Legal aid can be available for such issues if you qualify (see Chapter 1).

The applications that can be made to the court include a prohibited steps order, a residence order, an injunction and even making the child a ward of the court so that only the court can sanction the removal of the child from the country. The orders can be made without notice to the other parent, if necessary, and once granted are personally served on them so that they are aware of the court order.

Depending upon the urgency, such orders can also be made outside of normal court hours and this is where your solicitor is able to assist you in such an emergency. There are also applications that can be made under the Family Law Act 1986, which can be helpful in finding out the whereabouts of the child or having the child's passport returned to you.

You should also ask the police to issue a port alert. Depending on circumstances the court may need to order this before the police can take action (for example, when a child is over 16 or there is no clear order regarding residence). A port alert is only available if there is a real and imminent danger of abduction of a child (within the next 24 hours) and applies to all sea and air ports, which are notified of the details of the child immediately.

This used to be a significant power, but changes to EU border control means that a port alert is not so useful now. You can increase the chances of success of such a step by providing as much information about the child and parent as possible, including passport details, photographs and travel information if you have this.

Once the child has been taken out of the country the steps that you need to take vary depending on where the child has been taken to. If this is a country that has signed up to the Hague Convention then you should be able to get the appropriate authority in the country where the child is to take action to have the child returned.

If the country is not a signatory of the Hague convention, you will need to liaise with the Foreign and Commonwealth office and commence steps through the court to try and have the child returned. There are various actions and levers the court can try, but often the biggest hurdles can be finding the child and enforcing orders in the court in the country where the child now is. It is important that you have specialist legal advice as quickly as possible in these situations.

Preventing assets being disposed of

Sometimes one spouse/cp will try to prevent assets from being divided during divorce/dissolution proceedings by hiding or disposing of them. There are steps that can be taken to prevent such behaviour.

The court, unsurprisingly, does not give spouses/cps that take such action any leeway. As a result the court has power under legislation to prevent assets from being disposed of if they have sufficient notice, or undo transactions to get assets back if this is possible.

Making sure you act quickly if you believe your spouse/cp is about to do something to dispose of assets, or has already, is vitally important.

You need to decide if there is a risk of him/her acting in this way. Do you have reason to believe it is likely – have they made threats, do they have financial circumstance and arrangements they would not want the court to investigate? If they are particularly malicious or unscrupulous, and you have a real fear, you made need to take protective measures before you even separate.

Once assets or money are disposed of it is always more costly and difficult to get them back than it is to prevent them being used in the first place. Some of the actions you can take are practical and do not require the court's involvement, such as:

 Surrendering a tenancy
If you rent your home and your spouse/cp is a joint tenant with you or the sole tenant, he or she can surrender the tenancy to the landlord and you will not be able to get it transferred to you by a court order. If you want the opportunity to stay in the home you should get a formal undertaking from your spouse/cp that he or she will not make such a surrender. If this is refused, or if you fear that he/she will surrender it to spite you, you can seek an injunction to prevent this, which you can then serve on the landlord.

- **Joint accounts**. If you have joint accounts you should speak to the bank to put restrictions in place requiring joint authorisation from you both before money can be withdrawn.

If this is not possible the bank may freeze the account, which means that neither of you will be able to use or access the account until there is an agreement or order of the court. This can cause practical difficulties if the account has standing orders or direct debits that need to be paid, as the account will not be able to continue to make such payments if the bank has frozen it.

- **Joint credit cards**. The debts on joint credit cards will have to be assumed by one of you, and if you are concerned that the liability may be run up following separation you may want to take steps to prevent the card from being used further: you should stop the card with the provider as soon as possible.
- **Your home**. If you are married and your home is owned by your spouse/cp in their sole name, you need to register your rights (see page 50). If you are cohabiting there are still steps you can take at the Land Registry to protect your interest in the property and you should speak to your solicitor about this as soon as you can.

LEGAL OPTIONS

If the assets cannot be protected by the practical measures outlined above – for example, they are in your spouse's/cp's sole name – and you are concerned that they are about to be disposed of, you may need to make an application to the court. The application is for an injunction that will prevent your spouse/cp from disposing of that asset/s. This is a very complex area of the law where legal advice is required to ensure you protect your interest/assets adequately. To obtain such an order you need to tell the court sufficient information about your finances, and the risk of the disposal, to enable them to decide if the order is appropriate and necessary.

Injunctions can be expensive to obtain and your solicitor will need to review if incurring these costs is worth it, taking into account the value of the asset you are trying to protect. You may not have issued proceedings regarding your finances yet, and if you then need to make an emergency application you will have to file these as soon as possible after your emergency application has been made.

If the injunction is needed, the application can be made without any notice being given to your spouse/cp until afterwards, when the court order will be served upon them. This is to ensure that they do not have sufficient time to dispose of the asset before the court can make any decision about it.

The type of application is different if you are married or cohabiting. Spouses/cps are able to make applications under the Matrimonial Causes Act 1973, section 37, whereas cohabitants will need to use the civil court and the circumstances are more limited. Such applications can lead to assets being frozen, and so unable to be used for any purpose, and also, in specific (rare) circumstances, enable a warrant to be issued to allow a home or business premises to be searched.

Getting a divorce/dissolution

The Civil Partnership Act 2004 introduced procedures for the ending of a civil partnership that are virtually identical to those for ending a marriage. This section of the book applies to married and civil partner couples.

The law

This chapter outlines the law relating to divorce proceedings in England and Wales. For civil partners the procedure is the same, but the terms used are different; for example, divorce being called dissolution. To avoid duplication or confusion, this book uses the divorce terms and references to divorce apply equally to dissolution for cps.

LEGAL SEPARATION

If you and your spouse/cp are separated there is nothing you need to do to confirm this, as there is no official status to legal separation. You are able to confirm you have separated on documentation without having to apply to the court or complete any legal steps.

However, if you intend the separation to be long-term or permanent, you should consider having a separation agreement drawn up. This agreement will outline the arrangements for children, money and property following your separation and can be drawn up with the assistance of mediators or solicitors. The agreement is likely to have legal consequences, and so it is important that you have advice before signing it (see page 55).

If you are sure that your separation is permanent, but neither of you wishes to be divorced, you can apply for judicial

separation. This is rarely used anymore, but the details are outlined below.

JUDICIAL SEPARATION

If one spouse/cp does not agree that the marriage has irretrievable broken down, or does not want to get divorced for any reason, an alternative to divorce proceedings is to become judicially separated (or obtain a separation order if you are cps). The procedure for judicial separation is similar to divorce proceedings, but there is no Decree Nisi stage.

The facts that need to be proved are identical to divorce proceedings, and having gone through judicial separation proceedings you are not prevented from divorcing at any later stage and relying on the same fact (except for desertion).

A decree of judicial separation removes the obligation on spouses/cps to reside together and leaves you legally married,

The glossary on page 249 explains the jargon and indicates where there are different terms for civil partners.

Void/voidable

There are limited circumstances where a marriage does not need to be dissolved by divorce proceedings because it is void or voidable. This is a very technical area of law and rarely used. You should seek advice from a specialist family lawyer if you believe this may apply to you.

so neither are you are able to remarry unless your spouse/cp dies or you later divorce. Judicial separation does not affect your pension claims at retirement, or on your spouse's/cp's death and you would still be classed as a widow/widower in that situation, unlike following divorce.

An important consequence of judicial separation is that your claims after your spouse/cp has died are limited, as your inheritance rights are affected by treating you in the same way as a couple that has divorced.

Judicial separation proceedings are now uncommon, as they cost a similar amount to divorce proceedings and divorce proceedings may still be required later, which can mean there is a duplication of costs. The wish to maintain marriage status for religious reasons is less common than it has been, and as pension claims can be dealt with as part of the financial considerations within divorce proceedings, there is less benefit to judicial separation than there was in the past.

DIVORCE PROCEEDINGS

Divorce proceedings cannot be started until you have been married for a year. They do not need to be underway to enable you to apply for child maintenance (see Chapter 6), or to ask the court to assist you with issues regarding the arrangements for your children, such as residence or contact. Therefore there is no need to issue divorce proceedings until you are sure that this what you want.

Grounds and facts

There is only one ground for divorce in England and Wales, which is the irretrievable breakdown of your marriage. To show that the marriage has irretrievably broken down, you need to prove one of five facts. The five facts are outlined in the box below, and all apply to spouses and cps except for adultery (though sexual infidelity may form part of unreasonable behaviour for dissolution of a cp). Adultery is defined as voluntary sexual intercourse between a man and a woman.

Unreasonable behaviour is conduct of the Respondent that the Petitioner finds

The facts on which you can base a petition for divorce

1. Adultery.
2. Unreasonable behaviour.
3. Desertion for a period of two years.
4. Separation for a period of two years with consent of the other person.
5. Separation for a period of five years.

unreasonable, and to establish this the judge will consider the allegations that have been made by the Petitioner, and the impact and effect this behaviour has had. It does not need to be behaviour that a 'reasonable person' would find unreasonable, simply behaviour that the Petitioner finds unreasonable.

If you decide to cohabit as a married couple with your spouse/cp for six months (or for several periods that add up to six months) after the date of the last incident of unreasonable behaviour or adultery, you can no longer rely on that fact to establish your ground for commencing divorce proceedings.

Unless there is good reason not to, you should send a draft of the proposed petition to your spouse/cp before sending this to the court. This allows any issues about wording/contents to be resolved with the Respondent before the proceedings are started.

Even if you can establish one of the five facts in your case, you may still wish to enter into a separation agreement now and divorce on the grounds of two years'

separation (with consent of your spouse/cp) later, once you have lived apart for long enough. This can help keep things amicable with your spouse/cp as it is a divorce fact that does not apportion any fault or blame.

JURISDICTION

The court need to be sure that they have the power/ability (jurisdiction) to deal with your divorce before proceedings can be started. Our law has been changed so that we have the same rules as other European Union Countries about jurisdiction.

Either you or your spouse/cp need to be habitually resident or domiciled in England or Wales if you want to start divorce proceedings here. This is determined by where you live now, or where you are domiciled. Domicile is the country you are a national of or where you have chosen to live. Domicile is not affected by holidays/short trips away. It does not matter where you got married. If you are concerned about your ability to start divorce proceedings here, see a solicitor for advice.

Divorce proceedings

This section outlines the process of getting divorced or dissolving your civil partnership on a stage by stage basis, including the forms you need to complete and the steps that you will have to take.

WHICH COURT?

It is sensible to start the divorce proceedings at your local county court. Not all county courts deal with divorce, so you should check your local court does by telephoning them first. You may want to issue the proceedings in another part of England or Wales if you are concerned about publicity/sensitivity of your petition.

In rare case, where there are issues relating to finances or children that are extremely complex, your case will be transferred to the High Court. If you start the divorce in the London District Registry (called the Principal Registry of the Family Division) this is a High Court and a County Court.

If you are applying to dissolve a civil partnership, you should check that your local court is able to deal with this, as there are currently only 10 county courts that are designated to deal with dissolution of cps (including the Principle Registry of the Family Division in London).

STARTING THE DIVORCE

The spouse/cp that starts the divorce is called the Petitioner, and the other spouse/cp is called the Respondent. If you issue proceedings on the fact of adultery you can name the third party, who is then known as the Co-respondent, but this is not necessary.

Who chooses to be the Petitioner is normally the spouse/cp that feels most aggrieved about the breakdown of the marriage and sees it as their spouse's/cp's fault. However, if things are more amicable you should try and agree with your spouse/cp who is going to start the proceedings, and on what fact.

There are only two facts that allow divorce proceedings to be started immediately – unreasonable behaviour and adultery (although the latter fact is not available for cps). The other facts have in-built time delays for separation and desertion of at least two years. If you want to get divorced now, one of you will have to be the Petitioner and start the divorce by placing blame on the other spouse's/cp's unreasonable

When can you start?

It is not possible to start a divorce immediately unless it is on the basis of one spouse's fault (unreasonable behaviour or adultery) and it is not possible to start divorce proceedings together as a couple.

behaviour (or adultery of a spouse). This will not mean that the Respondent is viewed in a negative way by the court – judges are aware that there are no other immediate options available.

Whoever is the Petitioner will largely control how quickly the divorce progresses. They will also have more to do than the Respondent and will incur both the court fees and more legal costs than the Respondent. To compensate the Petitioner for this, it is possible for the Petitioner to ask the court to order that the Respondent should pay some/all of their costs (see Chapter 1).

UNDEFENDED DIVORCE

Most cases are undefended, which means they are dealt with purely on paper and there is no need to attend any hearings (unless there are separate issues about finances/children/costs). This means that the divorce follows a procedure called the 'special procedure' (which is so named because it used to be uncommon).

66 There is no public access to the divorce papers. 99

The judge at the county court will read through the forms that have been submitted and check that the fact is proved and the appropriate formalities have been complied with. This will happen in private, until the pronouncement of decree nisi, which is the first decree made in divorce proceedings. Decree nisi is pronounced in open court, but there is no need to attend on this date as it is simply the reading of your name from a list.

The stages that happen within a divorce are set out in the table on page 154, and if you instruct a solicitor they will do the tasks required to enable each stage to be passed through. If you do not use a solicitor, and decide to deal with the divorce yourself, you will be able to get the forms you need from your local divorce court, along with helpful leaflets. The forms and leaflets can also be downloaded from the Courts Service website.

FEES

Starting the divorce off, by sending the divorce petition to the court, currently incurs a court fee of £300. If you are eligible under the Legal Help scheme (see Chapter 1) you will not have to pay this fee, and if you are on a low income you can apply for an exemption from paying this fee by completing form EX160.

The other costs that the Petitioner will incur will be the costs of instructing their solicitor, if they choose to use one, and such costs should be estimated to you before the work is done. There is a fee for swearing an affidavit, which is normally between £5 and £10, and a further court fee of £40 when the Petitioner applies for decree absolute.

If other court applications are made during the divorce, such as ones relating to children or property, these are separate (and covered in the relevant section of the book).

Starting the divorce proceedings will require you (or your solicitor) to provide the court you wish to deal with the divorce with:

- The completed Divorce Petition (Form D8 for spouses, D508 for cps) in triplicate so that a copy can be served on the Respondent (and a Co-respondent if there is one)
- A completed Statement of Arrangements for Children (Form D8A) in duplicate, signed by you (and the Respondent if possible)
- A cheque or postal order payable to HMPG (Her Majesty's Paymaster General) to pay the court fee of £300, or a Form EX160 to apply for exemption from paying the court fee.
- Certificate with regard to reconciliation: this form is completed if you have a solicitor acting on your behalf on a private paying basis and confirms that they have discussed the possibility of reconciliation with you. If you are in receipt of Legal Help, or are acting without a solicitor, this form does not need to be completed.
- Your original marriage certificate or an official copy of it. A photocopy is not sufficient.

It is sensible to keep copies of all of these documents in case you need to refer to them later.

GETTING AN OFFICIAL COPY OF YOUR MARRIAGE CERTIFICATE

The easiest way to obtain an official copy is to go back to the Register of Births, Deaths and Marriages for the area in which you were married. It is sometimes possible to get a certified copy from the registrar or minister who married you, if they have not filed the records yet. You can apply there by post or in person and the certificate will cost you a fee, which can vary.

You can also apply for a certificate online at www.gro.gov.uk or by calling 0845 603 7788; you will still need to pay a fee.

Foreign marriage certificate not in English

You must have it translated and the translation notarised (which means that a special declaration is sworn by the translator confirming the accuracy of the translation). You should look in the Yellow Pages for a translator who can perform this service.

THE PETITION DOCUMENTS

There is a helpful leaflet called 'D8 Notes: Divorce Petition Notes for Guidance' (D508 Notes for cps) that is available from the court and the Courts Service website. This goes through the petition in detail and explains precisely what should go in each part of the petition form. If you are acting for

143

yourself in the divorce proceedings, get hold of a copy of this form and follow its instructions carefully. It is important to get all the parts of the petition form correct, because if you make a mistake the judge may refuse to grant the decree nisi until the error is put right, or further information filed at the court. This could cause you delay and inconvenience. Court officers may be prepared to help you with the forms, but they are not allowed to give you legal advice.

At a later stage in the proceedings you will have to swear an affidavit to say that the contents of your petition are true. If you feel that you have any doubts about, or difficulties with, completing the form, you should consult a solicitor.

Children

All 'children of the family', whatever their ages, have to be named in the petition. Children of the family are, in broad terms, those who are:

- Children of both of you
- Children adopted by both of you
- Step-children
- Other children who have been treated by both at any time during the marriage as part of the family, but these do not include foster children.

'Relevant' children, who need to be dealt with in the 'statement of arrangements', are those under the age of 16, or under the age of 18 and still in full-time education or undergoing training for a trade, profession or vocation (even if the child is also earning). If your child is over 16 and under 18, but is in full-time employment or is unemployed (that is,

no longer in the education system), it is important to say so, because he or she is no longer a 'relevant' child.

Petition requests

The last page of the petition asks the court for various things, which are very important:

- A prayer (request) for the marriage to be dissolved (ended).
- An order for costs to be made against the Respondent and/or Co-respondent. In a petition for adultery, unreasonable behaviour or desertion, it is usual to ask the court to make an order for costs against the Respondent, even if you propose to drop the claim if the petition is not defended.
- Under the heading of 'ancillary relief', orders for maintenance (called periodical payments), lump-sum payments, property adjustment and pensions; such applications are made in general terms at this stage, so you do not need to specify any amounts. **DO NOT** cross off the prayer or the claim for financial relief. If you do it may be complicated or even impossible to apply for it later. You would have to make a special application to the court for leave (permission) to apply later for any required order. Such an application may not be granted if it is made after a long time or if, for example, the Respondent says that he or she decided not to defend the petition only because of the absence of any request for ancillary relief.

Even if you have agreed with your spouse/cp that no financial claims will be made, you should still include them in the petition so that they can be formally dismissed by the court. In any event, the court cannot dismiss claims and make a full and final settlement order unless the claims were made in the first place.

To avoid misunderstanding when your spouse/cp receives the petition, explain to him/her that the claims are being included only so they can be dismissed by the court later. If you have no children, you can delete the part relating to their claims.

Costs

Similarly, you can include a request for costs even though you may agree or decide not to pursue this. What you are claiming here are only costs in respect of the divorce itself (not ancillary issues such as finance or claims about the children). These will be comparatively low, as they are worked out on a standard, limited basis, and are unlikely to cover the full costs of your solicitor.

In the case of a divorce based on periods of separation, the Petitioner and Respondent often agree that costs will be divided between them, so the Petitioner would seek an order for only half the costs to be paid by the Respondent. It is possible (but not usual) to seek costs against a Co-respondent, but it would still be wise to discuss this with a solicitor.

AT THE END

The last page of the petition should be signed by you if you are acting in person or receiving Legal Help, or by your solicitor if one is acting for you. You should also include the full names and addresses of the Respondent (and Co-respondent) for service of the petition, and your address. Home addresses can be used, but if solicitors are acting for either or both of you, their address(es) should be inserted here instead so that court paperwork is sent to them.

STATEMENT OF ARRANGEMENTS FOR CHILDREN

If you have relevant children you will need to complete a statement about the present and proposed arrangements for them (Form D8A). This form is available from the court office (or can be downloaded from the Courts Service website). You should try to agree its contents with the Respondent in advance of starting the divorce, and get his or her countersignature if possible.

If the Respondent has not signed the statement of arrangements some courts will want the Petitioner to confirm that he or she has tried to obtain the Respondent's signature.

This form is eight pages long and requires detailed information about the children of the family. Despite its length

Uncertain about the future
If your future is uncertain it may be difficult to complete the form fully. If so, just include as much information as you can, indicating where necessary which arrangements are yet to be decided upon.

it is fairly jargon-free. You will need to provide details about the home where the children currently live, their education or training, any childcare arrangements, what financial support is received for them, the arrangements for the children to see the other parent, their health and whether there are any other court proceedings about them.

If you do not agree with the current arrangements, any proposed changes should be set out. At the end of the form you are asked whether you would agree to attend conciliation (mediation) with your spouse/cp if arrangements are not agreed. You must then sign the form.

The reason the form is so detailed is to ensure you have considered the arrangements for your children and how these will change after the divorce. This may be the only information the court receives and considers about the children if no applications are made about them separately. In this situation it is understandable that the court wants to have as complete a picture as possible of the arrangements for the children.

SERVICE OF THE DOCUMENTS

The court posts to the Respondent, at the address given in the petition, one copy of the petition and of the statement of the arrangements for any children. They confirm this to you or your solicitor in writing, confirming the date the documents were sent and what your divorce case number is.

The court also sends with the petition an acknowledgement of service form (D10), which the Respondent has to complete and return to the court within eight days (although this time limit is, in practice, not always adhered to). If adultery is alleged and a Co-respondent is named, a copy of the petition is also sent to him or her, again with an acknowledgement of service form to be returned to the court.

The court has to be satisfied that the Respondent (and Co-respondent) has received the divorce papers or that all reasonable steps have been taken to serve the documents on him or her. The return of the acknowledgement of service form to the court is normally taken as proof that they received the documents. However, if the acknowledgement of service form is not returned, the Petitioner can apply to the court with another copy of the documents and arrange for 'personal service'. This means that somebody (normally called a 'process server') hand-delivers the documents to

Serving the petition
The Petitioner cannot personally serve the petition themselves. Any other person over the age of 16 can effect service by delivering papers to the Respondent personally and then completing an affidavit of service and sending it to the court.

the Respondent and then provides sworn evidence that this has been done.

If the Petitioner has had difficulty in serving the papers, he or she can apply to the court for the petition to be served by the bailiff of the county court for the area in which the Respondent lives, or can employ an enquiry agent to act as process server. You will need to provide a photo of the Respondent and pay the fee. This can prove very expensive and so it is worth trying other options first.

If the Respondent (or Co-respondent) fails to return the acknowledgement of service form, but has acted in a way that makes it clear that he or she has received the petition (for example, talking about it to people or writing to you or your solicitor about it), the Petitioner can apply to court for service of the petition to be deemed to have happened.

If service turns out, in practice, not to be possible, the Petitioner may be able to get an order dispensing with service.

THE RESPONDENT

It may seem very hard to be the person who is, on paper, being blamed for the marriage ending but, in practice, this will rarely affect the way in which the court treats the Respondent.

In issues concerning money the court will consider conduct only in cases where it is so very bad that it would be wrong to disregard it. A typical example would be where the husband attacked his wife so violently that she was unlikely to be able to work again as a result of her injuries. Adultery will generally not influence the court one way or the other.

DOCUMENTS THE RESPONDENT SHOULD COMPLETE

The Respondent receives a set of notes telling him or her about the implications of the answers on the acknowledgement of service form.

The acknowledgement of service form is used to prove that the Respondent has had the petition. If the petition is based on two years' separation, the Respondent is also asked to indicate that he or she consents to the divorce. If you have instructed a solicitor, he or she will sign the form. If you are admitting adultery, you have to sign as well.

If a prayer for costs has been made in the petition, the Respondent is asked whether he or she objects to paying the Petitioner's costs and, if so, why. The Respondent may have agreed with the Petitioner that no order for costs will be pursued against him or her, and a comment to this effect on the acknowledgement of service form should remind the Petitioner to delete that request in the next stage of the process.

If the Respondent does not agree with the proposed arrangements for the children, he or she should first make sure that what he or she is objecting to are actual proposals and not mere intentions, and should try to discuss them with the Petitioner. If there is underlying disagreement, the Respondent should send counter-proposals to the court by filing his or her own statement of arrangements.

All financial matters and any disputes about the children are dealt with as separate issues, irrespective of whether the divorce itself is defended or undefended. The Respondent has to sign the acknowledgement personally where an agreed statement of arrangements form has been filed, or if the Respondent wishes to annex a statement with concerns/comments about the arrangements for the children.

DEFENDING THE DIVORCE: CROSS-PETITIONING

Defending a divorce is difficult, largely because the sole ground for divorce is that the marriage has broken down irretrievably. If one party is so certain that the marriage has broken down that he or she has filed a divorce petition, it is virtually impossible for the other to say that the marriage is still in existence.

Defending a divorce is also costly. The court fee alone for a cross-petition or answer is £200. It is almost impossible to get legal aid for a defended divorce. Moreover, a full divorce hearing is done in public, which may be humiliating.

However, there are some cases in which the Respondent feels strongly, and can prove, that the breakdown of the marriage has been largely caused by the other person's actions, via adultery or unreasonable behaviour. In such cases, the Respondent can file a cross-petition. This can be coupled with an 'answer', or denial of some or all of the allegations. A cross-petition must be filed within 29 days of the petition being served.

In most cases, even when the Respondent feels that the petition is unfair, most solicitors would advise them to allow it to proceed undefended, because to do so would be cheaper and, in the long run, the Respondent will not be placed at any disadvantage in the rest of the proceedings.

Where an unreasonable behaviour petition has been filed, the acknowledgement of service form asks the Respondent: 'Do you intend to defend the proceedings?'. One way of reserving the Respondent's position is for him or her to answer: 'No. But I do not admit the truth of the Petitioner's allegations of behaviour made against me in the petition.' This is not a defence, but the Respondent can then feel that he/she has not admitted that the allegations are true.

Next steps

If a cross-petition is filed, the divorce goes ahead on the basis of the cross-petition (if the Petitioner does not dispute it), or cross-decrees (where each party gets a decree on the basis of the 'fact' that he/she has alleged).

If the Petitioner disputes the allegations made in the cross-petition, he/she can file a 'reply' at the court. The case cannot proceed under the 'special procedure' – instead, either party can apply to the court for 'directions for trial'. Normally, this means a private hearing at which the judge sees if any agreement can be reached so that the case can proceed undefended.

Only if these efforts fail will the judge allow the case to go forward to a hearing of the divorce where the court will decide which petition should proceed. In practice only a tiny number of defended divorces proceed to a full hearing.

The full divorce hearing will be in open court before a judge. Each party should instruct his/her own solicitor, who may instruct a barrister for representation in court. This is an expensive and time-consuming process that you should not enter into lightly.

GETTING BACK TOGETHER

Some couples realise that there is a way of saving the marriage when the divorce procedure is already under way, but feel that they are bound to continue with the court action until the end. This is not the case.

It is best to tell your solicitor and the court what is happening if you and your spouse/cp want to give the marriage another try. You can apply to the court to dismiss the petition when you feel the reconciliation is working. It is especially important to tell the court if you have obtained an order to get or keep your spouse out of the house and/ or not to molest you. Such an order will automatically lapse once you start living together again.

Studies of divorced couples suggest that some regret the decision to get divorced, and many start to feel uneasy about the process long before getting the final decree – but feel unable to stop it once it has begun. Remember that it is only you who can make these decisions, not your solicitor. If you are unsure about going ahead with a divorce you can bring things to a stop (if you are the Petitioner), as long as you do so before

decree nisi (although even a decree nisi can be rescinded by an application to the court).

You may want to consider whether some or all of the differences with your spouse/cp can be resolved with outside, non-legal help. A fresh viewpoint can often be useful. Such help can, for example, be obtained from a relationship counsellor (such as Relate); see also Chapter 4.

Stop if you want
The proceedings are not a rollercoaster – you can pause them or stop them altogether. You can do this if you feel at any stage that you both might like to give the marriage another try.

Continuing divorce proceedings

Once the Respondent has been served, the next stage in an undefended divorce is to apply to the court for a date for the decree nisi to be pronounced. This is done by completing a 'request for directions for trial (special procedure)' form.

SPECIAL PROCEDURE

The Petitioner can make this application only if he/she can prove that the Respondent and any Co-respondent have been served with the petition and have had the opportunity to defend it. Usually, the Respondent's filing of the acknowledgement of service is taken as proof of service.

The court will send a copy of the acknowledgement to the Petitioner together with a blank form of 'request for directions for trial' (form D84) and a blank form of affidavit (form D80 for spouses, D5804 for cps). The court has a helpful leaflet (D186 – or D196 for cps – 'The Respondent has replied to my petition – what must I do now?'), which can be downloaded from the Courts Service website.

The Petitioner must complete the 'request' and swear the affidavit and lodge them both with the court. In the 'request' form, the Petitioner should fill in only the top part by inserting the name of the court, the number assigned to the petition, the names of the Petitioner and

Respondent, and then dating and signing it. The rest of the form is completed by the judge and court staff.

AFFIDAVIT IN SUPPORT OF THE PETITION

The 'special procedure' affidavit is a fairly straightforward document, which is mainly in the form of a questionnaire. The questions refer to the petition, asking for confirmation that its contents are true and for any alterations or additions. You must answer all of the questions truthfully. (Knowingly giving false information is perjury, which is a criminal offence.) The Petitioner also has to state whether he or she is going to pursue any requests for costs made in the prayer of the petition.

There is a slightly different form of affidavit for each of the five facts on which a divorce can be based. It is important that you check you have the correct affidavit for the type of petition you issued.

If the Respondent has signed the acknowledgement personally, a copy of it must be 'exhibited' to the affidavit (attached and sworn with it). Similarly, if the Respondent has signed the statement of arrangements for the children, the signature must be identified. The fee for swearing an affidavit is £5 plus £2 for each document exhibited.

You can swear the affidavit in front of a solicitor (other than the one acting for you), a commissioner for oaths or the court office. Most solicitors' firms are very willing to offer this service and you can go to a firm convenient for you.

The completed affidavit, signed and sworn, has to be sent or taken to the court with the application form requesting directions for trial. You cannot do this until nine days have passed since the Respondent (and any Co-respondent) say they have received your petition.

You do not need to serve the Respondent, or notify him or her that you are doing this, but it is courteous to do so.

JUDGE GIVING 'DIRECTIONS FOR TRIAL'

Once you have filed these documents at the court they will be passed to the judge with your case file. Provided that the judge is satisfied that:

- The petition has been served on everyone concerned.
- An opportunity for defending the petition has been given.
- If the petition is based on two years' separation with consent, that the Respondent's consent has been given.
- That the paperwork is correct.

Then he or she will give directions for the case to be entered in the special procedure list.

" If the judge still does not accept that there is sufficient evidence for a divorce, he or she may direct that the petition be removed from the special procedure list. "

If the judge is not satisfied with the information in the petition or affidavit, the Petitioner (or a witness) may be asked to lodge a further affidavit or give additional information on the points of concern. A fresh application then has to be made for directions and for a date to be fixed for a hearing in open court before a judge.

When the judge is satisfied that there is sufficient evidence to support the petition, he or she will certify that the Petitioner is entitled to a decree nisi of divorce (or decree of judicial separation). The court office will then fix a date for the judge to pronounce the decree nisi.

If your petition was based on a five year separation, the Respondent can oppose decree nisi if they can show it would cause them grave financial hardship if the divorce were to proceed and that it would be wrong to dissolve the marriage. This application should be made before decree nisi and will lead to a review of your case to decide if it should be allowed to proceed.

About the children

At the same time that the judge looks at the divorce papers, he or she must also consider the arrangements for the children and decide whether an order is needed for the children. The rule is that the court will not make an order, unless it is plainly better for the children that one is made (see Chapter 5). If the judge is content with the information he or she has about the arrangements for the children, then a certificate of satisfaction will be issued, which means that the decree nisi pronouncement will go ahead.

However, if the judge has doubts or concerns about proposals for the children, or if there is a clear dispute between you, then further evidence will usually be asked for. This dispute is normally shown by the Respondent having made comments on the acknowledgement of service about the arrangements for children, or even having filed their own statement of arrangement form.

The judge can ask both of you to attend a special appointment at court, or for affidavits or a welfare report to be filed. In that case the decree nisi will usually be postponed until the judge is again satisfied that no court order needs to be made, or that a residence and/

or contact order will be made where appropriate in separate proceedings.

DECREE NISI (CP – CONDITIONAL ORDER)

You will both be sent a form with the date of decree nisi. The general practice is that the court will have a list of decrees to be pronounced on a particular day. This takes place very quickly, normally as the first court task of that morning, in a court that is open to the public. The court clerk simply reads out a list of the surnames and the judge utters a few brief words to pronounce all the decrees. You do not need to attend.

After the pronouncement the court sends a copy of the decree to you and the Respondent.

DECREE ABSOLUTE (CP – FINAL ORDER)

The decree nisi is only a provisional decree, and does not end the marriage. The effect of the decree nisi is to entitle the Petitioner to apply to the court for the decree to be made absolute (final) once a period of six weeks and one day has passed after the date of decree nisi.

In an emergency you can ask the court to shorten this time limit, but a formal application needs to be made at the time decree nisi is pronounced. The Petitioner will need to tell the Respondent about this application and will need to explain to the judge, normally in person, why the application is being made. An urgent application will only be granted in exceptional circumstances, such as enabling you to remarry again before a child is born.

! Issues over divorce costs
If there are issues about costs the judge will hear these in the same sitting as the pronouncement of the decrees. These arguments are normally quite short. You or your solicitor will need to be there if you have not sorted out who is to pay the divorce costs by this stage.

The procedure

To apply for a decree absolute the Petitioner completes the application form (form D36, obtainable from the court office) by:

- Inserting the date of the decree nisi.
- Dating and signing the application.
- Lodging this form, together with a fee of £40 (or an exemption from fees form, EX160) at the court office.

The court checks the file to make sure everything is in order, then issues the certificate of the final decree. It is sent to the Petitioner and Respondent, normally within a few days of receiving the application. If there are very urgent reasons for getting the decree absolute immediately, you can ask the court office if it will do this, explaining your reasons.

❝ It is important to keep your certificate of decree absolute in a safe place. You would, for example, certainly need to produce it for the registrar or priest if you ever wanted to marry again. ❞

made absolute, with an affidavit setting out the reasons why the Respondent is applying rather than the Petitioner. Notification will be given to the Petitioner. This will result in a hearing at which the judge will decide whether the decree should be made.

If decree absolute has not been applied for within 12 months of the decree nisi, the delay must be explained when the application for decree absolute is lodged, giving the reason for the delay and stating whether the couple have cohabited since decree nisi and whether any more children have been born to either party. A judge may require further explanation or even affidavit evidence before the decree is made absolute and final.

Abroad

If you want your decree absolute for use abroad – for a remarriage say – you will need to get the document specially signed by the judge so that the document can be legalised at the Legislation Office at the Foreign and Commonwealth Office in London.

If the Petitioner does not apply for the decree nisi to be made absolute when the time comes, after a further three months have elapsed (that is, six weeks and one day plus three calendar months after decree nisi), the Respondent may apply to the judge for the decree to be

Why wait?

It is sensible to wait until financial issues have been resolver before applying for decree absolute. If you have concerns about when to apply, you should speak to your solicitor.

Divorce: the legal steps

Follow these steps to see how the undefended divorce procedure works.

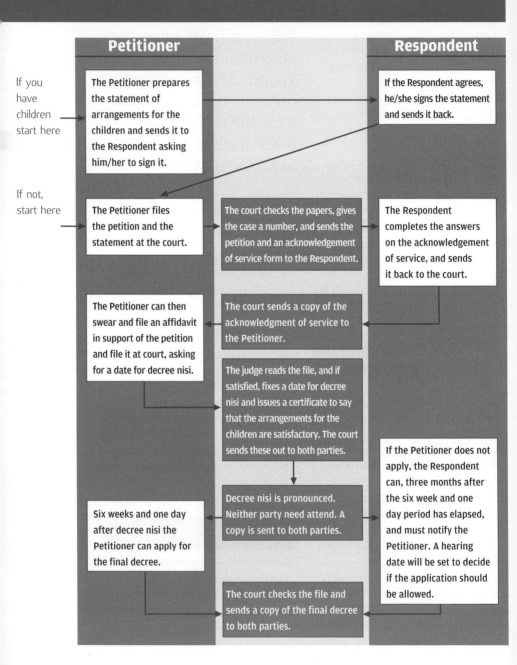

Petitioner

Respondent

If you have children start here

The Petitioner prepares the statement of arrangements for the children and sends it to the Respondent asking him/her to sign it.

If the Respondent agrees, he/she signs the statement and sends it back.

If not, start here

The Petitioner files the petition and the statement at the court.

The court checks the papers, gives the case a number, and sends the petition and an acknowledgement of service form to the Respondent.

The Respondent completes the answers on the acknowledgement of service, and sends it back to the court.

The Petitioner can then swear and file an affidavit in support of the petition and file it at court, asking for a date for decree nisi.

The court sends a copy of the acknowledgment of service to the Petitioner.

The judge reads the file, and if satisfied, fixes a date for decree nisi and issues a certificate to say that the arrangements for the children are satisfactory. The court sends these out to both parties.

If the Petitioner does not apply, the Respondent can, three months after the six week and one day period has elapsed, and must notify the Petitioner. A hearing date will be set to decide if the application should be allowed.

Six weeks and one day after decree nisi the Petitioner can apply for the final decree.

Decree nisi is pronounced. Neither party need attend. A copy is sent to both parties.

The court checks the file and sends a copy of the final decree to both parties.

Summary of terms

Acknowledgement of service Form sent by the court to the Respondent (and Co-respondent, if any) with the petition, with questions about his or her intentions and wishes in response to the petition; its return to the court establishes service of the petition.

Adultery Sexual intercourse by a husband or wife with someone of the opposite sex at any time before a decree absolute. Not applicable to cps.

Affidavit A statement in writing containing a person's evidence, made on oath or by affirmation.

Ancillary relief General term for the financial or property adjustment orders that the court can be asked to make 'ancillary' to a petition for divorce, dissolution or judicial separation.

Answer The defence to a divorce petition, denying the allegations in the petition or cross-petition.

Child of the family Any child of both the parties and any child who has at any time been treated by both the parties as a child of their own (but not foster-children). 'Family' in this context means married family.

Clean break A once-and-for-all order that deals with all financial issues between spouses, provides for the dismissal of maintenance claims and is not capable of subsequent variations even if circumstances change.

Consent order Order made by a court in terms agreed by both parties.

Contact (formerly called access) An order under the Children Act for the child to visit or stay with the parent with whom the child is not living, or to exchange letters, cards or telephone calls. Contact orders may also be made in favour of non-parents; for example, grandparents.

Co-respondent The person with whom the Respondent has committed adultery. Not applicable to cps.

Cross-decrees When a Petitioner is granted a decree on the basis of the petition and the Respondent on the basis of the answer.

Cross-petition When the Respondent puts forward different reasons for the breakdown of the marriage from the Petitioner's, and seeks a divorce on those facts.

Decree nisi (cp: conditional order) Document issued once the court is satisfied that the grounds for divorce or dissolution are established, allowing the Petitioner to apply to have the decree made absolute or final after a further six weeks and one day. Decree nisi does not end the marriage.

Decree absolute (cp: final order) the final order dissolving the marriage.

Summary of terms

Directions for trial The stage of divorce or dissolution proceedings when the judge considers the petition and affidavit in support, and requests further information if required, before giving his or her certificate for a decree nisi or a conditional order to be pronounced.

Petition The document that asks the court to end the marriage.

Petitioner The person who initiates divorce proceedings by filing the petition.

Prayer Formal request in the divorce petition, or answer, for the court orders that the Petitioner or Respondent seeks; for example, dissolution of the marriage, orders under the Children Act, costs, ancillary relief.

Respondent The spouse/cp who is not the Petitioner or the Applicant.

Special procedure In an undefended divorce or dissolution, the decree can be issued without either Petitioner or Respondent having to appear (or be represented) at the court. The facts submitted by the Petitioner in the petition and verified on affidavit are considered by the judge. When he or she is satisfied that the facts in the petition are proved and that ground for a divorce or dissolution exists, he or she issues a certificate to that effect and fixes a date for the formal pronouncement of the decree nisi by the judge. A copy of the decree is sent through the post to both the Petitioner and the Respondent by the court office.

Statement of arrangements Form that has to be filed with the petition if there are relevant children of the family, setting out arrangements proposed for them in the future; this should be agreed with the Respondent and countersigned, if possible, before the divorce or dissolution is started.

Undefended divorce Where the dissolution of the marriage and how it is to be achieved are not disputed (even if there is dispute about ancillary matters such as the children or finances).

Money in divorce

This chapter describes how you go about working out a fair division of your assets, the recent trends and the principles used by the court when making decisions about financial matters.

Working out who gets what

This section aims to provide you with some understanding of how assets can be divided following divorce/dissolution, and what guidance the law gives about the distribution.

There is no legal formula that can be applied to calculate how assets should be divided following a divorce, or how much maintenance should be paid (except for child maintenance where the Child Support Agency has jurisdiction – see Chapter 6). Instead, what exists is a list of factors the court should consider when making such decisions. These guidelines, and past cases, are what solicitors and judges have to apply to each situation to decide what is reasonable and assist couples in negotiating agreements to avoid the need for a fully contested court battle – or in the case of a judge, to determine what is the right outcome in the circumstances when they are making the decision at a final hearing.

It is not necessary for every case to go as far as a court hearing to decide this, and what happens in the majority of cases is that the parties, with the assistance of their solicitors or a mediator, attempt to negotiate a division that takes into account the legislative criteria and is fair, just and reasonable for both parties.

CONSENT ORDERS

If an agreement is reached without a court hearing, that agreement will still need to be drafted into a court order that is then reviewed and approved by a judge on paper only (i.e. without the cost or necessity of anyone attending court). This is vitally important to ensure the agreement is binding and the settlement is fixed as everyone intended.

This requirement alone makes it imperative for you and your spouse/ cp to have had independent legal advice to ensure you both understand the agreement/order and that it is drafted in a clear and concise way that can be relied on in the future with no dispute or misunderstanding.

SHARING ASSETS

There is no need for each and every asset to be divided down the middle and it may be that one spouse/cp keeps a particular asset on the basis that

❝ In most cases it is the couple together with the help of their mediators and/or lawyers, who work out the settlement of the finances. ❞

Financial advice
It makes sense to consult a solicitor about money, even if you feel that you can deal with the basic divorce proceedings yourself.

the other spouse/cp retains another. For example, a wife may keep the matrimonial home, while the husband keeps his pension, if this is creates a fair distribution of the assets. When deciding how the assets should be divided, the court are focused on who the children are living with and the needs of the children and parents in the short and long term, while bearing in mind the need for equality and a fair outcome. The judge is not looking to punish anyone for behaviour during the marriage and bad behaviour by one spouse/cp must be significant for it to have any impact on the financial distribution.

If there is a family business the court will look at the best way to value and treat this, depending on whether it is mainly an income stream or if it has a capital value that should be taken into account. It is important to ensure that the value of a business is included within the assets, but that the income/capital are not double-accounted for, as drawing capital out may have a significant impact on the available income.

❝ It is not necessary for a case to go to a court hearing for the result to be fair, just and reasonable for both parties. It is more likely that the outcome will be acceptable for both parties if they have agreed it together, rather than having an order inflicted on them by the court. ❞

Legal factors to be considered when assets are divided

Legislation outlines a list of factors the court must consider in deciding the division of assets following divorce/dissolution. These factors, and case law that exists from the past about how specific issues have been dealt with, are what your solicitor will be able to advise you upon to help you understand the likely outcome and hopefully reach an agreement with your spouse/cp.

THE FACTORS THE COURT MUST HAVE REGARD TO

No factor is given more weight than the other, but the first consideration must be the welfare of any child. The full checklist is summarised on page 163.

These factors are all relatively self explanatory, and are approached on a common-sense basis. However, it is helpful to be aware of the following points when reviewing the checklist.

Earning capacity

The court reviews how much both spouses/cps earn and could realistically increase their earning capacity by. This will take into account the need for some spouses to retrain if they have been out of the workplace for a long time, and the difficulties that increasing hours or responsibility could cause, such as childcare consequences.

The extent to which anyone may be expected to find employment if they have been out of the job market for a long time, will depend on the specific circumstances of that couple, for example the age, health and prospects of the spouse/cp, the background of the marriage and the other spouse's/cp's income.

There are circumstances where this can mean one spouse/cp is considered to have no earning capacity, which will have an impact on the type of order the court may decide is reasonable to ensure the needs of that spouse/cp are met in the foreseeable future. Earning capacity also affects the ability a spouse/cp has to contribute to a pension and the amount they will have on retirement, which may require provision to be made for them from the other spouse's/cp's pension assets.

If one spouse/cp is refusing to work to their earning capacity, without having good grounds for doing so, this is likely to have an impact on what provision the court consider should be made for them in the circumstances.

Conduct

The court are not looking to punish or penalise either spouse/cp for behaviour during the marriage, but will in very exceptional circumstance take the conduct of one spouse/cp into account as one of the factors to consider, if not doing so would be inequitable. This requires quite extreme behaviour by one spouse/cp to justify consideration (while the other spouse/cp must be largely blameless).

New relationship

If either spouse/cp has commenced a new relationship that has lead to new cohabitation, or is likely to in the near future, this will be important when considering the housing (and income) needs of each spouse/cp. If new cohabitation is on the cards or has already happened, the breakdown of the marriage is less likely to have such a financial consequence on that spouse/cp than it will on the other, as they will be pooling their income and sharing accommodation costs with their new partner.

Duration of marriage

The length of the marriage is a specific factor taken into account, meaning that short marriages can be treated differently to long marriages under the same legal framework. The amount of time you cohabited before marriage is also an issue that case law has grappled with,

and guidance suggests this should be added to the length of your marriage if the cohabitation flowed seamlessly into marriage, a child was born during the cohabitation and where it can be shown there was commitment and that finances were combined.

This issue could turn what would otherwise look like a short marriage into a long one, which may be particularly important in cp cases where a long period of cohabitation pre-dated the marriage, due to the inability to enter into a Civil Partnership until 2004.

ORDERS FOR CHILDREN

If you are the biological or adoptive parent to a child it is possible to apply to the court for orders in the children's favour, in limited circumstances. The

The information considered when deciding orders for children

- The gross income of each parent and any necessary expenses of his/her work that can properly be set against their gross income, together with any future earning capacity.
- The needs of the children, now and in the foreseeable future.
- The needs and outgoings of the two adults.
- The possibility of each adult being financially self-sufficient.
- The effect of tax on any proposed order.
- The effect of any order on welfare benefits entitlements.

CSA would normally have jurisdiction to determine the maintenance you should receive on for the child (see Chapter 6), but when they do not, such as when maintenance is sought for a step-child treated as a 'child of the family' or for a disabled child, or when the parent earns more than the CSA will take into account in their calculations, the court can assist and make orders.

The court can also make orders for payment of school fees and lump sum payments to be made for the children. In deciding what orders are appropriate, the judge will look at any CSA assessment and then the shortfall that exists between that amount and the needs of the parent in caring for the children. The court will consider the criteria outlined in the box on page 161.

TRENDS AND DEVELOPMENTS

Along with the legislation that exists, the court is assisted by a range of cases that they can rely on and refer to, to

> ❝ If a spouse/cp is felt to be unreasonably refusing to work when there are job opportunities available, their maintenance order might be reduced. ❞

Civil partnerships

The Civil Partnership Act 2004 introduced a new field of family law, but it is still too early to say whether the courts will apply existing case law to civil partnerships. In theory there is no reason why a distinction should be made. The factors that the court has to take into account and the powers of the court to make orders are the same as those for married couples. Any cps that have split up already have probably been treated as short marriages. However, many may have had a long period of cohabitation beforehand, which the court will generally take into account. Therefore, in general any established principles in the field of matrimonial law could be assumed to apply equally to cps.

help them decide issues that may have already been considered in another case with similar facts. Although there are no specific formulas outlined, case law does show a pattern and general attitude towards certain issues, which develops a general approach to those issues in the future. Such attitude changes over the last few years include:

- Looking to divide all assets that exist fairly, considering the needs of the parties, sharing of assets and compensation to one party (if relevant and there is income/assets to enable this to happen).
- Giving credit to a non-earning spouse/cp who has contributed to the marriage in another way.

- Trying to enable both spouses/cps to have comparable housing following the division.

These are general principles that have emerged through cases over the last few years, but if they would apply to you would depend on your particular circumstances. If applying an equal division would not meet the needs of one spouse/cp, particularly if they were providing a home for the children, then this would not be a reasonable or fair outcome the court is likely to follow. It would also seem unjust to end up with a 50:50 split if one party had brought in, or contributed, a much larger amount of the wealth than the other during the marriage.

The courts have looked to distinguish between assets that were clearly accumulated during the marriage, and other assets that existed before the marriage or after separation or were inherited. These issues have only been really relevant when the assets that exist exceed each spouse's/cp's needs.

The media has shown interest in some of the cases involving very rich couples, particularly those in the public eye. The extent to which the outcomes and decisions made in these types of cases can then be applied to a family of average wealth is limited. Quite often there is insufficient capital to meet the housing needs and living costs of both spouses/cps, and in such a situation achieving an equal division of the assets is more unlikely, particularly when there are children's needs to factored into the calculations as well.

The criteria that the court must consider

Marriages, Section 25 Matrimonial Causes Act 1973 (as amended); cps, Schedule 5 Part 5 Civil Partnership Act 2004

- **The property and financial resources of both spouses/cps and the income and earning capacity of both, now and in the foreseeable future, including any increased earning capacity that the court could reasonably expect either person to try to acquire.**
- **The financial needs, obligations and responsibilities of both spouses/cps, both now and in the foreseeable future.**
- **The standard of living before the breakdown of the marriage.**
- **The ages of both spouses/cps.**
- **The length of the marriage.**
- **Any physical or mental disabilities.**
- **The contributions of each spouse/cp to the welfare of the family, including any contribution in caring for the family or looking after the home, both in the past and in the foreseeable future.**
- **In limited circumstances, the conduct of either spouse/cp.**
- **The value of any benefit, such as a pension, which either spouse/cp would lose the chance of acquiring as a result of the divorce.**

How orders are worked out

This section aims to show how you as a couple can work out an agreement, what your lawyers will be doing when they advise you and what the judge will be doing if your case proceeds to a final hearing.

WORK OUT THE TOTAL FINANCIAL PICTURE

You both need clear and full information about each other's finances, as explained in Chapter 2. You are obliged to be honest as each of you is entitled to 'full and frank' disclosure from the other. If you don't provide this voluntarily, the court has powers to compel you to provide it, or force your spouse/cp to provide it.

All assets, however acquired and regardless of whose name they are in, need to be disclosed, as they form the matrimonial assets. That doesn't necessarily mean that they will be split between you, but they must be taken into account in reaching final settlement.

Once the financial disclosure is collated you are able to consider the options. It is best to draw up the joint financial summary into a table so that the information is easy to review.

WORKING OUT FUTURE NEEDS

For most divorcing couples, the housing arrangements following divorce/ dissolution are the biggest concern. Once decisions have been made about how both of your housing needs can be met,

many other issues will be decided as a result. This is because the deposit/equity you may need to re-house yourself may decide how capital should be distributed. It may also alter how much income you need (or have available for maintenance), depending on the income needs associated with your new housing arrangements.

Although your focus is likely to be housing, it is also important to consider your other needs and claims in the long term, as this is likely to be your only opportunity to make such claims against the assets of your spouse/cp. For example, there may be a significant difference in the amount of pension provision you both have, and the future amounts you are both likely to be able to contribute. Therefore it is important that you consider what will happen at various stages of your life, including retirement, and what claims should be made now to protect you, if appropriate.

NEEDS AND RESOURCES

Having made a schedule of the assets, liabilities and income you both have, and the needs you have both identified for the future, you can look to see how what you have can be divided to try and meet those needs. The factors the court must bear in mind during this exercise are summarised on page 163. Your overall aim is to reach an agreement that meets both of your needs as far as possible, while achieving a settlement that is fair.

FAIRNESS AND COMPENSATION

A fair agreement about how assets are divided does not mean an equal division of all assets. Although the court is looking for equality when possible, this is balanced against finding an agreement that is fair and reasonable in your specific circumstances, which may mean that splitting things down the middle is not right in your case. Factors that will affect how fair an equal split is will include:

- Where one spouse/cp has created most of the wealth or brought a large share of the assets into the marriage at the outset, for example by property they owned independently or assets they had inherited before marriage.
- If one spouse/cp is not able to be financially independent and needs support in the future.

The court also has to review if one party needs to be compensated for future financial provision or security they may have lost as a result of the divorce. For

example, if during a marriage a couple decide that the wife will give up her career to raise a family, it is likely that her pension contributions would stop, or be significantly less than her husband's, and getting back into employment may be difficult without costly retraining.

There is also an expectation in many marriages that one party will be able to rely on the other's pension on retirement, as the couple presume they will be together all their lives. So one party may not to invest as much in their own pension. This is not an unreasonable assumption and the court may factor in compensation for one party for loss of what they reasonably expected, particularly if the one party has lost a potentially high-earning career as a result of decisions made during the marriage.

In many cases the issues of fairness, sharing and compensation start and end with consideration of the needs of the parties. If consideration of these issues means that a spouse's/cp's (or child's) needs are not met, those arguments are unlikely to have any impact.

THE EFFECT CHILDREN WILL HAVE

If you have children, their needs are going to come first when considering how assets should be divided. The amount of maintenance that should be paid for the children is likely to be governed by the CSA formulas (see Chapter 6), although you can agree the amount of child maintenance without the CSA formally becoming involved.

Expectations
The assets that sustained one family cannot easily stretch to two. Both of you will probably be poorer, at least in the short term, than when you were together.

PRE-NUPTIAL/PRE-MARITAL/CP AGREEMENTS

'Pre-nups', as they have become known, are growing in popularity. This is largely due to their change in status over the last ten years. In many countries a pre-nup is a binding agreement that can be legally enforced if you divorce later.

However, pre-nuptial agreements are currently not binding between spouses/cps under English law and so are unenforceable, as the court is not bound to any agreement that prevents them from deciding how assets should be divided on divorce. Having said this, recent case law has developed the standing of these agreements and there are increasing calls for the government to legislate to allow pre-nups to be binding, or at least strongly persuasive, in the future.

If certain conditions are met, the court is likely to give more consideration to the pre-nup when making their decisions. These criteria include there being no

If you have no children

A couple with no children who are financially independent of each other may find it easier to divide their assets. If the marriage is relatively short a couple might expect to each take what they brought into the marriage, divide any jointly acquired assets evenly and achieve a clean break. The longer the marriage, and the more finances have been intermingled, the greater the tendency to an equal division will be, provided this means that the needs of each are met.

children involved at the time of divorce, both parties having given full and frank financial disclosure, both having had independent legal advice, and the terms of the agreement having been reached without any duress or pressure on either party, with fair and reasonable provision (without significant injustice to either) being made for each spouse/cp.

Pre-nups need to be made at least 21 days before the marriage ceremony takes place and should be reviewed regularly following marriage to ensure they stay appropriate and fair. Case law

Post-nuptial agreements

Agreements can also be entered into after the marriage has taken place. Subject to conditions being met these are binding, as long as the usual contractual principles have been met.

has given some pre-marital agreements significant weight in deciding what is an appropriate outcome when there is an international element to the marriage (and the agreement would be binding in that jurisdiction), where the marriage is short in length and there is independent wealth on both sides. Such agreements can therefore save legal costs and disputes later in some situations.

This means that such agreements are starting to become another factor the court is taking into account (depending on the circumstances) when deciding what outcome fair, along with the legal criteria outlined on page 163.

A 'CLEAN BREAK'

The court is required to try to achieve a 'clean break' order if possible. Most couples would generally prefer this sort of arrangement if it is practical and feasible in their specific circumstances. A clean break is an order where the couple are not left with any continuing future obligations to each other. This means that there cannot be any maintenance payments, other than for children. It is not possible to have a clean break for child maintenance.

When thinking about a clean break, you have to consider whether one of you has a maintenance claim against the other. If so, the order will need to 'compensate' for the loss of the maintenance by increasing her or his share of the capital, if this is possible.

A clean break agreement gives you both the freedom to act as you choose with your income, capital and pension in the future, with no risk of your former spouse/cp coming back later, as all claims you have against each other as a result of your marriage are terminated at the point the clean break order is made.

In most circumstances, where it is not practically possible to achieve a clean break, an end is brought to claims such as capital, property and pension as the order will normally conclude those claims once and for all. The only issue that will be left, for either spouse/cp to come back to review or vary in the future, will be the amount of maintenance paid by one spouse/cp to the other. The amount of maintenance is always open to variation on a change of either

Clean break order
This should include a provision to prevent each of you from having a claim on the estate of the other after death under the Inheritance (Provision for Family and Dependants) Act 1975.

spouse's/cp's circumstances and at any point can be capitalised. This means that the payer feels financially able to 'buy-off' the person to whom the maintenance is paid, by paying a one-off lump sum instead of ongoing maintenance, which will bring the maintenance claims to an end and create a clean break, despite this not having been possible at the time the original agreement was made. If you cannot agree to the amount that would have to be paid to do this, the court can decide it.

GETTING TO THE 'RIGHT' AGREEMENT

Coming up with an agreement that meets the legislative criteria, the needs you both have (and those of any children), and which is fair and reasonable, is not always easy to achieve. The more assets that are available, the more likely it is that such an agreement will be possible. Sometimes what is emotionally valuable to one spouse/cp can be worth as much to them in negotiations as an asset that has far more significant financial value.

It is also important to keep in mind the legal costs you are spending in dealing with a dispute, compared to the value of the issue that is in dispute.

Potential financial orders

When you are trying to work out a financial settlement you have to consider the various orders that the court can make. This section sets out the powers of the court and the usual ways in which such orders are made.

POTENTIAL FINANCIAL ORDERS

It is important than any settlement you come up with is enforceable by a court order, and so it must be something the court has the power to order under legislation. The orders the court can make are:

- A property adjustment order or order for sale of a property or assets
- A periodical payments order (more commonly known as maintenance) for a spouse/cp, or in some circumstances for a child. Periodical payments can be limited in various ways, made pending suit (i.e. made before decree absolute is obtained), or secured if appropriate.
- A lump sum order for a capital amount to be paid by one party to the other.
- An order requiring Pension Fund Trustees to pay part or all of a pension fund to the other spouse in accordance with specific rules.

This chapter will examine each of the types of order and how they can work in practice. These orders cannot be made until after Decree Nisi/a Decree of Judicial Separation/Conditional Order has been pronounced (except for maintenance pending suit, see page 175).

**"The court has the power to order the sale or transfer of any capital asset, but in doing this there has to be consideration of what is sensible to divide or sell, and what the available resources are.""

Property orders

When you own property the court needs to ensure that the property has been considered appropriately and distributed so as to meet your housing needs, and any surplus money is divided between you.

Whose name your joint home is registered in, or how the legal ownership of it has been defined between the two of you, is able to be varied and reviewed by the court on divorce. The court is able to transfer the property from one person to the other, from joint names to one name, or order it to be held in different shares to how it is currently. These powers relate to the home you live in and any other property that is owned by either of you.

If you rent your home, you should take specific steps to protect your interest in the tenancy (see Chapter 7).

Sale

The court has the power to order the sale of a property or assets, although this is not often wanted by either party because of the potential costs of sale through estate agents and solicitors.

In some cases, there is no choice but to sell the home to release money to enable both parties to re-house themselves in suitable accommodation. Or if there are debts that need to be cleared, sale of the home may be the only way to do this.

When ordering a sale, the court can also set how the sale should occur: how the sale price will be set, who will market the property and which solicitors will deal with the conveyancing.

Types of orders for property

The orders that a divorce court can make about the family home are:
- Immediate sale with division of proceeds.
- Postponed sale – usually until children complete their education, but sometimes beyond that. House then to be sold and proceeds divided in specified proportions.
- A transfer of one person's interest to the other with a lump-sum adjustment.
- Outright transfer of one person's interest to the other.

 See Chapter 7 'Emergencies', about preventing the surrender of a tenancy.
For more information on Capital Gains Tax see: www.hmrc.gov.uk/cgt/index.htm

Order for postponed sale

This chart outlines the options for how you can hold your property pending a sale.

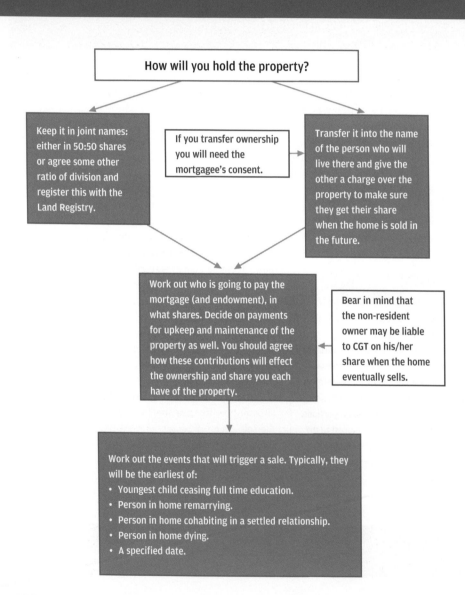

How will you hold the property?

Keep it in joint names: either in 50:50 shares or agree some other ratio of division and register this with the Land Registry.

If you transfer ownership you will need the mortgagee's consent.

Transfer it into the name of the person who will live there and give the other a charge over the property to make sure they get their share when the home is sold in the future.

Work out who is going to pay the mortgage (and endowment), in what shares. Decide on payments for upkeep and maintenance of the property as well. You should agree how these contributions will effect the ownership and share you each have of the property.

Bear in mind that the non-resident owner may be liable to CGT on his/her share when the home eventually sells.

Work out the events that will trigger a sale. Typically, they will be the earliest of:
• Youngest child ceasing full time education.
• Person in home remarrying.
• Person in home cohabiting in a settled relationship.
• Person in home dying.
• A specified date.

Delayed sale

There may be a number of reasons why selling the property at the time of reaching settlement is not the best solution, so one party agrees that they will wait to receive their share of the property until a certain event in the future triggers the sale. The circumstances where such a delay may be appropriate include where the house value is low due to the economic climate, where the property is in a negative equity position due to low value and high mortgage, or where the home needs to be retained as the home for the children for the time being.

If there is going to be an order for a postponed sale, there will need to be decisions made about how the property will be registered/owned between now and the future sale. You also need to decide the arrangements for paying the outgoings and when the sale will happen. The chart on page 170 outlines some of these issues.

There are a number of risks associated with delayed sales, both for the spouse/cp who remains in the property and the spouse/cp who is delaying receiving their share. These include:

- Capital Gains Tax that may be payable by the spouse/cp who has delayed receiving their share of the property instantly. This may be the case where that spouse/cp has bought another property while waiting for the home to be sold, and in this situation can only have one property registered as their principle residence for tax purposes. The amount of CGT that will be

Charge for the non-occupying person

If the home is in one person's name, the non-occupier can protect his or her interest in the eventual proceeds of sale by having a 'charge' put on the property. This means that their interest is registered at the Land Registry on the title deeds, so that anyone dealing with the property can see that they are entitled to a share in the proceeds of sale.

payable at some point in the future may be difficult to quantify, and if the amount is more than had been expected, this could have a significant impact on the overall fairness of an agreement.

- Actually achieving a sale of the property may not be as easy as the spouse/cp waiting for their share may want. Although the triggering events could have been agreed, the house will still only sell as quickly as a buyer can be found and so they may be waiting for their money longer than they had anticipated.

- The spouse/cp who remains at the property may not plan ahead as well as the other spouse/cp, and could find that when the property sells they do not have sufficient capital or mortgage capacity to buy another home. Selling in that situation can be very difficult to face, but will still have to happen as it is not possible to go back to the court later if things do not work out as you had hoped. This is why thinking about your future needs is so crucial.

- The negotiations will lead to either a new way for the ownership of the property to be divided, or a specific amount being paid to one spouse on sale. The decision of if a percentage sum or fixed amount should be agreed can be very tricky, as no one can guess how the property value will fluctuate during the period until sale. Considering property price increases and decreases and how this will affect your share on a fixed basis or percentage will help you assess the amount of risk you are taking on in each scenario.

- Deciding how costs associated with the property will be dealt with, until sale, can also have an impact on each share. For example, if significant works are needed at the home to maintain it or conduct repairs, or if one spouse/cp develops and improves the property, is this going to be compensated?

Case Study   Ann and Mitch

Ann and Mitch split up and decided that Ann would stay in the home with their three children until it was sold. They then decided to divide the net proceeds of sale so that Ann would get 67 per cent, and Mitch the rest (the house was in their joint names). They decided it would be best to transfer it into Ann's sole name so that Mitch could take out another mortgage on his new home – the building society said that they wouldn't give him a mortgage if he already had one. However, their existing building society said that Ann did not have enough income to take over the existing mortgage as it was more than two and a half times her salary. Ann was sure that she could manage to pay it with what she was getting in wages, tax credit and what Mitch was paying for the children. However, the building society would agree to the mortgage if Mitch guaranteed the payments – which means he would have to pay them if Ann didn't. Mitch gave the guarantee and Ann, in the court order, gave him an indemnity that said that she would reimburse him if he did have to pay the mortgage.

Getting the consent of the mortgagee

If you are going to change the shares in which you hold the home, or transfer the home into one person's name, you will have to get the consent of the mortgagee (the bank or building society).

Although you can have a court order for the transfer of a property which is subject to a mortgage, the court has no power to order the bank or building society to agree. Without their consent the transfer can't go ahead, so it is important that you have explored the idea with the mortgagee and established what they would be happy to do before you either agree a settlement or go to court.

If there is nothing specified within the agreement one spouse/cp may find that they are out of pocket for expenditure that could have increased the value of the property for the benefit of the other spouse/cp.

It is possible for the court to order the spouse/cp that stays in the home to pay an 'occupation rent' to the other spouse/cp, due to the benefit they have by remaining at the property and to compensate the spouse/cp whose money is tied up in the property. However, this is uncommon in most situations, unless the home has no mortgage on it.

Transfer

The court can order that a property is transferred into one person's name with a charge to protect the other person's interest, or to order that the property should be transferred outright to one spouse/cp. In either of these situations, if there is a mortgage on the property the transfer will not be possible unless the mortgage company agree, you find a new mortgage company who is prepared to let you have the mortgage in your sole name, or find a guarantor who is willing to guarantee that the mortgage payments are made.

The court can order that in the situation of an outright transfer of the home to one spouse/cp, there is a simultaneous capital payment to the other spouse/cp to compensate them for the interest they are giving up in the property. This may be possible if there are sufficient other funds to do this,

or if one spouse/cp has a mortgage capacity that would be large enough to take over the existing mortgage on the property and raise a further sum to give to the other spouse/cp when the property is transferred.

In some situations the court will order that an interest in a property is transferred from one spouse/cp to

Endowment mortgages

If you have an interest-only mortgage, which you plan to repay at the end of its term by an endowment policy you are contributing to, or a similar repayment scheme, it is important that when you decide how the house is be transferred you also decide who is going to pay for the endowment policy/investment and who will have the benefit of that asset when it matures. It is possible to transfer an endowment policy, and most investments that may support the mortgage, or there are options to surrender or sell, too.

It is worth getting some independent financial advice about what is the best option depending on the type of mortgage/investment/policy you have and how it is performing.

another with no lump sum payment to be made or charge registered. This would be where other assets are being retained by the other spouse/cp, making such an order fair just and reasonable in the circumstances.

Sale and transfer

The powers of sale and transfer apply to any assets that have a monetary value, not just a property/your home. This power does extend to overseas assets, unless the court where those assets are held would disregard the order.

If there is a mortgage on the property the court would not realistically be able to make an order for transfer unless the mortgage company had confirmed that they would agree to the transfer happening.

RENTED PROPERTY

A property transfer order can transfer the tenancy of most rented homes. If your spouse/cp, rather than you, is the tenant, you must ask the court for a transfer of tenancy order before the divorce decree is made absolute. This is because the occupation of the accommodation by the non-tenant spouse is keeping alive the protected, statutory, secure or assured tenancy arising from the 'deemed occupation' rules.

Once the marriage is ended on the final decree of divorce, these rules no longer apply, and the tenancy will lose its protected, secure or assured status, or, in the case of a statutory tenancy, will simply cease to exist. If a protected, statutory, secure or assured tenancy no longer exists, there is nothing for the court to transfer.

The general rule is that a transferee spouse/cp cannot get better tenancy rights than the tenant spouse/cp, so if the home is rented on a short-term basis the court will not be able to extend the term of the tenancy, and if rent payment debts have been built up then these would be passed on to the transferee. Although it is not often used, the court has the power to compensate the person transferring the tenancy by ordering the other person to make a payment to them.

Maintenance orders

The media has shown great interest in some 'big-money' divorces where wives have been awarded high maintenance, above what they would appear to need. It is not usual for one spouse's/cp's income to be high enough to be beyond what is required to meet the needs of two separate homes in a standard similar to that when they lived together on that income. In most cases, decisions about maintenance are focused on what each spouse/cp needs to live on, and how this can be afforded. In situations where there is a surplus, the court are guided by case law where consideration of equality, sharing, and compensation come into play (particularly where one spouse/cp has given up the chance of a successful career as a result of the marriage).

MAINTENANCE PENDING SUIT (MPS) (CP: PENDING OUTCOME)

MPS is maintenance paid from one spouse/cp to the other before the final decree of the divorce is made. It is often called 'interim maintenance', although this can be paid beyond decree absolute, unlike a maintenance pending suit order. This can be dealt with in a court order, or can be done by agreement to save going to court. Due to the cost involved, and timing, these applications are quite rare.

PERIODICAL PAYMENTS (MAINTENANCE)

Periodical payments are the name given to maintenance paid by one spouse/cp to the other. Maintenance is considered for children initially, then reviewed for the adults.

For the children

If the CSA do not have the ability to decide the maintenance that should be paid, or the amount is agreed between you, this can be dealt with by a court application (or a consent order).

In these circumstances maintenance for children is normally stated as an annual or monthly sum, paid weekly or monthly, in advance or arrears. It is broken down as an amount for each child and is paid until each child reaches the age of 17, or can go on until 18 if the child is still in full-time education. In some instances the maintenance can also go beyond 18, if the child is still in full-time education. The CSA formula is useful to the court, but they are not bound by it and the amount awarded will be based on needs of the children and resources available.

Children within the CSA	Children outside the CSA
If your children come within the jurisdiction of the CSA, then you can only make a court order by consent. Most parents will agree an amount, rather than use the CSA. You will generally use the CSA formula as a guideline. The court does have power to vary an order that was originally made by consent, so you can later argue a change in the amount before the court, unless the CSA has become involved.	Examples of these cases are: • Children who are not yours by blood or adoption. • Children who are, or whose parent(s) are, habitually resident abroad (and not employed by a UK-based company). • Disabled children who need more than the CSA formula provides. • Where one parent earns more than the CSA limit. The court can hear a contested application for their maintenance, if you cannot agree it.

For the spouse/cp

This maintenance is again normally expressed as an annual or monthly sum paid monthly or weekly. The amount of maintenance is not decided by any formula or specific guidance and is decided on the particular circumstances of each case. It is normally for a fixed sum rather than a percentage of the payer's income, but this is possible. The maintenance can also be self-varying by stating that it increases in line with the retail prices index (RPI), or such other guide as may be considered appropriate.

It is possible for the maintenance to be set at a nominal amount of something like 5 pence per year ('Nominal Maintenance'). This is simply to provide an option for the person who has the benefit of the order to apply to have that increased to a substantive sum if they need to in the future. This is often used where there are young children and

the court are concerned about imposing a clean break on a single parent who may need help in the future, or where there is a plan to reduce the amount of maintenance paid each year, specified in the order, the last step being nominal maintenance. This could deal with a situation where maintenance has been paid during a spouse/cp's retraining, and then nominal maintenance is in place for the period where that spouse/cp is establishing their career. This is seen as 'safety net' that the court can decide if to invoke if an application is made in the time period specified.

The order requiring the maintenance to be paid will state for how long this payment should be made. This could be:

● Until a specified date that cannot be extended (called a non-extendable term order).

● Until a specified date, but this is extendable if an application is made before the date and there are exceptional circumstances to justify it (extendable term order).

- For life, not ending until the death of either party (joint lives order).

Spousal maintenance will automatically end if the party receiving maintenance remarries, or if either party dies. The court can also terminate the maintenance if they consider it appropriate at any stage. Once a term order has ended there is no option to seek maintenance again.

The type of maintenance order will depend on the reason the maintenance is being paid. For example, if maintenance is to help with young children, it may be linked to the timescale in which the parent who provides full-time care plans to return to work. Retraining can also be a factor that effects how long spousal/cp maintenance should be paid for. If there is a risk that the spouse/cp receiving the maintenance is not going to be financially independent by a specified date, they may need the option to apply back to the court during the term to extend it.

If it is decided that a joint-lives maintenance order is appropriate, it is important to consider how the recipient will be protected if they do not remarry and the maintenance payer dies first. To ensure they are maintained after the death, there will need to either be a life policy of sufficient value to cover the maintenance, or pension provisions made. In either case, how the costs of such protection will be met during the lifetime of the parties also has to be decided. The amount that is paid under any type of maintenance order is always open to variation (see page 196).

If there is a risk that the maintenance that has been ordered will not be paid, the court can order that the amount of the maintenance payments should be 'secured' against a capital asset of the paying party. This would mean that the asset could be sold if the maintenance is not paid. This is sometimes used as a method of enforcement if other options are not suitable. Secured maintenance orders of this type can only be made where there is sufficient available capital, and it is best to seek legal advice before requesting this option from the court.

Capitalisation of maintenance

In some cases, it can be agreed or ordered that the maintenance should be paid as a one-off lump sum. The benefit of this is that it gives both parties a clean break. However, the amount to be paid to end the maintenance claim cannot be calculated until what the right of maintenance is has been agreed. Then there are various calculations and formula/tables that can be used to calculate how much capital would be required to compensate one party for the end of the maintenance. This is not necessarily a straightforward calculation and you should seek advice from your solicitor and a financial advisor.

Capital orders

When the court looks at capital orders – sale, lump sum and transfer of property – it first has to consider the available resources, and how they can be sensibly divided up.

The court has the power to order the sale or transfer of any capital asset, but in doing this there has to be consideration of what is sensible to divide or sell, and what the available resources are.

ORDERS FOR SALE

The court can order sale of any asset that has a monetary value (such as property, see page 169) This type of order could also apply to a family business; for example, requiring the proceeds of sale to be divided equally. However, this might not make economical sense if the business is providing valuable income but has minimal capital value.

LUMP SUM ORDERS

A lump sum order is an order requiring one spouse/cp to pay a capital sum to the other. This can be a one-off payment by a specified date, or a payment in instalments to be paid by a specified date. This can also have interest payable.

This type of order is common when it is agreed that one party is to retain specified assets, but that they will raise funds (by mortgage/loan, etc) to buy

off the other party's entitlement to a share of those specified assets. Lump sum orders can also be made when maintenance is being capitalised (see page 177).

Lump sum orders payable in instalments can be varied and it is important this is considered carefully when accepting such an agreement.

TRANSFER OF PROPERTY ORDERS

Property is not limited to bricks and mortar by this legislation and can include any asset that has a monetary value. This could be shares, policies, council tenancies and many other assets that may be held.

The order can require one spouse/cp to transfer all of their interest in the asset to the other, or part of their share to the other so that the proportion of the assets held by you both is altered. This type of order can only be made against a spouse/cp and cannot force a third party to make a transfer (or a mortgage company to co-operate with a transfer).

Pension rights

Pensions are assets that are often misunderstood and overlooked. As they are rarely assets that are realisable during the divorce, they have less short-term importance. However, in the long term they can be valuable assets that must be considered carefully.

The law relating to pensions is complex due to the interaction between pension law, family law and tax law. The pension claims that exist on divorce are designed to compensate one spouse/cp who has inadequate or insufficient pension assets, which unless they consider at the time of the divorce proceedings they may not have a chance to rectify later when they go to draw their pension.

This is a particularly important issue when one spouse/cp has made minimal pension contributions during the marriage and is unlikely to have the income to make significant contributions in the future, unlike their spouse/cp. Or when there has been a long marriage and the party with then lower pension will not have time following marriage to build their pension fund up, losing them the opportunity to have a reasonable income in their retirement as they had expected.

The purpose of the pension options are to ensure pensions are assets considered in the overall distribution, and are therefore governed by the same decisions about what is fair, just and reasonable in the circumstances.

The age of the parties and the duration of the marriage are often pivotal

What orders you can have about pensions

- Giving one of you a bigger share of other assets to offset your loss of interest in your spouse/cp's pension.
- Giving one of you a lump sum to compensate you for the loss of specific benefits, such as the right to receive a widow's pension.
- Earmarking part or all of a future lump sum payable on the death of one of you for payment to your spouse/cp.
- Requiring one of you swap part of the pension for a lump sum at retirement (called 'commutation') and earmarking part or all of that lump sum to the spouse/cp.
- Earmarking part of your pension (either a future pension or one currently being received) to be paid to your spouse/cp (only in England and Wales, not in Scotland).
- 'Pension sharing' – in other words, transferring part of one person's pension rights to the other.

in deciding how pensions are dealt with. If a pension is already in payment – one spouse/cp is already being paid their pension – implementing an earmarking or pension sharing order will immediately reduce the income they are receiving from their pension. Depending on the circumstances, simply looking at the value of the pension may not be appropriate to decide how the fund should be divided. Expert assistance to look at what income at retirement would be payable under each of the options detailed below may be necessary.

The types of order that can be made offer varying solutions to how pensions can be treated during divorce/dissolution, and each are explored below.

Offsetting

This option does not involve sharing or transferring any pension, but instead giving one spouse/cp more of another asset as compensation for giving up the claims they have to the pension fund. The amount that is provided from another asset (such as cash, home or policies) is not necessarily the same as the cash value of the pension for a number of reasons. This includes the fact that getting the money now holds less risk than waiting for the money to come from a pension at retirement, which involves fluctuations within the fund between now and retirement that cannot be foreseen or anticipated.

The tax treatment of how the offset asset is used is different to the tax treatment of the pension commencement lump sum (which is normally tax free) and so how the cash is invested by the receiving party may make them open to Capital Gains Tax and Income Tax, reducing the longer-term value for them.

Earmarking

The court has the power to allocate some of a spouse's/cp's pension to the other spouse/cp in the future, which can be a proportion of the pension income or the commencement lump sum, as a form of maintenance order. This can be expressed as a fixed amount or a percentage and is paid directly to the other spouse/cp, by the pension trustees when the fund commences payment to the pension member. However, there are a number of issues/risks with earmarking orders that result in them being rarely used compared to the other options, see below.

Problems with earmarking your pension

- **No clean break is possible, because you are still tied together financially**
- **The person with the pension can manipulate what the other spouse/cp gets (by changing the contributions), and when.**
- **Earmarked rights will be lost if the person with the pension dies before retirement.**
- **The earmarked rights will be lost if the person receiving the earmarking sum remarries.**

It is also important to bear in mind that, for the purpose of tax, the income a spouse/cp receives under an earmarking order is the same as if it were deferred maintenance or death benefit. If the recipient of the earmarking order is in receipt of legal aid and a proportion of the pension commencement lump sum is earmarked for their benefit, the statutory charge will apply to this sum once the order is implemented (see Chapter 1).

Pension sharing

Since 1 December 2000 the court has had the power to share or split a pension. This is a useful option that avoids the problems of earmarking as it allows the parties to still have a clean break, is not affected by death or remarriage (once the order is implemented against the fund), and allows both parties to have pension assets invested in their own names to deal with as they please. This option can apply to a number of types of pension and rights but does not apply to basic state pension, widow/widower benefits and lump-sum death benefits. It is not possible to have an earmarking order and a pension sharing order against the same pension fund.

The pension scheme administrators can charge for implementing a pension sharing order, and those costs can be divided between the parties in such proportion as is agreed or ordered by the court.

A pension share can only be effected if there is a court order (either by agreement in a consent order or by an order made by the court at a hearing), and must be expressed as a percentage of the fund that is being taken from the member's fund and re-invested in a separate fund in the name of the spouse/cp. This does not need to be a half share, and the percentage to be transferred will depend on the merits of the spouse's/cp's claim to the pension fund in the circumstances. Also, it is not limited to the extent of the pension that was contributed to during the marriage. Note that different rules apply in Scotland.

There are two types of transfer that can happen under a pension sharing order:

- **Internal transfer.** This means that the spouse's/cp's share under the order is invested within the name pension scheme in their own name, and the rights and rules that apply are the same as the member's whose pension was shared. This is usually the case for unfunded schemes in the public sector, due to the effect having to provide cash to another scheme would have on the scheme itself.
- **External transfer.** This enables the spouse/cp to move their share to a scheme of their choice; for example, to one they may already belong to, if that is possible.

Choices such as these can affect when the spouse/cp is able to draw their share of the pension, depending on the rules of the scheme where the fund is invested for them.

In some cases there may be a significant delay before one party can obtain their pension under a pension sharing order: for example, if they are younger than their spouse/cp and the rules of the pension fund require them to be a certain age before they can have the pension lump sum or income.

This is why obtaining specialist pension advice is so important, as you do need to understand the risks/alternatives because these can have a significant financial impact on the pension that will be available at retirement.

VALUING PENSIONS

Pensions are not an asset that can be used immediately in most cases, and so are difficult to value in a way that makes them comparable to other assets, or even other pension funds. The information required in most cases is a calculation of the Cash Equivalent Transfer Value (CETV) of the pension, which can be obtained from the pension provider. A member is usually entitled to one CETV without charge, in any 12 month period, for divorce purposes. However, you should check this with your pension provider to avoid incurring unnecessary costs.

The CETV needs to be less than 12 months old to be of any use in negotiations/court proceedings, and is an indicator of how much capital would be needed to buy a pension at retirement producing the same income/benefits as the pension fund currently has. This valuation is not always accurate and the calculation usually favours the person giving up the pension, to the cost of other spouse/cp.

A CETV ignores how the fund may change between now and retirement – the effect future increases in earnings may have – and does not include the value of death in service benefits. There can also be issues if a pension is under-funded that may effect the valuation.

It is possible to seek expert advice from an actuary or pension expert about the value of the pension, which instead of focusing on a CETV may also look at other valuation methods. Such reports and advice can consider what impact the pension share will have in real terms on the pension income each party will receive. Many people are surprised to find out that a 50/50 split of the pension will not necessarily bring in the same income for both spouses/cps at retirement, which is why specialist pension advice can be so important.

If an expert is to be used this should be by joint appointment with your spouse/cp, or by court order, to ensure the report is of use to everybody without incurring the cost of multiple reports that may favour one party and so give varying answers.

State Pension information, The Pension Service (part of the DWP): 08456 060265: www.direct.gov.uk/en/pensionsandretirementplanning/state pension. Society of Pension Consultants, St Bartholomew House, 92 Fleet Street, London EC4Y 1DG: 020-7353 1688: fax 020-7353 9296: www.spc.uk.com

FOREIGN PENSIONS

The court can make orders against foreign pension schemes, but enforcement of these can be difficult and if they will be implemented will depend on the rules of the individual pension scheme. Expert advice should be sought if you or your spouse/cp have pension assets held abroad.

STATE PENSION

Divorce/dissolution may impact your entitlement to a full state pension. You should make enquiries of the Department of Work and Taxes to ascertain what effect this could have on your state pension entitlement.

UNDERTAKINGS

The court's powers are specific and are defined by the legislation dealing with divorce/dissolution. There are circumstances where other issues need to be resolved or dealt with that the court cannot order, and in this situation you will need to agree with your spouse/cp what is going to be done, and make an undertaking about it.

An undertaking is a binding promise that is stated at the start of a court order as background information and once approved is enforceable (but in a different way to a court-ordered action).

Undertakings are useful to deal with financial issues or assets that may not have significant financial importance, but may have sentimental or emotional value to you. This can include dealing with how specific items of contents of a property are to be divided, which if they are of low value are unlikely to justify a court application or argument. Undertakings are often used to oblige a spouse/cp to clear a debt, maintain medical insurance cover, take out a life policy, resign as director in a family business or obtain a Get (Jewish divorce).

The benefit of an undertaking is that it can be very specific and clearly shows the basis upon which the overall financial agreement was entered into. Undertakings can also give great security, and increase trust between spouses/cps when they relate to promises, such as not to apply to the CSA for a certain period of time, or to leave their assets in a certain way under the terms of their will. Undertakings are often given by both spouses/cps and are part of the bargaining that goes on in negotiating the financial settlement in a divorce/dissolution.

The Pensions Advisory Service: 08456 012923:
www.pensionsadvisoryservice.org.uk

Applying to the court for an order

Even if you agree everything about the finances between you, you will still need a court order so that the agreement is binding. This will be an order made by consent. This section tells you how the court procedure works for spouses and cps.

THE GENERAL POSITION

Many couples start out with some level of disagreement that will mean that you need to make a court application to settle those issues.

PERFECT TIMING

Sorting out your finances in a divorce is a separate matter from the divorce proceedings themselves. However, the timings have to coincide at certain points. You cannot actually make a financial application until the divorce petition has been filed (though this does not stop you starting to negotiate about finances beforehand).

A final financial order cannot be made by the court until after decree nisi, but often the terms of such an order are agreed before decree nisi and submitted to the court for approval at the same time as the decree. The final financial order cannot take effect until decree absolute (the final decree of divorce), and in fact the order may not be resolved or finalised until after decree absolute has been pronounced.

❝If an application is made to the court, the judge will try and assist you in reaching an amicable agreement, or refer you to mediation if this is appropriate.❞

❝Only a small percentage of cases go all the way to the final hearing.❞

FINANCIAL APPLICATIONS

You can sort out the financial issues between you at any stage. Sometimes these are sorted out with relative ease and no applications are made to the court, a consent order is simply submitted for the court's approval. More often, a financial application will be filed at the court, seeking assistance to resolve certain issues. The application will then proceed until both of you feel comfortable enough with the information that you have obtained about each other's finances to be able to reach a settlement. Sometimes such a settlement is not reached until the day of the final hearing, 'at the court door'. Only a very small percentage of cases actually end up before a judge at a final hearing, who will then decide how the assets are to be divided.

The court takes more control over the progress of the financial application than it does the divorce process. There is a strict timetable for the progress of cases regarding financial issues. The court also keeps a close eye on the level of costs you are both incurring so that they do not escalate unreasonably. You are encouraged, and even obliged, to be frank about your negotiating positions, rather than play tactically. For the same reason, simultaneous exchange of information is prescribed. The content and format of the initial exchange of financial information is also laid down by the legislation and this is explained on page 187.

❝The parties themselves can decide at any point to settle the matter.❞

Final orders
The rules about when final orders can be made do not stop interim orders for maintenance or maintenance pending suit orders being made, if necessary pending decree absolute.

Making the application

This section sets out the court procedure you have to follow when you make an application for a financial order (called ancillary relief). Full details are supplied below as to which forms you will need to complete and where you can obtain the necessary paperwork.

THE APPLICATION FORM

Either spouse/cp can start the financial process off. If you want to apply to the court for an order, you start by filling in a Form A, which is available from the court or the Courts Service website and filing it (with two copies) at the court where the divorce proceedings have started. The fee is £210 (the usual exemptions apply). The form simply notifies the court and your spouse/cp that you intend to proceed with the financial application.

You do not have to file evidence of your financial position at the time that you make the application. This comes later (see below).

It is important to bear in mind that once you have filed Form A you are on a tight timescale, with which you must comply. It is sensible to make sure that you are going to be able to get together all the financial evidence that you need to meet the court timetable before you start.

THE 'FIRST APPOINTMENT'

Once the court receives Form A it will fix what is officially known as a First Appointment. This must take place between 12 and 16 weeks from the date on which the court gets Form A.

Once the date has been set for the First Appointment, the court will not exchange it unless your spouse/cp agrees or the court gives permission. This permission is only granted if the reason for the date change is significant and not trivial. If there

---

Filling in Form A

On this form you tick boxes to show which of the orders you intend to apply for:
- An order for maintenance pending suit.
- A periodical payments order.
- A secured provision order.
- A lump sum order.
- A property adjustment order.
- A pension sharing/attachment order.

If you intend to make an application for periodical payments for the children, you have to tick boxes to show why the court has jurisdiction (and the CSA does not).

---

are dates you know you cannot make, before you issue the Form A (for example, holidays, hospital appointments or work commitments), you should make the court aware of them so that you do not have to rearrange the court date afterwards, which may not be approved unless they believe the reason is good enough.

BEFORE THE FIRST APPOINTMENT

When the court set the date for the First Appointment, they will also notify you of a list of directions (requirements) that you need to comply with. Along with dealing with these directions, you should also send a copy of the Form A to any pension providers you may be asking to make a pension sharing order so that they are aware of this.

Form E – Financial Disclosure

Five weeks (35 days) before the hearing date, you and your spouse/cp must

exchange sworn Form Es. A Form E is a very long and detailed court form that requires full financial disclosure about your income, capital, pension and needs, and documentation to support your answers, where this is stated or where you think it would be helpful to attach it. It is important that this form is completed accurately and thoroughly, and although it may seem as though you have a long time to do it (sometimes up to 11 weeks depending on when the court set the First Appointment for), you should start it as soon as possible, as getting information and documentation from some of the financial institutions can take a long time (particularly pension information).

Without full financial disclosure from you both, the process can be delayed and this could lead to costs orders being made against one spouse/cp if the delay is unjustified. Missing information can prevent a settlement being reached, delay the process and incur unnecessary legal costs for both spouses/cps.

Documents required with your Form E

- A valuation of your family home or any other property you own (if you have obtained the valuation in the last six months).
- Evidence of the amount of mortgage outstanding on any property you own.

 Go to the Courts Service website for details of the forms you need to apply for an order: www.hmcourts-service.gov.uk

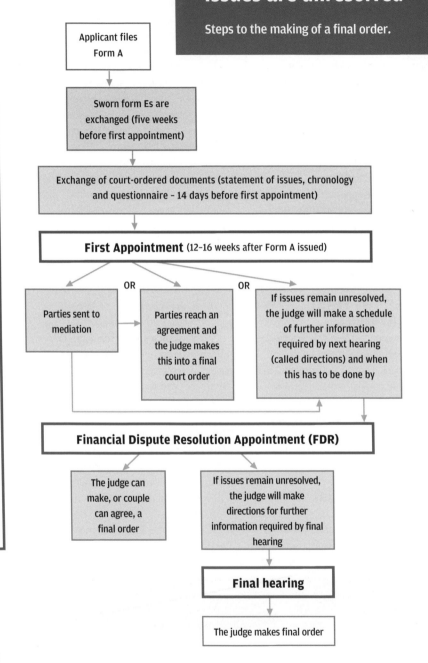

Financial procedure (ancillary relief) when issues are unresolved

Steps to the making of a final order.

Applicant files Form A

Sworn form Es are exchanged (five weeks before first appointment)

Exchange of court-ordered documents (statement of issues, chronology and questionnaire – 14 days before first appointment)

First Appointment (12–16 weeks after Form A issued)

Parties sent to mediation

OR

Parties reach an agreement and the judge makes this into a final court order

OR

If issues remain unresolved, the judge will make a schedule of further information required by next hearing (called directions) and when this has to be done by

Financial Dispute Resolution Appointment (FDR)

The judge can make, or couple can agree, a final order

If issues remain unresolved, the judge will make directions for further information required by final hearing

Final hearing

The judge makes final order

Parties can reach an agreement to settle at any point during this process

- Bank statements for the last 12 months for all accounts in which you have an interest (held in your sole name or jointly with someone else).
- Surrender values of any life insurance policies you hold.
- Current valuations of any investments.
- Business/partnership accounts for the last two years if you have an interest in that business/partnership, and any evidence of how you have calculated valuation of the business/partnership.
- Your last three payslips and most recent P60 and P11D, or if you are self-employed, your last tax assessment.
- Pension Cash Equivalent Transfer Value (CETV) outlining a valuation of your pension rights and benefits.

The court produce helpful information to assist you in completing this form (Form E – notes for guidance), which can be downloaded from the Courts Service website or picked up from your local court. Try to complete as much of this form as you can in advance and collate the information to save a lot of your solicitor's time, and so save you money.

Once you have completed the Form E and have all of the documentation you can obtain, this document needs to be sworn on oath, in front of an independent solicitor, to prove its accuracy.

Once your Form E is ready you/your solicitor should contact your spouse/cp/ their solicitor to agree a date to exchange the Form E's, which is normally done by post. A copy also has to be sent to the court. You can do this as soon as you are both ready and you do not have to wait until the deadline.

Other documents required before the first appointment

Fourteen days before the date the First Appointment is set for, you and your spouse/cp must also prepare the following documents, which you will send to the court and to each other:

- **Statement of Issues**. This provides the court with a concise description of the financial issues that are in dispute between you and your spouse/cp.
- **Chronology**. This gives the court details of the history of your relationship/ marriage, including significant events such as the start of your cohabitation, the date you married, dates of birth of your children, house purchases, job changes, date of separation.
- **Questionnaire**. This will arise as a result of the Form Es you have exchanged. Once you have read through your spouse's/cp's Form E you may have some issues/more information you want to know. This document is where you ask questions or request further information you require from your spouse/cp, or clarification of things they have said in their Form E. You can request further documents from your spouse/cp in this document if these are necessary. If there is nothing you want to ask or no further documents you wish to see, you should state this so that the court know there is nothing else needed by you. This is the last opportunity you may have to seek further information, as no further evidence of finances can be filed or sought without special permission of the court (which will

only be granted if you can show that the information will make a material difference to the outcome of the case).

- **Form G**. This must be completed to confirm if you think you have enough information to use the next hearing (First Appointment) as a Financial Dispute Resolution Appointment (FDR). If you both agree that you are ready, the court will be able to use the hearing as an FDR, which will skip a stage in the process (see chart on page 188) and save you and your spouse/cp time and legal costs. If you do not think you are ready to have an FDR, the court will set the date for the FDR at the First Appointment.

- **Form H**. This is a cost estimate of the work that has been done so far in dealing with the financial issues following the breakdown of your marriage and is completed by your solicitor. The court will be checking that the legal costs you have spent so far are proportionate to the issues you have.

THE FIRST APPOINTMENT

You and your spouse/cp will have to attend court for this hearing, but neither of you will have to give evidence. Your solicitor (if you have one) will attend with you. If you do not attend, there can be orders made against you for wasted costs as a result of you not attending.

The purpose of the First Appointment is to define the issues you both have and attempt to save costs in deciding how the case should proceed to the next stage (the FDR hearing). The judge will give directions (orders) about what should be done by when. For example:

- Questions that must be answered with further documents where relevant.
- Valuations that should be obtained (normally jointly).
- Expert evidence that may be needed (normally jointly, such as pension reports).
- Any other evidence that may be needed from either party (which can include further pension information in a standard format called Form P).
- When the Financial Dispute Resolution (FDR) hearing should be (see below).
- Adjourning (i.e. holding) the application to enable you to both attend mediation or negotiate, or for other reasons as may be appropriate

If you reach an agreement with your spouse/cp before or at this hearing, the judge can then turn that agreement into a Final Order. The hearing can go on for longer than is planned, depending on the court timetable that day and the issues that the judge needs to resolve.

Joint valuations and experts

If valuation evidence or expert reports are needed, the court are likely to order that these should be requested jointly by you and your spouse/cp to prevent two lots of evidence being filed, which may be partisan and increase the areas of dispute/costs. You will need to agree the identity of the valuer/expert together, and will instruct them jointly (and probably share the fee).

Third parties

You may feel evidence from a third party, such as your spouse's/cp's new partner is necessary. Your spouse/cp cannot be compelled to produce this evidence, and could claim they do not know the information. Nobody else can be obliged to file a Form E, as they are not a party to the proceedings. The court does have the power to require a third party to attend with documents that can be inspected. This is called an 'Inspection Appointment' and to obtain one you will need to file an affidavit explaining what documents you want to see and why they are relevant and necessary. The judge will review your request, and decide if the appointment is appropriate in the circumstances.

FINANCIAL DISPUTE RESOLUTION APPOINTMENT (FDR)

Both parties will be required to attend this appointment, but neither will be required to give evidence to the court. The objective is for the judge and parties to try to see if an overall agreement can be reached about the financial issues.

This hearing is informal and the structure of it will depend on the style of the judge helping you. The intention is to give you an opportunity to negotiate and discuss the issues and settlement with your spouse/cp and seek guidance from the judge on issues where there may be a stalemate.

The judge will try to help you with different views you and your spouse/cp may have about a fair outcome, and try to assist you in finding an overall agreement that suits you both.

This appointment can go on for several hours, as negotiations often take some time. There are likely to be periods where you are in with the judge and time where you are negotiating outside the courtroom, before going back in to see the judge.

Any offers and proposals that you have made or received before this hearing should be sent to the court at least seven days before the FDR. The judge is able to see these offers if they were 'open' or 'without prejudice', and this will help him or her see what points may be close to agreement and how far negotiations have progressed. The judge at the FDR is not able to be the judge at your final hearing, as seeing these proposals (which would otherwise be privileged and so hidden from the court) would make it inappropriate for them to deal with the final hearing.

If matters do not settle at this hearing, the copies of the offers and proposals are returned to you, so that the judge at any final hearing does not see them.

At the end of this appointment the judge will either:

- Make an order outlining the agreement that you have reached with your spouse/cp, which is called a consent order. This will bring the financial negotiations and issues to a conclusion. If the court ran out of time, or consent of a third party (such as a mortgage company) is required before the order can be made, the solicitors will draw up a document called a Heads Of Agreement, which everyone will sign and the judge will approve. This will then made into a court order at a later date, or a further hearing will be scheduled if the order cannot be finalised on the basis of the Heads Of Agreement.

- Give further directions where a settlement has not been reached, with details of any further information/clarification needed, and fix a date for a final hearing.

THE FINAL HEARING

A final hearing is quite rare, as it is only needed where you have not managed to reach an agreement at any earlier stage.

At least 14 days before the final hearing you must send the court (and your spouse/cp) a statement of 'open' proposals (seven days later if you are the Respondent). This statement will outline the amounts and terms of agreements that you have suggested, and the order that you have suggested the court make. You will also need to complete an updated Form H and send this to your spouse/cp and the court.

At least two working days before the final hearing, trial bundles (folders of documents set out in a specific format) must be sent to the court and copied to the other spouse/cp by the Applicant. Ideally the contents of these bundles should be agreed with the other spouse/cp beforehand.

At the hearing you will both have an opportunity to outline your position and what you think is the right outcome. This will normally be done by your solicitor or barrister (unless you are acting in person). You and your spouse/cp must attend this hearing and be prepared to give oral evidence on oath if needed.

Tips on giving oral evidence

- Always listen carefully to any questions put to you and answer clearly.
- Remember that the person to convince is the judge, not the lawyers.
- Speak slowly: often the other party's solicitor and the judge (as well as your solicitor, if instructed) will take notes.
- Avoid becoming heated or emotional in response to the questions, the judge will want to stick to the facts.

You will be asked questions by your spouse's/cp's solicitor/barrister, which is called cross-examination. Whoever started the application will give evidence and be cross-examined first, followed by the other spouse/cp.

The judge will make a decision about what orders they are going to make based on the evidence they have heard and the documentation that they have seen in the trial bundles. Their decision will then be made into a court order that will be binding upon you and your spouse/cp.

Negotiating a financial settlement

Very few cases end up going as far as a final hearing to resolve the money issues. This section explains the steps that you can take in negotiating and reaching an agreement at any stage in the process.

Reaching an agreement avoids expensive, and often hostile, court proceedings. The Law Society has published guidance that solicitors are obliged to follow to try and help parties to deal with disclosure and negotiations of settlement without the need for a court application. This is known as the Family Law Protocol.

Once the ancillary relief procedure has been started (by the issue of a Form A),

it can be stopped at any point if an agreement is reached between you and your spouse/cp. This could be very early on in the divorce – before court proceedings have even been commenced regarding the financial issues, at some point during the financial process, or even on the day of the final hearing before the judge has made a decision.

Mediation can be used at any stage (see Chapter 4) that helps reach resolution of the financial issues, hopefully avoiding the costs and time court proceedings involve.

Advantages of an agreement

Whenever an agreement is made, the family as a whole is likely to save significantly on legal costs. There are rare cases where a spouse/cp pretends to make an agreement while in reality he or she is determined to drag out the process of resolution, but as a general rule making agreements will save you money. The earlier you can do so the more money will be saved on legal fees and the less stress/upset there will be involved in the whole process.

CONSENT ORDERS

Although you have the option of keeping your agreements oral and informal and relying on your spouse/cp's sense of honour, the problem is that such agreements have a habit of unravelling over time, as one or other of you claims no longer to be able to 'remember' the terms. So, to protect yourself properly, an agreement should be drawn up in the form of a separation agreement or deed (see page 55) or, better still, a consent order made by the court.

If you have reached a settlement through mediation, this will usually be drawn up in the form of a 'Summary' or 'Memorandum of Understanding'. This again should be translated, usually by solicitors, into a court order that you seek approval of from the court to make the settlement financially watertight and binding.

PROPOSALS

Once you are satisfied that you have a clear view of the overall financial picture and that both of you have fully disclosed your financial circumstances to each other, you can put forward proposals for settlement on a 'without prejudice' basis. This means that if the proposals do not result in settlement and litigation does follow, they cannot be referred to at a final hearing before a court (but, as described earlier, they must be disclosed at the FDR to the judge).

Any 'open' offer (as opposed to one that is 'without prejudice') that you make to your spouse/cp can place you in a vulnerable position, in that your spouse/cp could later use in court any admissions you have made in this offer. Accordingly, if your solicitor is conducting negotiations for you, he or she will normally mark proposals with the words 'without prejudice'; if you are conducting negotiations yourself, you should do the same.

Usually it is the spouse/cp who will be paying maintenance and/or a lump sum who puts forward the first proposals; frequently (but not always) these result in counter-proposals from the other spouse/cp. Generally, the eventual agreement will fall somewhere between these two sets of proposals, if that results in a fair and reasonable outcome.

FINANCIAL AGREEMENTS AND DIVORCE

If couples agree a financial order, rather than have one decided by the court, it is known as a 'consent order'. An application for a consent order involves drawing up the draft court order that you would like the court to make: this is usually called by lawyers 'minutes of agreement and consent order' or 'minutes of order'. This is tailor-made to fit your own requirements (and so can often suit an individual family far better than a court order made by the court after a battle).

One of the main reasons why lawyers emphasise that a court order should be drawn up, instead of leaving an oral or written agreement as it stands, is the issue of a clean break. You may have amicably agreed to a clean break, that you will divide your assets to give one of you a greater share to compensate her or him for giving up claims for maintenance. But unless the

 To ensure that the form of a proposed consent order is as watertight, tax efficient and comprehensive as possible, you should instruct a solicitor to draw up the document.

court has formally ordered a dismissal of the maintenance claims, they can still be activated at a later stage. If circumstances changed you would still be able to make a further claim for maintenance (unless you had remarried). Capital claims that have been listed in the 'prayer' of the divorce petition continue, even after remarriage, unless dismissed by the court.

Making a clean-break order by consent will not preclude a future application for child support via the CSA. You cannot ever have a clean break as far as claims for children are concerned.

DRAWING UP A CONSENT ORDER

A consent order typically starts with an outline of the basis of the agreement and background information. Then it lists undertakings: solemn and binding promises that you make to each other. These can cover aspects of the settlement that the court cannot formally order, such as promises by one of you to provide medical insurance for the children. The main part of the document outlines the court orders that state everything that has been agreed, including any agreement about costs.

The consent order needs to be signed by you and your spouse/cp (and solicitors where you have them). You will also both need to complete a form called a 'Statement of Information for a Consent Order' (Form D81), which is a very short form requiring a condensed summary of your income, capital and pension provision and details

of your future plans. This form needs to be completed and sent to the court with the consent order as it also helps the judge review if the agreement is fair, appropriate and reasonable in the circumstances. The consent order needs to be sent to the court in triplicate, along with Form D81 and the court fee of £40.

At any time within the divorce proceedings you can apply for a consent order for maintenance pending suit (temporary maintenance payments made to a spouse until the decree absolute) and for interim periodical payments for the children.

You cannot apply for a final consent order (lump-sum, property adjustment or periodical payments) to be made a court order until the decree nisi has been pronounced. The order will then not become effective and enforceable until decree absolute has been made.

MAKING OF THE CONSENT ORDER

Once the consent order and fee have been lodged at the court, the judge will review it. Provided the judge has sufficient information to be satisfied that the proposed terms are reasonable and both parties are in agreement, he or she is likely to accept the agreement and issue a formal consent order as requested.

If the agreement is put forward by solicitors on each side, the judge may approve it without either of you having to attend in person, but if you are acting for yourself, the judge may make an appointment to discuss the proposed order with you and your spouse/cp, and may require further evidence, especially if no Form E has been filed. Approval by a judge is not a rubber-stamping procedure. In certain cases, where the judge feels that the order is unfair to either party, he or she may refuse to make it or may ask for more information to help him or her decide if it is fair and reasonable, and will then review it again.

EFFECT OF A CONSENT ORDER

Consent orders, once made, are as effective as orders made by the court after a full hearing. The undertakings can be enforced as well as the actual orders. You cannot appeal a consent order, because that would be logically impossible. However, you can apply to have it 'set aside', but only on limited grounds of:

- Fresh evidence that could not have been known at the time.
- Fundamental mistakes, such as wholly erroneous information, on which all parties, including the court, relied.
- Fraud (which may include evidence that the other party had no intention of ever abiding by the terms of the order).
- Lack of full and frank disclosure, if such disclosure would have resulted in an order substantially different from the one that was made.
- In certain rare circumstances, where the fundamental basis on which the order was made has been destroyed.

What to do with your court order

If you are acting for yourself, the court will send the court order to you. If you have a solicitor, he or she will be sent the copy and will send it on to you. This is not necessarily the end of the process.

CHECK IT

The first thing to do is check it through carefully. Sometimes errors creep in even if the order was made by consent. If there is anything that is the result of a typing or transcribing error, the court can put it right under what is called the 'slip rule'. If there is anything that you do not understand in the order (with a consent order this is unlikely to happen because you should have seen it before it went to the court), you should discuss it with your solicitor straight away – or go back to the court if you are acting for yourself.

MAKE SURE THE ORDER IS CARRIED OUT

You need to make sure that you keep to any promises that you have made or things that you have been ordered to do. There may be time limits that you need to comply with. You do not want to find yourself in breach of the order simply because you have overlooked part of it or have forgotten to do something by a certain date. You also need to check that your spouse/cp keeps to his or her part of the order. No one else polices the

> **❝ The longer maintenance is unpaid, the harder it is to recover, so be alert at this stage. ❞**

order for you; the court does not have a supervisory role, and your solicitor will not get involved in the implementation of the order unless there is something legal to be done, like the transfer of the home. Therefore you should ensure the steps that have been ordered actually happen.

Arrears of maintenance can quickly build up after an order is made, unless the payer makes immediate arrangements and the payee makes sure that payments are made on the correct dates.

Keep the order safe

You must keep the order safe. It would be a good idea to take a photocopy and put the court copy away securely. Some orders have a long-term effect – such as orders where the sale of the home is postponed until the children grow up – and you will need to refer back to them later.

After the order

You may need to vary or enforce an order once it has been put into effect. This section will show you the range of different factors that you might need to consider when and if you have to do this.

Even after an order has been made, there are occasions where you may have to ask the court for further assistance or make another application.

APPEALING THE ORDER

If you are not happy with an order you can appeal against it to a judge by filing a notice of appeal within 14 days. The fee for this is £100. The notice setting out the grounds for an appeal should ideally be prepared by a solicitor as it can be complex and the grounds have to be clearly stated.

VARYING THE TERMS OF AN ORDER

After an order has been made circumstances may change, so the original order may need changing (see box right).

Only some orders can be varied. Transfer of property and lump sum orders cannot be changed, except if a lump sum is payable by instalments – then the court can change the payment timing, but not the overall sum. Maintenance orders can be changed, and so can deferred pension attachment lump sums. If the original maintenance order was for a fixed period, you can apply to extend it, if you apply before the term runs out.

In the case of either the recipient's or the payer's change in financial circumstances,

an application can be made to vary a maintenance order if one of you is feeling the pinch. Usually, the court will look at the actual needs and resources of the parties and will be concerned to try to share out the more limited finances fairly. If this relates to retirement there are tax allowances available for those over 65 that could help financially. Review and variation of child maintenance paid via the CSA is only done by the CSA (see Chapter 6).

Typical reasons for an application for a variation

- A change in financial circumstances of the payer or payee, including retirement.
- remarriage of the payee (a periodical payments order ends automatically, so normally no application is necessary).
- Cohabitation of the payee.
- Remarriage or cohabitation of the payer.
- Death of either party.
- Either party becoming disabled.
- Children becoming significantly older and no longer financially dependant.
- Length of time elapsed since the making of the last order.

Varying an order in the divorce proceedings

Relevant law	Matrimonial Causes Act 1973 Section 31	Civil Partnership Act 2004 Schedule 5 Part 11
What the court must consider	All the circumstances, with particular regard to the children's welfare and any changes in the factors that were relevant when the original order was made.	
What the court can do	• Change the amount to be paid, up or down. • Extend or reduce length of time over which the payments are to be made. • Substitute a lump sum for a spouse's/cp's maintenance.	
How do you apply/what is the process?	Same way as you apply for an original financial order in the divorce proceedings. The fee is £210.	

What happens if the spouse/cp getting the spousal maintenance...

Remarries	Cohabits	Dies
Right to maintenance ceases immediately and cannot be revived against the spouse/cp, even if she or he subsequently divorces, separates or is widowed. If you are receiving spousal maintenance and do not tell your former spouse/cp you have remarried, you can be made to pay the maintenance back.	Rights to maintenance do not end automatically, but there might be grounds for asking for a variation. The court won't automatically treat a new partner as having an obligation to support their cohabitee, but it will be a factor the court looks at when balancing the needs of both former spouses/cps.	Maintenance stops.

Children's maintenance is not affected

What happens if the spouse/cp paying the spousal maintenance...

Remarries	Cohabits	Dies
He or she may be able to apply for a variation, but the court will treat the claims of the first spouse/cp as taking precedence over a new partner.		Maintenance stops, unless it has been secured. The recipient may be able to claim against the estate unless claims have already been dismissed in the divorce proceedings. You should seek urgent advice about this if the order is not clear.

Enforcing a court order

Payments of maintenance.
Need permission from court if arrears are over 12 months old.

Lump sum payments

CSA maintenance	Attachments of earnings order	Registration in Magistrate's Court
With a CSA assessment, the Child Maintenance and Enforcement Commission will apply their own enforcement procedures.	If payer is in regular paid employment the court can order an employer to deduct payments direct from wages. The court may reassess the amount payable.	You can apply to have a maintenance order registered at the magistrate's court. Once this happens the court can enforce the order, by attachment, seizure of goods or committal to prison. The court can also reassess the amount payable.
	Form: N337 Fee: £100 Affidavit setting out the debt.	Form: D151 Fee: £35 Certified copy of the order.
www.childmaintenance.org 08457 133133	EX323	EX327

Information leaflets available

	Property transfer

Warrant of execution	Committal by way of judgement summons	Charging order
Court instructs bailiff to seize goods, which can be sold to produce the amount owed. Only worth doing if there are enough assets. County Court up to £5,000; if more, transfer to High Court.	If you prove the payer has the means to pay, the court can order him/her to be committed to prison for up to six weeks if they don't pay.	The court can impose a charge on the debtor's property and, if the debt is not paid, order the sale. Court can execute the sale document if debtor does not cooperate.
Form: N323/N293A Fee: £100 or £50 Affidavit setting out the debt.	Form: N78 (collect from court only) Fee: £80 Affidavit setting out the debt and the means to pay.	Form: N379 Fee: £100 Affidavit setting out the details.

EX322

EX325

from the Courts Service

UNFORSEEN EVENTS

After a consent order has been made an event can happen that makes the order unfair. If this event happens within 12 months of the order having been made, and is something that was both unforeseen and unforeseeable that invalidates the fundamental assumptions upon which the order was made, it is possible to ask the court to set aside the order and re-consider the matter. This needs to be a significant event.

If you find yourself in this situation you should obtain urgent legal advice to see if your circumstances would justify an application on this basis, and then make it quickly as time is of the essence.

BANKRUPTCY

If following the making of an order, your spouse/cp (or you) is made bankrupt, their assets and property vest in the trustee in bankruptcy. If there is any question that the transfers that occurred between you during the divorce/dissolution were made at an undervalue (i.e. for less than they should have been), the trustee may apply to have that transaction set aside.

Case law reviewing this has found that orders made in ancillary relief proceedings should not be set aside, but in some circumstances the trustee has been able to force a sale of a property, and so each situation must now be considered on its own specific circumstances. If there is a risk that you/your spouse/cp will be made bankrupt, you should discuss this with your solicitor to ensure the order deals with such an eventuality.

ENFORCING MAINTENANCE PAYMENTS

Whether you actually receive maintenance following a court order or CSA assessment often depends on the continuing ability of your ex to make the payments.

Should the payer fall into arrears there are several channels for enforcement, none of which are entirely satisfactory. If arrears are allowed to accumulate, they may prove impossible to recover: a court will not generally enforce arrears that are more than a year old. The chart on pages 200–201 sets out the main enforcement procedures that you can use.

APPLICATIONS TO ENFORCE AN ORDER WHEN YOUR SPOUSE/CP HAS DISAPPEARED

If you have an order to enforce and your spouse/cp has disappeared, you can make a court request for help from government departments to find an address for them. If you have bank or employer details there may be enforcement options you can take without an address, but these may not be enough. In that case you can make the application for information, which is then requested by the judge for the purposes of enforcing an order against a person who cannot be traced.

You will need to complete a form outlining as much information as you can about your spouse/cp. The request is made to the DWP and if they can trace your spouse/cp, the address will be given to the court. It is also possible to seek information from agencies such as the Passport Agency or Ministry of Defence.

Cohabiting couples

The law for cohabitants is very different to that for married couples. Despite proposals being drafted, there is still no specific legislation to protect cohabitants. As it stands there are no rules or obligations about how cohabiting couples should separate, and the law that does exist is limited. This chapter outlines that law, and applies to heterosexual and same-sex couples.

PART 3

10

Splitting up

When a cohabiting couple split up there is no legal process to follow as for married couples. Instead the law only applies to some of the practical consequences that follow the decision to separate.

The proportion of cohabiting but unmarried couples has increased significantly; it is projected that by 2031 the number of cohabiting couples will be 3.8 million (about 1 in 4). This emphasises the need for a change in the law and for options for cohabitants to expand. However, new legislation is unlikely in the near future and so we presently have a complex mix of law for cohabitants on separation.

There is a misapprehension that after you have lived together for a number of years you have automatic rights by being a 'common law spouse'. This term has no legal meaning and is regularly used in error by the public to classify couples who have lived together for a period of time (often quoted as two years). No period of cohabitation gives automatic financial rights or status under existing law to unmarried couples, including claims for maintenance, capital or other assets, such as pensions. In limited circumstances claims may be made through a court application on a cohabitant's death.

COHABITATION AGREEMENTS

Agreements between cohabitating couples are now more common and confirm the rights and responsibilities both partners will have if the relationship breaks down. If the cohabitation agreement (sometimes called a living together agreement) is in the form of a deed, it is a legally enforceable document that you and your partner can rely on

Jargon buster

Cohabitation Agreement Sometimes called a 'living together agreement', this outlines the financial arrangements of a cohabiting couple and what will happen if they separate.

Declaration of Trust Document registered against the title of a property confirming the contributions that have been made on its acquisition and how the proceeds of sale will be divided.

 For further reading on Living Together Agreements: www.advicenow.org.uk and follow links to the living together pages.

if general contract requirements and principles have been met.

A cohabitation agreement should be supported with full disclosure of financial and other circumstances.

INCOME

If you and the partner you are separating from have children, there are claims that can be made on behalf of the children for maintenance (see Chapter 6). In certain circumstances this can include an element of your costs if the children live with you.

If you do not have children there is no right or mechanism for a cohabitant to claim maintenance against the other cohabitant, in any circumstances, other than by voluntary agreement. If you can reach an agreement, this should be put into a maintenance agreement/deed if you wish it to be binding on you both. It will only be enforceable if it is specific and clear and drafted as a deed, so you will need legal advice.

Maintenance agreements

A maintenance agreement needs to include:
- **Clear details of the amount.**
- **Whether it is to be paid weekly or monthly or at another interval.**
- **How it is to be paid.**
- **If it is to be paid in arrears or in advance.**
- **If it is to be increased and by how much.**
- **What events might cause it to end.**

If you are not specific, it can be hard to enforce an agreement even if it has been made as a deed.

The breakdown of your relationship may have an impact on your income due to the effect separation can have on tax and benefit entitlements. You should notify the benefits agency and HMRC as soon as you stop cohabitating. This does not necessarily require you to live under separate roofs, but does need you to live as separate households for cleaning, cooking, eating and financial arrangements.

YOUR HOME

If you and your cohabitant had a declaration of trust or cohabitation agreement when you purchased your home and you agree with the terms of those documents, there is nothing else you should need to do; the agreements will be sufficient to regulate what happens next in most circumstances.

If there was no declaration of trust or cohabitation agreement, then there is no one single piece of law that applies to assist you with how your home should be divided. As well as the legislation that exists there are also a number of cases that provide some assistance (but each case is fact specific), and the common law and equity principles, which have been established over centuries.

How your home will be treated by these combined principles will vary depending on if the property is owned jointly or solely, or rented.

Jointly owned property

If you both agree what shares you have in the property and there is no dispute, there is no need to take further action;

your agreement will regulate what happens next. More difficulty comes when there is a dispute about what the agreement was, or what you meant, or if your situation/contributions have changed.

When you first purchased/transferred the property in joint names you would have been asked how you wished to own it. This would include if you wanted a declaration of trust drafted, which is a document outlining the contributions you made and how the ownership of the property would be shared.

There are two ways of legally owning joint property; as joint tenants or as tenants in common. How you register your ownership from these options has an impact on the way the property would be treated on your death, as well as having consequences regarding the general ownership of the property in the future. Your solicitor should have discussed these options with you at the time of the purchase/transfer of the property, and if they did not there may be claims you could have against that firm (see box right).

You can end a joint tenancy by taking steps to 'sever' it, which then converts the joint tenancy into a tenancy in common in equal shares. You should seek advice about the effect and consequences of taking such a step before doing it.

The way the property was registered when it was purchased (or subsequently) is the legal starting point for determining how it will be shared. The registration can be checked by looking at the Land Registry title and reviewing

Correct advice at time of purchase?

Do you have a remedy against the solicitors who helped you buy the home? If you bought the home jointly, or transferred it into your joint names, you ought to have been given sensible advice by the solicitors who dealt with the purchase so you knew the implications of what you were doing. The Court of Appeal has said in one case that it was probably negligent if the solicitor did not find out and record at the time of the conveyance what the joint purchasers' shares of the property were agreed to be.

If your solicitor failed to do this and you end up having to pay legal costs to establish your rights in the home, or you end up with a court case where you end up losing part of the property, you may be able to recoup some of your loss from your original solicitor. You can explore the possibilities with your current solicitor – unless of course you are still using the same one. If this is the case then you will need to take advice from another firm.

documents that were completed by you both at the time. If those documents declared that you would officially own the property jointly so far as the Land Registry were concerned, then unless certain facts can be shown, the presumption is that you will both own the benefit of the property equally in financial and practical terms.

In this situation, if you cannot reach an agreement with your former cohabitant about what shares you both have in the property – either directly, through mediation, or through solicitor negotiation – it will be necessary to apply to the court to ask then to determine the shares you both own of the property, and how these should be realised.

If you wish to argue that the property should not be owned equally, the burden is on you to show why your share of the equity in the property should be different to the legal title. There are limited options to try to prove this:

- Identifying an issue about the way the conveyance (transfer into joint names) happened and the original terms of the purchase; for example, there was mistake at the time. This is rare and can be difficult to prove. The judge has to review the facts of what happened at the time and the burden of proof is on the person who does

not agree that the legal title should be followed. Unless they can show there was a problem with the original agreement, the judge will declare that your shares in the home should remain as the legal title states.

- By showing that there was a subsequent agreement. This could be a formal document – such as a subsequent declaration of trust document – or a more informal agreement, such as a verbal agreement or what you thought was a mutual understanding that you relied on. Again, there would need to be a review of the facts of what happened between you to establish if this is sufficient to overturn the legal title as registered.

- By showing that events or actions since the transfer make the legal title illogical. This would need one of you to have acted in such a way that your behaviour was completely

Jargon buster

Joint tenancy Under a joint tenancy each person's interest in the property is not quantified: you own the whole of the house (or flat) jointly. When one of you dies, the whole property automatically passes to the survivor, irrespective of any provision the former may have made in a will. The law assumes a 50:50 split regardless of the contributions you have both made to the property.

Tenancy in common Under a tenancy in common the interests of each person are fixed (usually on a 50:50 basis, but it can be in any proportion) and separate, so that each person can separately dispose of his or her share by will. If you don't state the shares, the law assumes a 50:50 split. This ownership is often confirmed and defined by a Declaration of Trust, which outlines each person's share of the property and their rights and responsibilities.

inconsistent with equal joint ownership. For example, each owner agreeing to share the purchase costs and mortgage, but then one paying little or nothing towards the property improvements, repair or mortgage. In this situation, it would seem illogical that you both still intended to share the property equally. The court will look at what has actually happened and what is fair in light of the terms of the original agreement you had. Unless one of these three grounds can be established and proved, the presumption remains that the beneficial ownership follows the legal title.

Property owned in the sole name of one person

The strict legal position is that if a property is legally registered in one person's name, no-one else has an interest in it. However, this common law position can be overturned by 'equitable principles' that exist in our legal system, allowing the common law to be overridden if fairness requires it. To do this there are particular circumstances that need to be shown, which have been laid down by previous cases seen as precedents for this type of claim.

TRUSTS

For the person who is not the legal owner of the property to be able to make a claim against the property, they will need to show that a form of trust has been created that would mean the legal ownership is in one cohabitant's name, but that a trust exists that requires the value/benefit of the property to be shared or divided to give them a share (which does not necessarily mean an equal share). There are two types of trust that can be identified:

- **An Express Trust**. This means that the agreement has been expressed or stated in some way, such as a cohabitation agreement or declaration of trust. An express trust would be binding unless superseded by a later agreement or propriety estoppel (see below).

- **An Implied Trust**. This could be that a trust is presumed to exist due to the way that you have both acted. An example of this would be if you both contributed to the purchase

Contribution

A key factor in determining how property should be shared is the circumstances surrounding the costs and contribution towards the property during the relationship. This includes a review of the contributions (in money or kind) made towards the purchase or improvement of the home. One party obtaining a council house discount can be seen as a contribution towards the purchase price. The contributions at the time the property was transferred and subsequently throughout the period of joint ownership, highlight the common intention of the cohabitants and how they envisaged the equity in the home would be shared.

price and mortgage payments on the property. The contributions necessary to show an implied trust do not need to be direct and can be evidenced by other contributions, such as payment of utility bills. Each claim is decided by a review of the facts to establish what both parties' true intentions were, not by just looking at financial contributions.

To establish that a trust exists and that you have a claim in the property, there needs to be a review of the events that have taken place to show what was agreed or implied. If you and your cohabitant do not agree these events, the judge will consider the evidence and decide which version of events is more probable. This will require a great deal of evidence about what was said, in detail, and what has happened. The court will look at your whole course of conduct to establish if a claim is justifiable. The test is often seen as clarifying if there was a common intention about the ownership of the property, and then seeing if the non-owner had relied on that common intention to their detriment.

It is also possible to seek a share of the property if you can show that 'proprietary estoppel' applies. This means that the owner has behaved in such a way that you were led to believe that you would have rights in the property (either to live there or have a financial interest in it), and that based on this belief you acted to your detriment and relied on what you believed.

Engaged couples

If you have been engaged to your cohabitant there is specific legislation that can apply to you – which is quite specific and requires a substantial contribution to have been made. This can still be defeated by a contrary agreement (see page 216).

Proving you have acted to your detriment

Detrimental acts can be making direct financial contributions, such as making payments towards the property purchase or mortgage, or indirect contributions enabling the owner to use their money to pay for the property. Detriment can also shown by non-monetary contributions, such as developing or improving the property.

Proving that you have acted to your detriment requires evidence of you having an effect on your own circumstances, but again this does not need to be financial. It could be shown by you giving up your own home or a particular opportunity, which you did on the basis that you had been promised that a share of the property, or a home would be provided for you, for life, by your partner and so you acted in a way that relied upon that assurance.

Once the court has decided if the non-owner was successful in showing there was a trust, or proprietary estoppel applied, this would determine if they had a beneficial interest in the property. The next stage would be to establish the extent of that interest.

IN A HOME THAT YOU RENT

The legal position regarding rented accommodation depends on the sort of tenancy that you have (see Jargon Buster, right). The following is only a very brief guide and you will need to take specialist advice about your position. See *The Which? Essential Guide Renting and Letting* for more information. In most cases the court has power to transfer a tenancy between cohabitants, as long as the tenancy has not already been terminated by a notice to quit.

What the court can do

The court can decide whether you ought to have a share in the home, (and how big that share ought to be) or whether you have the right to live in the home for a fixed period, or for life.

Jargon buster

Types of tenancies. Your tenancy agreement may state what sort of tenancy you have. If it is not clear look at the explanations below:

Assured shorthold tenancy and assured tenancy If it started on or after 28th February 1997, unless the landlord has stated in writing that it is an assured tenancy. If it started from 15th January 1989 to and 27th February 1997 it will be an assured shorthold tenancy if the landlord stated it to be so on a legal form when it first started. If he did not, then it is an assured tenancy. Housing Association tenancies from 15th January 1989 generally come into this category.

Regulated or protected tenancy If your tenancy started before 15th January 1989 it will generally be a regulated or protected tenancy.

Secure tenancy Most council tenancies unless they are in temporary accommodation. Housing Association tenancies that started before 15th January 1989.

Periodic tenancy Periodic tenancies have no fixed end date when you sign the original agreement and simply continue from week to week, or month to month (depending on how you pay your rent), until either you or the landlord gives the appropriate notice.

Fixed term tenancy A tenancy for a limited period – six months is typical.

Statutory periodic tenancy A tenancy that continues after the fixed term ends.

Sorting out your shares when you own the family home

Is the home in joint names or one person's name?

Sole

Joint

Non-owner can make a claim if he/she can show that a trust has been created, explicitly or implicitly:
• Owner has promised a share in return for a contribution.
• Owner has made promises that have made the non-owner act to his/her detriment.

Is it a tenancy in common or a joint tenancy? (see Jargon Buster on page 207).

TIC

JT

You are entitled to the home in the shares in the original deed. If none stated, 50% each.

You are entitled to 50% each.

Cost rules

Applications relating to property for cohabitants are part of civil law rather than family law and as a result the cost rules are different – see page 217.

However, there are factors that might alter the legal shares, such as:
• An agreement between you.
• A change in circumstances that changes the original understanding.

Your interests in other assets

There are no legal proceedings designed to allow cohabitants to make claims against each other to sort out ownership of possessions. This means the court treats you as they would any two people who have a dispute over ownership.

The fact that you have had a family relationship is all but irrelevant. The only exception to this is if you are a male-female couple and have been engaged. This brings you within the scope of the Married Women's Property Act 1882, and the court can say who owns disputed items of property (including your home) if you apply within three years of the termination of the engagement.

In any other circumstances, if you did not have an agreement about the things that you bought together and need to sort them out now, try to do it together. You can make a list of all the items and then try to agree who should have what. You can decide how you want to do this. You may want to divide on the basis of the price that you paid for them, or you may want to look at their value now, rather than at the date of purchase. You may want to achieve a rough equality in the sorts of things that you have, so that one has the sitting room suite, and one the dining table and chairs, for instance. You can decide that the fairest way is to take it in turns to choose, or discuss items room by room. It really does not matter how you do it, provided you find a way of reaching an agreement. If you cannot do this without help, you could seek assistance from a mediation service.

The law on items such as purchases/contents of your home is often referred to as 'chattels'. The law governing ownership of chattels is the Law of Property Act (section 188). In disputes there is a review of if the item has been gifted, where the purchase money came

Cost warning!
You need to think carefully about starting a legal claim. Few domestic assets have such value that you can justify the amount that you will spend in legal costs sorting out a dispute over them. You will probably spend far more on lawyers than the value of the item.

Rules about ownership: the legal position outlined

- If you bought something, and you alone paid for it, it belongs to you.
- If you bought something out of joint funds, without distinguishing in what shares you contributed, you own it jointly and equally.
- If you bought something and contributed unequally, then you own it in the shares in which you contributed to its purchase.
- If one of you gave the other something, it belongs to the person it was given to. This includes engagement rings, even if you never marry. The exception would be if at the time of the gift it was specifically stated that the item should be returned in the event of a break up.

from, if there was an express agreement or arrangement or understanding, and if any items of sole ownership were put in by way of 'part exchange' in the purchase.

In most cases, you will not be able to establish ownership by referring to documents. For example, a car may be registered in a person's name, but that is not conclusive proof of ownership; in the absence of a gift or a promise, the car would belong to the person who paid for it.

These rules can be upset by what you do or say to each other. If you buy something with your money but say to your partner, 'this belongs to both of us',

"Try to list your personal items together so that you can work out the best way to divide them. "

or 'this is yours', and behave as though you mean it, then a court can hold you to your promise. You can be regarded as having created 'a trust' over that item or asset. You might do this consciously – as you do if you enter into a living together agreement. Or a court can find that you have created a trust by implication; your behaviour or what you have said lead to the conclusion that the item should, for reasons of fairness, be shared or even transferred to your partner.

However, there does have to be a shared, or communicated, intention to share the property.

BANK AND OTHER ACCOUNTS

On the face of it, if you have a joint account with your partner, you hold it in equal shares and things that you buy from it are owned jointly and equally. But this is not always the case. If only one of you puts money into the account, though you can both draw on it, the strict legal construction would be that that money and any purchases made from it would belong to the person putting the money in. The strict legal position can be over-ridden by an agreement between you, or by your behaviour giving rise to a trust, as described above.

PREVIOUSLY-OWNED POSSESSIONS

These will be your own individual property unless you have made gifts of them to each other. There could also be circumstances in which you have started to treat such items as belonging to you both and you have both contributed to their maintenance. For example, if you helped to restore and maintain a classic car that was owned by your partner prior to the relationship. You may have contributed financially, as well as giving up your time. When you split up you could justify a claim to a share of the car on the basis that you had been led to believe that you had an interest in it and had acted to your detriment in helping restore it.

WHAT IF YOU ARE STILL PAYING FOR THINGS WHEN YOU SPLIT UP?

If you have bought things using a credit card, hire purchase agreement or loan, the person who made the credit agreement is liable for the repayments as far as the lender is concerned. You are jointly and severally liable if you took the loan out together.

The logical position ought to be that if you are paying for something, you ought to have it, unless you have said to your partner that you are buying the thing for him or her and, in effect, have already made a gift of it. If you were buying something jointly you will have to decide between you who is going to go on

making the payments and who will have the object.

The credit company will not be bound by your decision that only one of you is going to be responsible for the payments, but it would be worth explaining to them the arrangement that you have made in any event, and telling them your new address(es). The reason for this is that if your partner says that he or she will take on the repayments and does not make them, the company can take debt recovery proceedings, and will name both of you. You do not have to be personally served with the proceedings; they can post them to your last address. You might find that a judgment had been obtained against you without your having had the chance to defend the proceedings. Judgments like this can affect your credit rating. Therefore it is important that as long as your name is linked to that credit arrangement, you are aware of what liability is still outstanding and that repayments are being made in accordance with the initial agreement.

Applying to the court for an order

As there is no umbrella legislation to protect cohabitants, you have to use a number of laws to bring claims to court.

This book can only give a brief outline of procedure in each case. You will need specialist legal advice if you intend to proceed with a claim. We strongly advise you to consider using mediation to reach a settlement (see Chapter 4), as court applications on these issues can often be very expensive and time consuming.

Applying for a share in an owned home

Relevant law	**Trusts of Land and Appointment of Trustees Act 1996, section 14.**
What the court must consider	• The intentions of the person or persons who created the trust. • The purposes for which the property subject to the trust is held. • The welfare of any child who occupies or might reasonably be expected to occupy the home. • The interests of any secured creditor or of any beneficiary.
What the court can do	• Declare who owns the home and in what shares. • Order a sale of the property. • Order one person to pay the other a sum of money in return for their assessed share.
How do you apply	On form N1 (Part 7 claim form) or N208 (Part 8 claim form) with evidence set out in a sworn statement. You have to serve any mortgagee as well as the owner. County Court Fee: £150. (Exemption form EX160.)

If you want the home for you and any children, you can combine this claim with one for them under the Children Act 1989. If you don't succeed on your own account, you might be able to keep a home for the children.

 Courts service: www.hmcourts-service.gov.uk Leaflet N208a.

Applying for a transfer of property order for the children

Relevant law	**Children Act 1989, Schedule 1.**

What the court must consider	• Your income, earning capacity, property and other financial resources, now and in the future.
	• Your needs, obligations and responsibilities.
	• The children's needs.
	• Any income or other financial resources that belong to the children.
	• Any physical or mental disability of any child.
	• The way in which the child was being brought up and educated.
	• If the order is against a person who is not the child's parent, the court must also consider:
	  o To what extent that person has assumed responsibility for the child.
	  o Whether he or she knew that he or she was not the child's parent.
	  o Whether there is anyone else who is liable to support the child.

What the court can do	As well as maintenance and lump sum payments the court can order a transfer of property order, either to the person who applies for the order for the benefit of the child, or to the child him or herself.
How do you apply	On Form C1 and C10 in the county court with a statement of means form on C10A. Fee: £175 (county court). (Exemption form EX160.)

Under a Children Act application the court will generally not transfer a home to a parent outright. Instead, you might get the right to live in the home while the children are still in full-time education. You should consider combining an application under this Act with one for yourself for a transfer of tenancy or a declaration of your interest in the home.

Courts Service : www.hmcourts-service.gov.uk
Leaflet CB1.

Applying for a transfer of a tenancy

Relevant law	**Part IV of the Family Law Act 1996, Schedule 7.**

What the court must consider	• The circumstances in which the tenancy was originally granted.
	• Each person's housing needs and those of any child living with you.
	• Your financial resources.
	• The likely effect if the court orders, or does not order, on the health, safety and wellbeing of each of you and of any child.
	• If only one of you is the tenant:
	  o The nature of your relationship.
	  o The length of time you have lived together.
	  o Whether you have any children.
	  o How long it is since you separated.

What the court can do	• Transfer a tenancy between you. • Order (if appropriate) the person who gets the tenancy to pay the other a lump sum. • Order who is liable for any unpaid debts.
How do you apply	On Form FL401 in the county court (The landlord must also be served a copy of this) and Form N285. Fee: £80 (county court). (Exemption form EX160.) HMCS information leaflet FL700.

COSTS

The rules about how costs are awarded are not the same as the rules in the context of divorce, as they form part of civil law rather than family law. The various procedures described in this chapter are more adversarial. Costs can be awarded against the 'loser' in the case and this can have a significant impact on your general financial position if you do not win. You and your solicitor will have to think carefully about the way you negotiate and the offers that you make to settle. If you receive proposals for settlement you must consider them carefully. If you refuse to settle and the case goes to court you will need to get a better order than the offer or risk being liable for costs.

When you get a court order

See Chapter 9 about what to do with your order and enforcement.

Ownership of property if you have been engaged

This only applies to male-female couples. The Civil Partnership Act has not amended the law to include a couple engaging to enter into a civil partnership. This may be open to a challenge but there is, as yet, no established law on the point. 'Property' includes ownership of a home, so if you have been engaged it may be helpful to combine this with a TOLATA application. You must apply within three years of the termination of the engagement.

Relevant law	**Married Women's Property Act 1882, section 17.**
What the court must consider	Principles of ownership as they exist in common law – established rules and case law.
What the court can do	• Say who is entitled to property and in what shares. • Order property to be sold. • Order payment of a lump sum. • Prevent disposal of an asset.
How do you apply	In form M23 in the county court with a supporting sworn statement. Fee: £200. (Exemption Form EX160.)

Application to sort out ownership of disputed property

Relevant law	**Common Law.**
What the court must consider	Principles of ownership as they exist in common law – established rules and case law.
What the court can do	• Say who is entitled to property and in what shares. • Prevent disposal of an asset
How do you apply	In the small claims court if the item is under £5,000, otherwise in the county court. The fee depends on the item or amount. (Exemption Form EX160.)

Courts Service: www.hmcourts-service.gov.uk
Leaflets on how to bring a claim and court alternatives EX301 and EX302.

Other parts of the UK

This chapter highlights the differences in the law in Scotland and Northern Ireland, each of which is a separate legal jurisdiction from England and Wales.

11

Scotland

For your convenience, this has been arranged to highlight the difference chapter by chapter in the rest of the book. The Civil Partnership Act 2004 is in force in both Scotland and Northern Ireland. As in England and Wales, it mirrors matrimonial law in both jurisdictions.

CHAPTER 1 LEGAL COSTS

If there is no agreement as to divorce expenses, the court will apportion them at the end of the proceedings. The main factors that influence the court are which spouse/cp won and whether each spouse/cp conducted the proceedings in a responsible way. For example, if you make exaggerated claims or are uncooperative, thus forcing your spouse/cp to litigate unnecessarily, you could end up paying most of your spouse's/cp's expenses as well as your own. Often no award is made, so each spouse/cp is left to pay his or her own expenses. The courts are reluctant to order a legally aided spouse/cp to pay the other's

 The Family Law (Scotland) Act 2006 which came into force on 4th May 2006, has brought a number of changes to Scottish family law including 'DIY divorces'.

expenses. If an award of expenses is made against a legally aided party, they then have the ability to ask the court to modify that award, usually to zero.

It is common for consent to be given to a one years' non-cohabitation divorce on condition that the consenting spouse/cp will not be liable for the other's expenses.

It is possible to obtain an award of expenses in a divorce action. However, in many divorces the court will be asked to adjudicate on several different matters (divorce, money, maintenance, children, etc). In such cases there is frequently mixed success; one party may not get as much money as they want, but the other party may not get as much contact as they want. This will often result in the court deciding that each party should bear their own costs.

Even if your spouse/cp pays your expenses you will almost certainly be out of pocket, as the court's award is unlikely

 Scottish Legal Aid Board: 0131 226 7061: www.slab.org.uk

to meet the costs of the litigation, let alone all consultations with your solicitor and other extras that your spouse/cp is not required to pay for.

Legal aid

Legal aid is available for court proceedings: divorce, financial claims and matters concerning the children or housing, whether with the divorce proceedings or separately. Your solicitor will help you apply for legal advice and assistance, or legal aid. The Scottish Legal Aid Board runs both schemes.

The Scottish Legal Aid Board deducts the amount of your expenses from money the court awards you, or property that the court orders to be transferred to you, if it cannot recover the sum in full from your contributions or from your opponent. However, no deduction is made from any aliment (money paid periodically for a person's support), or periodical allowance, or the first £5,338 of any capital sum, or transfer of property awarded (as from 6 April 2010).

CHAPTER 2 FINANCIAL PLANNING

The Matrimonial Homes (Family Protection) (Scotland) Act 1981 gives you certain rights if you do not own the home and your spouse/cp is the sole owner. You are entitled to continue to occupy and live in the home. Moreover, your consent is required for any sale or other disposal, although the court can dispense with your consent if it is being withheld unreasonably. These rights are automatic: you do not have to register them in the Land Register for Scotland or the Register of Sasines (public registers of property and its owners).

You can renounce your occupancy rights, but it is seldom in your interest to do so. A renunciation must be in writing and signed and declared before a notary public.

CHAPTER 3 GETTING LEGAL ADVICE

The Family Law Association in Scotland has a comprehensive list of solicitors who practice in family law. The Law Society of Scotland have a list of solicitors who are accredited as specialists in Family Law. Alternatively, your library or CAB should have lists showing which local solicitors undertake divorce work and whether they will act for clients on legal aid. The Law Society of Scotland will also help you find a solicitor.

 Married co-tenants and spouses/cps of sole tenants have similar protection against the tenancy of the home being given up.

CHAPTER 5 CHILDREN

The Children Act 1989 does not apply to Scotland; the legislation applicable is the Children (Scotland) Act 1995. In Scotland parents have various legal responsibilities towards their children, such as safeguarding them, advising them and acting on their behalf in legal transactions; and various rights, such as deciding where they are to live, controlling their upbringing and having contact with them.

These responsibilities and rights cease when the children reach 16. The children can then live where they like, look after their own money and generally make their own decisions. A child under 16 can consent to medical treatment if the doctor thinks that he or she can understand what the proposed treatment involves, and in such a case the parents cannot overrule the child.

While parents live together they share parental responsibilities and rights. Each can act alone, neither can veto the other's actions, and any irreconcilable disputes have to be resolved by the court. On divorce the court may, on application, reallocate these responsibilities and rights.

Orders may be unnecessary if the parents are going to cooperate or if the non-resident parent will not interfere with the day-to-day decisions of the parent looking after the children. Otherwise the parent who is going to be looking after the children may need to apply for a residence order, which will give him or her the right to have the children living with him or her in addition to the other responsibilities and rights. The other parent retains these except in relation to the children's residence.

If the parents cannot agree which of them the children should live with, the court will decide on welfare grounds, taking any views expressed by the children into account. Children of 12 years and over are presumed able to form a view, and the court rarely goes against firm views of 14- or 15-year-olds. Children below 12 years can also give the court their views, which will be taken into account, but they may not be regarded as conclusive.

CHAPTER 6 CHILD MAINTENANCE

The CSA now assesses maintenance for children up to and including 18 years of age who are still in secondary education. Currently the court has no power to deal with claims for aliment made for these children. Certain categories of children as described in Chapter 6 are not within the Agency's remit and can still be awarded aliment by the court. Children have to look after themselves once they reach 25, as the parental obligation of aliment ceases then. A formal registered agreement for child maintenance (aliment) has the same effect as a court order in England, and excludes the CSA jurisdiction.

The amount of aliment a court can award depends on what the person paying it can afford and what the child needs. The previous level of support the child enjoyed is also important. A child over 11 years old can apply to the CSA for an assessment of his or her own maintenance. Children over 18 years who wish aliment via the court must claim themselves. Below that age a parent may claim on their behalf.

CHAPTER 7 EMERGENCIES

You can be protected from harm by obtaining an 'interdict', which you may need to combine with an exclusion order (see boxes below).

An interdict orders the Defender not to assault, threaten or harass the Pursuer. It can also be used to protect children.

Interdicts

Married couples/cps 'matrimonial interdicts'	Cohabiting couples 'domestic interdicts'
'Child' is a 'child of the family' and includes any child or grandchild of either spouse/cp – and any person who has been brought up or treated by either spouse/cp as if they were a child of that spouse/cp, whatever the age.	'Child' is any child in the permanent or temporary care of the Pursuer, and is thus restricted to children under 16 years.

Exclusion orders

Married couples/cps	Cohabiting couples
You have rights of occupancy whether or not you are the owner or tenant of the home.	You do not have automatic occupancy rights unless you are the sole or joint owner/tenant of the home.
Your spouse/cp cannot legally exclude you from the house, and the police will help you get back in if you are evicted.	You can apply for occupancy rights at the same time as you ask for an exclusion order.
You can apply for an exclusion order that generally lasts until the marriage ends on divorce. You can apply for this order as part of the divorce proceedings.	If you are the sole owner/tenancy, you do not need to apply for an order unless your partner has already been granted occupancy rights: you can simply tell them to leave. If they don't you can get a summary ejection order.

It can restrain the Defender from coming near your home.

If you need to exclude your partner from the home you will need to apply for an exclusion order as well.

If the court is satisfied, first, that the (interim) exclusion order is necessary to protect you and/or the children, it then has to consider whether it is reasonable for him or her to be excluded. Your spouse/cp must be sent a copy of your application for an (interim) exclusion order and given an opportunity to oppose it. You will have to back up your claim with as much evidence as you can, such as affidavits from your doctor or neighbours about your health and past incidents of violence, reports by the police if they have been involved, and evidence of your need for the home and the unsuitable nature of your present temporary accommodation if you have been forced to leave home.

The Protection from Harassment Act

This 1997 Act (Sections 8 to 11) applies to Scotland. There is no necessity for there to be any defined relationship between Pursuer and Defender. For example, this could be used after a divorce. A person must not pursue a 'course of conduct' that amounts to harassment. There must be at least two occasions on which the conduct has taken place. There is no provision for interim Non-Harassment Orders, and therefore interdict and interim interdict are often sought in the same action, if immediate protection is required.

However, the Defender cannot be subject to the same prohibitions in an interdict and a Non-Harassment order in the same action. Breach of a Non-Harassment Order is a criminal offence.

Power of Arrest

A power of arrest can be attached to an interdict where protection from abuse was sought. Once the power of arrest is granted you must inform both the defender and the Chief Constable of the local Police Force. A constable can then arrest the defender without warrant if he has reasonable cause for suspecting that there has been a breach of interdict and that he considers that, if the person was not arrested, there would be a risk of abuse or further abuse. Criminal proceedings may be brought. If not, the Sheriff, after enquiry, can still order the Defender's further detention for up to two more days.

Child abduction

The Scottish provisions of the Child Abduction Act 1984 are different from those for England and Wales. A parent commits a criminal offence by taking a child out of the UK only if:

- The other parent (or someone else) has a residence order (or in old cases, was awarded custody) and has not agreed to the child's removal, or,
- The court has interdicted removal.

If your spouse/cp is likely to take the children abroad, you should at once apply for a residence order or an interdict. You can do so even without applying for divorce, but if you have started divorce proceedings the application has to be made in the context of those proceedings. In an emergency you can obtain an interdict at any hour of the day or night. Once you have an interdict or a residence order, you can ask the police and sheriff officers to trace the children and prevent their removal from the country. You should also ask the police for a Port-Stop Order.

CHAPTER 8 GETTING A DIVORCE / DISSOLUTION

Jurisdiction: One or both of you needs to be habitually resident or domiciled in Scotland.

Judicial separation

The court granting a judicial separation has no power to award a capital sum or order a transfer of property: it can only award aliment for you. You and your spouse/cp remain married to each other, so neither of you can remarry. There is limited legal point in getting a judicial separation, because now you can get aliment from the court without asking for separation, but a few couples still opt for a judicial separation for religious reasons.

A husband does not inherit any of the property the wife acquired after judicial separation if she dies without having made a will. There is no equivalent rule disinheriting a separated wife.

Grounds for divorce

There is no minimum period you have to wait after marriage before you can bring divorce proceedings.

In Scotland divorce is initiated by initial writ (Sheriff Court) or summons (Court of Session).

There are only four facts on which you can base an application for divorce to show that the marriage has irretrievably broken down. Cps have only three facts, as adultery is not available to them. You can also have a divorce on the basis that an interim gender recognition certificate has been issued to one of the parties after the marriage. This is a certificate that allows a transsexual to be legally recognised in their acquired gender.

 DIY court forms are available from the courts or Citizens Advice Bureau (CAB), or go to: www.scotcourts.gov.uk to download them. Help leaflets are also available.

Which court?

Most divorces are dealt with in the sheriff courts. These are local courts situated in most major towns in Scotland. You can bring proceedings in the court for the area in which you or your spouse/cp have been living for the past 40 days; you would usually choose your own local court. Divorces are also heard in the Court of Session in Edinburgh. Divorces are usually heard in the Court of Session if the case is more complex, difficult or if large sums of money are involved.

There are no decrees nisi or absolute in Scotland. The court grants a single decree of divorce that is immediately effective, although a certain period (14 days in the sheriff court, 21 days in the Court of Session) is allowed for an appeal.

Getting a divorce

There are two types of procedure: the simplified procedure (usually called a DIY divorce), and the ordinary procedure.

Ordinary procedure

This is more complex and you are strongly advised to get a solicitor to act for you. Most divorces are heard in the sheriff courts, so only that procedure will

 You do not need a solicitor for a DIY divorce. However, it is a good idea to get legal advice before you start in order to make sure that you are fully aware of the consequences and that you are not losing rights in ignorance.

Fees for swearing an affidavit

Before a notary public – most solicitors – (for a fee)

Before a justice of the peace (free)

DIY Procedure

One year + non-cohab with consent	Send completed form to court with:	Two years + non-cohab with consent
Complete part 1 of form. Spouse/cp completes part 2 of form. You swear affidavit on part 3 of form.	• Marriage certificate • Court due £95 (exempt if you are on legal aid). Court tells you when divorce is granted, usually about two months.	Complete part 1 of form. You swear affidavit on part 3 of form.

be described here. The Court of Session procedure is slightly different.

Proceedings start with your solicitor lodging the initial writ in court. This document sets out briefly the facts of your case and details the orders you are asking the court to make. A copy of this writ is then served on your spouse/cp. You are called the Pursuer and he or she is the Defender. A copy also has to be served on any person (a Co-defender) with whom you aver your spouse has committed adultery.

The children may be sent a notice telling them about the court proceedings (if a parental rights order is sought), unless the court considers it inappropriate because of the children's age, and they will be invited to express their views either in person or in writing.

In a divorce action based on either one or two years' non-cohabitation, your spouse/cp is also sent a notice warning of the possible financial consequences of divorce (for example, loss of pension or inheritance rights). The notice alerts your spouse/cp to the financial and other applications he or she can make to the court.

In your initial writ you can apply for various interim orders, or you can add them on later (which will incur extra court fees). Interim orders last until the divorce is granted, when the position is reviewed and fresh orders made. Examples of interim orders are:

- Interim aliment for you. The CSA deals with maintenance for the children, unless the parent against whom the order is sought is out of the UK.
- Interim residence for and contact with the children.
- An interim interdict (order) against violent behaviour or disposal of assets.
- An interdict against taking the children out of Scotland. Your application for this need not be intimated to your spouse/cp, so that he or she may get no warning at all.
- An exclusion order excluding your spouse/cp from the family home.

You can also apply for these remedies separately; they are available not only in divorce proceedings. If you cannot apply for a divorce as soon as you and your spouse/cp split up, you may need to use separate proceedings.

DIY divorces – only on the fact of non-cohabitation facts 3 & 4

Conditions:

- No children of the marriage under 16 years of age.
- No financial claims by you or your spouse/cp.
- No other legal proceedings affecting your marriage waiting to be heard.
- The divorce is not defended.
- Neither you nor your spouse/cp are suffering from a mental disorder.

Defences

A notice of intention to defend must be lodged within 21 days (42 if the Defender is abroad). The court will then specify the date defences have to be lodged by and the date of the options hearing (see below). In your defences you can oppose your spouse's/cp's claims and/or make claims against him or her. Each of you will then adjust your case to meet the other's.

An options hearing will then be held during which the court will clarify the issues in dispute and decide how to proceed. You and your spouse/cp and your respective solicitors are required to attend, but on application you or your spouse/cp may be excused. Some courts involve the couple in the discussions, others listen only to the solicitors.

It is unusual for the divorce itself to be defended. More commonly your spouse/cp will defend your application for financial orders or matters relating to the children, or will apply for similar orders. Where the divorce is defended, the case is heard in court with each side and their witnesses giving evidence.

Where only financial aspects are at issue, the divorce itself can be disposed of on the basis of sworn statements (affidavits) from the Pursuer and a corroborating witness giving details of the evidence to be relied on to prove the grounds of divorce.

Reconciliation

You and your spouse/cp can still try to save your marriage even though divorce proceedings have started. The court will, if asked, stop proceedings for a reconciliation. If this does not work, you can ask the court to let the proceedings continue from where they were stopped.

Affidavits

An affidavit is accepted by the court as evidence of the facts contained in it. You, your spouse/cp and others can give evidence by affidavits instead of attending court, but this is not advisable unless the action is undefended or the evidence is uncontroversial. Your solicitor will prepare your affidavit from the information you give, and you will then swear it before a notary public (who may be your own solicitor). The information must be up to date, complete and accurate; otherwise further affidavits or oral evidence will be called for.

Deliberately concealing facts, or making false statements, is regarded as a very serious offence for which you could be imprisoned.

The children

You should show that satisfactory arrangements have been made for any children of the marriage who are under 16 years of age. Most couples reach agreement about who is to look after the children. You or your spouse's/cp's affidavit will state who is going to look after the children, how they are going to be looked after, and what accommodation will be available for them. In addition, the court requires an affidavit from a relative or a person (such as a neighbour) who knows the children well. If these affidavits are satisfactory, the court will accept the arrangements without interviewing the couple or the children.

If you or your spouse/cp apply for an order in relation to the children, a child welfare hearing will be fixed. This hearing takes place on the first convenient date three weeks after lodging the notice of intention to defend. You will both be expected to attend; the children may attend and may be given an opportunity to make their views known.

The court may decide the matter there and then, it may refer you both to mediation, or it may postpone the matter to a later date for more thorough consideration. If the outcome is the last of these, the court may ask an independent person to prepare a report. The reporter is often an advocate or solicitor, but sometimes a social worker is used. The court will consider this report along with all the evidence from witnesses and other sources before deciding what option is best for the children's welfare.

Joint minute

If you and your spouse/cp can agree on the financial aspects and future arrangements for the children before proceedings start, you can ask the court simply to make the appropriate orders and your spouse/cp need not defend. An alternative, which is sometimes adopted, is for a formal enforceable agreement to be prepared covering these matters (this is commonly known as a minute of agreement and is similar to a separation agreement). In these circumstances, you can then apply to the court for divorce – divorce being the only order sought. In some cases a DIY divorce may be possible. However, in many cases agreement is reached only after proceedings have started, as a result of negotiation or mediation.

You and your spouse/cp will then arrange for your respective solicitors to submit a joint minute to the court (note that this is not the same document as a minute of agreement). This joint minute either sets out the orders that you and your spouse/cp request the court to grant, or asks the court to make no orders because the matters are covered by a written agreement. The terms of the joint minute should be checked carefully. Once it has been lodged in court it is normally impossible to change your mind and ask the court to do something else.

Where the proceedings are undefended or a joint minute is submitted, the court will normally grant the orders sought without further enquiry. The court may, however, demand further information in matters affecting the children.

Decree

A decree is a formal document containing the orders made by the court. The financial orders are almost always granted at the same time as the divorce, although it is possible, in certain circumstances, to have these left over for a later hearing.

The court will notify you that decree has been granted and also notify your spouse/cp if his or her address is known. There is a 14-day period allowed for appeal (21 days in the Court of Session). After that, an extract (certified copy) of the decree, which details the orders the court made, can be obtained from the court. You will need an extract to show that you are divorced if you plan to marry again, and also to enforce the orders if your spouse/cp refuses to pay.

CHAPTER 9 MONEY IN DIVORCE

Financial orders

The court can grant several financial orders together. The main financial orders the court can make on divorce are:

- Ordering one spouse/cp to pay a lump sum (a 'capital' sum) to the other, and/or,
- Ordering one spouse/cp to pay the other a periodical allowance – a regular sum each week or month, and/or,
- Ordering a spouse/cp to pay aliment for the children of the marriage, but only if the CSA cannot assess maintenance, and/or,
- Transferring the ownership of property

from one spouse/cp to the other, and/or,

- Ordering one spouse/cp to split their pension with the other.

It is possible, but unusual, for the court to grant a divorce and postpone the financial orders to a later date if disagreement is holding up the divorce.

The court can also order the house to be sold immediately or at a later date and/or say who is to occupy it and to have use of the contents. Where the house is rented, the court can transfer the tenancy from one spouse/cp to the other.

Either the Pursuer or the Defender can apply for financial orders. You have to state in your initial writ or defences exactly what orders you seek from the court and give evidence of your and your spouse's/cp's needs and resources to demonstrate that they are reasonable claims. The court also needs to know the amount of aliment currently being paid.

Making exaggerated claims is a bad tactic, as it will merely get your spouse's/cp's back up and possibly have a bearing on any sympathy the court may have with you or your spouse/cp. This may result in you having to pay your spouse's/cp's legal costs. Almost inevitably a couple's living standards drop after divorce. A fair settlement should result in this drop being shared between the spouses/cps.

A claim for a lump sum or transfer of property must be made before the divorce is granted. You can claim periodical allowance afterwards but you are very unlikely to get it then, because the principles required to justify an award (principles 3 to 5 below), generally speaking apply to your situation at the time of divorce. You cannot claim periodical allowance later if at the time of divorce you and your spouse/cp made a formal agreement that you would not claim.

The Family Law (Scotland) Act 1985 sets out a series of principles to guide the court in making financial orders, as follows.

1. Sharing matrimonial property
This includes:
- the home and its contents, savings, investments and other assets which you or your spouse/cp own and which were acquired between the date of marriage and the date of final separation.
- The home and contents are also counted as matrimonial assets if they were acquired before marriage as a family home for the couple, even if the house is in the name of one spouse/cp only.
- Lump sum payable on retirement and pensions.

Matrimonial property should be shared equally unless there is a good reason for unequal division, which may be ordered where, say, your parents helped you buy the home or where you run a business that cannot be divided.

2. Balancing economic advantages and disadvantages
The court has to take account of your financial and non-financial contributions to your spouse's/cp's wealth. Examples include helping with the costs of the home, sacrificing a career to care for children, or working in a spouse's/cp's business at an artificially low wage.

 Assets given to you or inherited by you are not regarded as matrimonial property.

3. Sharing childcare
Future childcare costs are to be shared. These include your loss of earnings while looking after the children and the expense of keeping up a larger and more expensive house than you would need if you were living on your own. If maintenance for the children is assessed by the CSA, it includes an amount for childcare costs; the court will then take account of this principle only for extra costs.

4. Financial dependency
Under this principle a party who was financially dependent upon their spouse/cp during the marriage is entitled to apply for maintenance for up to three years after divorce to enable them to become self-supporting.

5. Severe financial hardship

If you are unlikely to be self-supporting after divorce (for example, you are too old or too ill), you may need financial support for many years (the rest of your life, perhaps) to avoid severe financial hardship.

Court orders

Principles 1 and 2 can be satisfied only by the award of a lump sum and/or a transfer of property. The lump sum may be payable all at once, shortly after divorce or at a specified later date, or by instalments. Principles 3 to 5 should be satisfied by a lump sum or transfer of property if possible, otherwise by a periodical allowance. If you are looking after young children you may be able to get a periodical allowance under principle 3 as compensation for loss of earnings, or the childcare costs if you work.

If a periodical allowance at the time of divorce cannot be justified by principles 3, 4 or 5, a spouse/cp will not be awarded one. The court will not award a nominal periodical allowance on divorce with the intention that it could be increased later if the recipient's financial circumstances get worse.

Change in circumstances

After divorce your or your ex's financial circumstances may change. You may be able to go back to court to get your orders changed, depending on the type of order involved.

Lump-sum order

You cannot apply for a lump-sum order after divorce. If you were awarded a lump sum on divorce the court cannot generally change the amount payable. The only exception is a rare one. If the true facts were concealed from the court or lies were told to obtain the original order, the court can make a new order. Apart from this exceptional case, all the court can do is to alter the way in which the lump sum is paid, perhaps by ordering payment by instalments or giving more time to pay.

Property-transfer orders

You cannot apply for a transfer of property order after divorce. If you were awarded a transfer on divorce, the court cannot alter the property to be transferred except in the circumstances mentioned above. All it can do is to alter the date set for transfer.

Periodical allowance

You can apply for a periodical allowance after divorce, but it would be awarded only in unusual circumstances. You cannot apply if you agreed not to do so as part of the divorce settlement.

You or your ex can apply to the court for the amount to be increased, decreased, terminated or made payable only for a certain number of years more. For example, if you lose your job or now work part-time, your allowance could be increased. If your ex's business is not doing so well, your allowance could be decreased or even terminated. Your allowance, which was awarded on grounds of severe financial hardship, could have a time limit put on it if you were offered a retraining course with a job at the end. If you were awarded an allowance on financial dependency grounds (principle 4), it cannot be extended beyond three years after divorce.

Your remarriage terminates your periodical allowance automatically. A woman's periodical allowance is usually terminated by the court if she lives with another man even if he is not supporting her, but not all courts take this attitude.

Your ex's remarriage can result in your periodical allowance being reduced or terminated if the court thinks his or her commitments have increased. Your periodical allowance should not be reduced if your ex lives with another adult partner. But if they have children, the court will take these new liabilities into account.

When you die, your periodical allowance comes to an end automatically. But the death of your ex does not mean that your periodical allowance comes to an end automatically. The executors have to apply to the court for it to be terminated. Occasionally the court will then order payment at a reduced rate or set a time limit on the allowance, rather than terminate it.

Any variation the court awards can be backdated to the date of the application, or to the date when the circumstances changed, as long as there was a good reason for the delay in applying for the variation.

Another variation the court can be asked to make is to substitute a lump sum (payable by instalments, perhaps) for a periodical allowance. You and your ex should weigh up the advantages and disadvantages carefully, because once the substitution order is made it cannot be reversed.

Aliment for children

In exceptional cases (see above) the court may still award aliment and can vary the amount awarded subsequently. Apart from these cases, if aliment is payable under a court order that was made in proceedings commenced, or a written agreement entered into, before April 1993, the court retains power to vary the amount.

A variation of aliment can be applied for if the circumstances of the child or those of the paying parent change. The amount of aliment is not reduced merely because the paying parent, or the parent looking after the children, remarries or cohabits. Aliment ceases automatically when either the paying parent or the child dies.

Enforcing maintenance

Legal enforcement methods are called diligence. You do not have to go back to the court, but you will need a solicitor's help. The legal aid certificate for your divorce covers the cost of diligence for up to 12 months later. After a year, or if you are applying for your ex to be imprisoned for failure to pay, you will have to apply for legal aid or legal advice and assistance.

Where your ex is employed, the best diligence to use is a current maintenance arrestment. You (or your solicitor) send a copy of the court order to your ex and if, not less than four weeks later, three or more instalments are in arrears, a current maintenance arrestment can be served by a sheriff officer on your ex's employer. The employer thereafter automatically deducts every payday the maintenance due to you for the period since the last payday and sends it to you or your solicitor. A current maintenance arrestment does not enforce arrears, but you can use an earnings arrestment or another diligence at the same time to recover the arrears.

The following diligences enforce arrears only, although the threat of repeating them may make your ex keep up regular payments in future.

- Earnings arrestment: a sheriff officer serves a notice on your ex's employer, who deducts every payday an amount that varies with the earnings payable then. The deductions are sent to you or your solicitor and stop when the arrears are paid off.
- Arrestment of a bank or building society account: a sheriff officer serves a notice that freezes the money in your ex's account. You then have to apply to the court for an order requiring the bank or building society to pay you, unless your ex agrees to release the money.
- Attachment and sale of goods: a sheriff officer goes to your ex's home or business premises and makes a list of his or her goods and their

value. The court can then order these 'attached' goods to be auctioned to pay the arrears.

- Imprisonment: if the court is satisfied that your ex's failure to pay was wilful, he or she can be imprisoned for up to six weeks. Imprisonment is available only for failure to pay aliment; you cannot use it to enforce payment of your periodical allowance.

Effect of divorce on your inheritance rights

After divorce, you have no rights to your ex's estate if he or she dies without a will or leaves you nothing. The Inheritance (Provision for Family and Dependants) Act 1975 does not apply to Scotland.

Legacies or other provisions for you in your ex's will are not cancelled by divorce/dissolution after the date of the will. Generally speaking, you are entitled to take them unless the will makes it clear that you are not.

Your ex's will is not cancelled by his or her subsequent remarriage. If you sign a separation agreement setting out the arrangements for dividing your matrimonial assets, it normally includes a clause giving up your automatic rights of inheritance upon your ex's estate, although the usual provisions contained within the Separation Agreement do not over-rule the terms of an existing will. You should always remember to review the terms of your will in the event of separation.

After divorce, you and your ex should review any existing will. You will probably want to cancel any bequest to your ex, but other changes may also be desirable.

Most married/cp couples who own their home together have in the title deeds that the property will go to the survivor when one of them dies. This is another thing that ought to be changed on or before divorce/dissolution. A solicitor's help will be needed to change the title deeds.

CHAPTER 10 COHABITING COUPLES

In May 2006, the Scottish Parliament introduced limited legal rights for Scottish cohabitants.

COHABITANTS' RIGHTS

The Family Law (Scotland) Act 2006, which came into force on 4 May 2006, brought in significant, although limited, rights for unmarried cohabitants for the first time in the United Kingdom.

Former cohabitants in Scotland are now, in some circumstances, able to make financial claims against a former partner in a way that is almost akin to seeking financial provision on divorce, or claim certain succession rights on the estate of a former partner following their death where they have left no will. These rights may also be open to Scottish cohabitants who live or have lived in England. The law regarding jurisdiction for those former cohabitants is complicated and advice should be sought from a Scottish family lawyer.

The 2006 Act sets out certain broad principles to be applied in the event that a cohabitating couple split or one of them dies without leaving a will. However, at the time of writing, there is little guidance on how the court will apply these principles. Some applications are now being made to the court but as yet none have been decided.

The new rights afforded in terms of the 2006 Act apply only to those who ceased cohabitation by reason of separation or death after 4 May 2006, when the legislation came into force.

Definition of cohabitation

To make a claim, it first needs to be shown that the couple concerned would be regarded as 'cohabitants' for the purposes of the Act. A cohabitant is defined as a person who is or was living together with another person as if they were husband and wife or civil partners. In other words, the Act covers male-female and same-sex couples. There is no minimum period of cohabitation.

However, the Act also goes on to state that in determining whether a person is a cohabitant, the court will have regard to the length and nature of cohabitation, the extent to which the cohabitant is financially dependent on

Part 4: Other parts of the UK

For more information see Which? Essential Guide *Wills and Probate* and Which? Essential Guide *Giving and Inheriting*

the other and whether the cohabitants have a child of whom they are the parents. Therefore, it seems possible that a couple who are living together as husband and wife/cps could be deemed not to have been cohabitants if, for example, they had not been living together for long or if their finances had remained completely independent of each other.

Financial provision on relationship breakdown

Assuming that you are able to show that you were cohabitants for the purpose of the Act, a number of claims for financial provision can now be made following the breakdown of a relationship (by reason other than death).

1. Right to a share in certain household goods.

There is a presumption that each of you has a right to an equal share in household goods acquired during the period of cohabitation. This would not apply for any household goods acquired by either of you by way of gift or inheritance and does not include money, cars, caravans, road vehicles, securities or domestic animals. Household goods would be regarded as any other goods kept or used for joint domestic purpose in any residence in which the cohabitants live or have lived together.

2. Right to a share in certain money and property

Unless there was any agreement to the contrary – for example, in terms of a Cohabitation Agreement – a former cohabitant can claim an equal share of any money or property deriving from any allowance made by either of the cohabitants for the joint household expenses or for similar purposes, and any property acquired out of such money. 'Property' specifically excludes any sole or main residence, but could include cars, other motor vehicles, policies etc, providing those items were purchased using household allowance or money from a joint account.

3. A claim for payment of a capital sum

A former cohabitant can claim for payment of a capital sum, to be paid by way of a lump sum or in instalments, for their own benefit and/or for a further amount to reflect the additional burden they have of caring for a child of the parties or a child accepted as being a child of the family. Where a claim is being made in respect of a child, that would be most likely to have to relate to the capital cost of obtaining suitable accommodation for the person making the application and the child to live in. Maintenance payments for any child would still be dealt with by the Child Support Agency.

A former cohabitant making a claim for payment of a capital sum would have to show that the former partner had derived an economic advantage from the contributions (financial or non-financial) that they, the claimant, had made, and that they, the claimant, had suffered an economic disadvantage in the interests of either the former partner or of any children of the relationship. They would also then need to show an imbalance in any respective advantages and disadvantages suffered.

In looking at whether an economic advantage had been gained or an economic disadvantage suffered, the court would look at gains and losses in respect of capital, income and earning capacity.

Your partner has died without leaving a will

A claim by a former cohabitant can only be made against the former partner's estate upon death if the deceased partner died without leaving a will. A claim can only be made if at the time of death, the deceased was domiciled in Scotland and cohabiting.

Any application must be made to the court by the surviving cohabitant within six months of the date of death. The court will consider various factors, including the extent and nature of the deceased's estate and any other claims on that estate. Such a claim will not affect an existing spouse's/cp's claims against the estate, but could act potentially to prejudice any claim by the children of the deceased.

If the financial provisions in the 2006 act do not apply to you

There are a number of reasons that the rights afforded by the 2006 act may not be available to you. Some examples of such reasons are:

- You may have ceased cohabitation or your partner may have died before 4 May 2006.
- You may wish to apply for a capital sum but cannot show an economic imbalance in respect of the contributions made by you and your partner.
- You may not have made an application to the court in time, that is to say within 12 months of the end of your relationship, or six months after the date of your partner's death.
- You may have entered into a Cohabitation Agreement waiving your right to make such claims.

In circumstances such as these, if you have not entered into a Cohabitation Agreement regulating what is to happen regarding finances in the event of your separation, all that you can rely upon is joint property law or the law of unjustified enrichment.

In terms of the law of joint property, if there is a house that has been purchased

 Any claim following on from the breakdown of a relationship must be made to the court within one year of the date of the couple's separation.

in the joint names of yourself and your partner, or a joint bank account, you will each be entitled to a half share of any equity in the property or a half share of the funds held in the account. This may or may not produce what you would consider to be an equitable result.

If you have made financial contributions towards a heritable property that is owned in your former partner's sole name, or title has been taken in proportions that are not reflective of your respective financial contributions, your only possible right of claim may be to rely upon the law of unjustified enrichment. However, the law of unjustified enrichment is complicated and the results highly uncertain. The cost of legal fees in making an application under the law of unjustified enrichment are likely to be extremely high with little guarantee of success.

Northern Ireland

To a large extent, divorce in Northern Ireland mirrors that in England and Wales. The most important differences are highlighted in this section.

CHAPTER 4 - MEDIATION AND COLLABORATIVE LAW

There are limited mediation services available in relation to children's issues, but these are rarely available in relation to financial matters. There is a collaborative law website in operation: www.afriendlydivorce.co.uk.

CHAPTER 5 - CHILDREN

Until 4 November 1996 Northern Ireland did not have any legislation in place equivalent to the Children's Act 1989. However, the Children (Northern Ireland) Order 1995 brought the legislation in relation to children in line with the rest of the UK and created the concept of 'parental responsibility'. Where parents are divorcing and there are children of the marriage, the court in Northern Ireland will no longer make custody or access orders, but will make what are termed 'article 8' orders, most important of which are residence and contact orders.

CHAPTER 6 - CHILD MAINTENANCE

In Northern Ireland the equivalent body to the Child Support Agency (CSA) is the Child Maintenance and Enforcement Division (CMED): 0800 028 7439. www.dsdni.gov.uk

CHAPTER 7 - EMERGENCY MEASURES

In Northern Ireland a spouse/cp or a cohabitant can apply under the Family Homes and Domestic Violence (Northern Ireland) Order 1998 to a court for protection. The protections are the same as the law in England and Wales, though there are some local variations in procedure.

CHAPTER 8 - GETTING A DIVORCE/DISSOLUTION

Divorce proceedings cannot be brought within the first two years of marriage.

The 'special procedure' for undefended divorces does not apply to Northern Ireland. The Matrimonial Causes (Northern Ireland) Order 1978 does provide that the Court can dispense with oral testimony where there are special

 Jurisdiction
One or both of you needs to be habitually resident or domiciled in Northern Ireland.

reasons to do so. The Petitioner has to apply to the court for leave to proceed on this basis and such leave is only granted in exceptional circumstances.

Petitioners must appear in person before a judge and formally prove the ground upon which the petition is based, whether in the County Court or the High Court. The judge hears the Petitioner's evidence in private (known as 'in chambers'), and most undefended divorce hearings are relatively brief (about ten minutes).

CHAPTER 9 - MONEY IN DIVORCE

While there is legislation in Northern Ireland equivalent to that in England and Wales, a separate body of case law has been created in Northern Ireland that can result in a slightly different approach being taken. Decisions from the Court of Appeal downwards in England and Wales are not binding on the Northern Irish courts, though they are of persuasive authority.

The court cannot order the capitalisation of spousal maintenance.

The ancillary relief procedure in Northern Ireland was revised and a new procedure was implemented on 1 May 2006 that has some similarities to that existing in England and Wales, but there are also many differences. Reference should be made to the Ancillary Relief Guidance Notes for applications to the High Court at www.courtsni.gov.uk

WHICH COURT?

In Northern Ireland divorces can be brought in either a county court or the High Court. There is at least one county court for each of the six counties in Northern Ireland, including Recorder's Courts in Londonderry and Belfast. Whether the divorce petition is to be heard in a county court or the High Court is a decision for the Petitioner's solicitor. By and large, for petitions that are likely to be defended or in which there are sizeable assets to be taken into account, the High Court is considered the more appropriate venue. If a divorce that is issued in the county court becomes defended then it must be transferred to the High Court (see Chapter 9).

Fees

Stamp duty payable on a divorce petition is £200 in the County Court and £200 in the High Court. To set the divorce down for Hearing in the County Court there is a fee of £250 and £300 in the High Court. The application for a Decree Absolute in either Court costs £75. The position in relation to dissolution proceedings is exactly the same as set out for divorce proceedings.

Family Mediation NI: 028 9024 3265
Relate NI: 0870 2426091: www.relateni.org
Law Society of Northern Ireland: 028 9024 1614: www.lawsoc-ni.org

Appendices

APPENDIX A1: APPLYING CURRENT CHILD SUPPORT AGENCY FORMULA (THE 2000 REGIME)

Step 1 Work out the net income of the non-resident parent (NRP)

Weekly income – including regular overtime, bonuses, commission and tax credits if their income is higher than the PWC's income (half if the same, none if PWC earns more) less:

• Income tax   • National Insurance   • Pension contributions

If the NRP is self-employed the CSA work out average weekly earnings for the most recent tax year then make the above deductions.

Ignore:

• Child benefit   • Housing benefit
• Council tax benefit   • Student loans and grants
• Income from lodgers (unless it is a significant source of income)
• Non-contributory benefits for people with disabilities (such as disability living allowance and attendance allowance)

> The CSA is able to calculate maintenance on the net income of the NRP only up to £2,000 a week. If the income is higher than this, you may be able to get a top up order from the court.

Step 2 Decide whether it would be appropriate to apply any variation

For detailed information see: CSA leaflet CSL108 Child support variations: Help for exceptional circumstances. You can get a reduction or seek an increase if:

• You have costs relating to keeping in contact with a child for whom you are paying maintenance.
• You have extra expenses because a child who lives with you has a disability or a long-term illness.
• You are paying boarding school fees for a child for whom you are paying maintenance.
• You are paying a mortgage, loan or insurance policy to repay a mortgage or loan on the former home, you no longer have an interest in it and your (former) spouse/partner and the children still live there.
• If the NRP has assets (money or property) worth more than £65,000 (except for their home or assets they use for their business).
• If the NRP has taken steps to reduce the amount of income the CSA can take it into account by diverting it to someone else for another purpose (for example, into a business or pension).
• If the NRP controls their own income and receives an income of more than £100 per week from a company or business (for example, dividends).

Step 2   (continued)

- You are still paying off a debt that you took on for the family before you separated.
- Where the NRP's lifestyle suggests they have a higher income than the income the CSA have used to work out child maintenance.

If the costs mentioned above amount to £10 or less and your net income is below £200, or £15 or less where your net income is £200 or more, then you will not get a reduction (though this restriction does not apply to expenses for a sick child or a child with a disability).

You will also not be able to use a variation to reduce the maintenance to less than £5 per week or, at the other end of the scale, if your net weekly income is more than £2,000 and would still be over that amount once the variation was deducted.

Step 3   Apply the appropriate rate: basic, reduced, flat or nil.

If the NRP has other children for whom he receives child benefit (these are known as 'relevant children', such as children from another marriage), the rate of maintenance is calculated by applying the basic rate percentages to the net income after first deducting a similar percentage for the relevant child(ren) .

Nil rate

The NRP does not have to pay any child maintenance if they have an income of less than £5 per week or who are:

- Students or young people in full-time education. • Prisoners.
- 16- or 17-year-olds on income support/income-based jobseekers' allowance.
- People in residential care or nursing homes receiving help with fees. • Are under 16 years old.

Flat rate

Maintenance is paid at a 'flat rate' of £5 per week, regardless of number of children, if the NRP's net weekly income is between £5 and £100, or if he or she is in receipt of certain benefits, such as:

- income support   • jobseeker's allowance   • state pension
- incapacity benefit • bereavement allowance   • contribution-based jobseeker's allowance

A full list of the benefits that apply can be found at www.csa.gov.uk. In these cases the maintenance is normally taken directly from the benefit. This assessment can be applied to be varied if the NRP has other weekly income of more than £100 that would normally be taken into account.

For more information go to:
www.csa.gov.uk

Step 3   (continued)

Reduced rate

If a NRP's net weekly income is more than £100 but less than £200 you take:
• A flat rate of £5 per week, **plus**
• A percentage of the net weekly income over £100.
The percentages used are shown in the Reduced Rate table below.

Reduced rate %		Qualifying children		
		1	2	3
Relevant	0	25%	35%	45%
other	1	20.5%	29%	37.5%
children	2	19%	27%	35%
	3	17.5%	25%	32.5%

Basic rate

If NRP has a net income of £200 to £2000 per week, the percentages used are shown in the table on the right.

Number of children	% of NRP net income
1	15%
2	20%
3 or more	25%

Step 4 Make any appropriate deductions for shared care

Shared care – basic and reduced rate

If you share the care of the child(ren) so that from time to time they stay overnight with the NRP, this will decrease the amount of maintenance payable. You have to look at the number of nights that the children have spent with the NRP over the last 12 months or, if the break-up is new, the projected number of nights in the next year. Reductions are:

Number of nights	Subtract
52 to 103	one-seventh
104 to 155	two-sevenths
156 to 174	three-sevenths
175 or more	one-half

Maintenance payments
Note that maintenance is worked out on a weekly basis to the nearest whole pound. Amounts of 50p and over are rounded up.

If there is more than one child and you have different amounts of staying time for the different children, calculate the reduction by adding the appropriate fraction for each child, and dividing the total by the number of children.

If the NRP looks after a child for 175 nights or more each year, you have to make an additional reduction in the maintenance of £7 for each child.

The lowest limit to which the maintenance can be decreased is £5 per week.

(If there are children with different PWCs, the £5 minimum would be divided.)

Shared care – flat rate

If the child(ren) spend(s) at least 52 nights a year with the NRP, who would otherwise be paying at the flat rate, then the maintenance reduces to nil.

Children with different PWCs – apportionment

If a NRP has children who have different PWCs the amount of child support payable will be apportioned between the different PWCs. The amount payable will be divided by the number of children and shared depending on how many children each parent with care has, so that the same amount is paid for each child.

APPENDIX A2: APPLYING NEW CHILD MAINTENANCE FORMULA
(the 2008 Regime, anticipated to be introduced in 2011, subject to any changes made in the interim)

Under the new rules the upper age of a child will be 20, rather than 19, subject to other conditions being met.

Income is calculated as the gross income of the NRP using the latest available tax year information from the HMRC.

There are still reductions made for other relevant children living with the NRP that allow a deduction of their gross income by the following percentages, before the child maintenance calculation is applied.

Relevant children	Reduction applied to gross income before calculation is done
1	12%
2	16%
3 or more	19%

Four rates of maintenance will exist
Basic rate
This rate applies if the NRP has gross income of £200 per week to £3,000 per week.

Gross income of	Number of qualifying	Amount of gross income payable
between £200 and	1	12%
£800 per week (i.e. up	2	16%
to £41,600 per annum)	3 or more	19%

Gross income of	Number of qualifying children	Amount of gross income payable
between £800 and	1	9%
£3,000 per week (i.e.	2	12%
up to £156,000 per	3 or more	15%
annum). Basic rate is		
applied to first £800		
then these percentages	Any income over £3,000 gross per week is not taken into	
of remainder of the	account in calculations, but could lead to an application to	
gross income.	the court for a top-up order.	

Reduced rate
A reduced rate applies where the NRP's gross weekly income is between £100 and £200. The amount to be paid has yet to be prescribed by regulations.

Flat rate
A flat rate assessment under the new rules is that flat rate of maintenance is paid of £7 per week if the NRP earns between £7 per week and £100 gross per week or receives certain benefits.

Nil assessment
No maintenance is payable in the same circumstances as under the current rules, except that the gross income bracket is below £7 per week (rather than £5 per week as under the current rules).

Shared care Reductions for overnight stays remain as with the 2000 regime (see page 243).

Length of assessments In most cases assessments will apply for a fixed period of 12 months unless there is a fundamental change in circumstances or an income change of 25% or more.

Appendices

APPENDIX B: YOUR RIGHTS IF YOU SHARE A RENTED HOME

Private tenancy or Housing Association tenancy since 15.1.1989 in one person's name.	Private tenancy or Housing Association tenancy since 15.1.1989 in joint names.		Council tenancy or Housing Association tenancy before 15.1.1989 in one person's name.	Council tenancy or Housing Association tenancy before 15.1.1989 in joint names.
	Assured tenancy or statutory periodic tenancy.	Regulated or protected tenancy.		

↓ ↓ ↓ ↓ ↓

| Tenant can give other person notice to quit. There is no protection for the non-tenant. If the tenant leaves, you can ask landlord to assign the tenancy but you can't compel him to do so. | In a periodic tenancy either of you can give notice to quit, ending it. You can stop your partner doing it (see box below). You must get a new tenancy granted to you. In a fixed tenancy you need the landlord's consent to end it or stay liable. | If one of you leaves the other can stay, and, by giving notice, prevent the other one from returning. | Tenant can give other person notice to quit. The non-tenant has no rights to stay. Tenant can assign the tenancy by 'deed'. If tenant leaves, the tenancy ends, but you can ask council to grant tenancy to person who stays if she or he shows housing need. | You must decide who will stay, unless you both decide to leave. Either can give notice to quit, which will end the tenancy. You can stop your partner doing this (see box below). You must get a new tenancy granted to you. |

↘ ↓ ↓ ↙ ↙

Under Schedule 7 of the Family Law Act 1996 you can ask the court to transfer the tenancy to one of you. The court will not be able to do this if the tenancy has been ended by one tenant giving notice to quit. If you need to you can get a court order to prevent the notice being given. If you have children you can also apply for a transfer of the tenancy under Schedule 1 of the Children Act 1989.

Useful helplines and websites

Alcoholics Anonymous
National helpline: 0845 769 7555
www.alcoholics-anonymous.org.uk

Asian Family Counselling Service
Tel/Fax: 020 8571 3933/020 8813 9714
www.asianfamilycounselling.org.uk

Association for Shared Parenting
Tel: 0116 254 8453
www.sharedparenting.org.uk

Cafcass
Tel: 0844 353 3350
www.cafcass.gov.uk

Childline
Helpline: 0800 1111
www.childline.org.uk

Child Maintenance and Enforcement
Commission
Tel: 0800 988 0988
www.cmoptions.org

Council of Mortgage Lenders
www.cml.org.uk

Dawn (South Yorkshire Surviving Separation
and Divorce)
Tel: 01709 309130
www.dawnproject.org.uk

Department for Work and Pensions (DWP)
www.dwp.gov.uk
For general queries contact your local office

DirectGov
www.directgov.uk

Divorce Aid
www.divorceaid.co.uk

Families Need Fathers
Helpline: 0300 0300 363
www.fnf.org.uk

Family Action
Tel: 020 7254 6251
www.family-action.org.uk

Family Law Association of Scotland
www.familylawassociation.org

Jewish Marriage Council
Counselling line: 020 8203 6311
www.jmc-uk.org

Law Society of Scotland
Tel: 0131 226 7411
www.lawscot.org.uk

Law Society of Northern Ireland
Tel: 028 9024 1614
www.lawsoc-ni.org

London Lesbian and Gay Switchboard
Tel: 020 7837 7324 (10am–11pm)
www.llgs.org.uk

MALE (men's advice line and enquiries)
Tel: 0808 801 0327
www.mensadviceline.org.uk

National Children's Bureau
Tel: 020 7843 6000
www.ncb.org.uk

National Debtline
Tel: 0808 808 4000
www.nationaldebtline.co.uk

National Family Mediation (NFM)
Tel: 01392 271610
www.nfm.org.uk

National Housing Federation
Tel: 020 7067 1010
www.housing.org.uk

Northern Ireland Housing Executive
Tel: 028 9024 0588
www.nihe.gov.uk

Northern Ireland Legal Services Commission
Tel: 028 9040 8888
www.nilsc.org.uk

Northern Ireland Women's Aid Federation
Helpline: 0800 917 1414 (24 hours)
www.niwaf.org

NSPCC
Tel: 0808 800 5000
www.nspcc.org.uk

One Parent Families/Gingerbread
Lone Parents Helpline: 0800 802 0925
(Mon–Fri 9am–5pm, Weds 9am–8pm)
www.gingerbread.org.uk

Lone Parent/Families for Scotland
Helpline: 0808 801 0323
www.opfs.org.uk

Principal Registry Of the Family Division
Tel: 020 7947 6000

Refuge
Tel: 0808 2000 247
www.refuge.org.uk

Relate
www.relate.org.uk (for local office telephone
contact number)

Relationships Scotland
Tel: 0845 119 2020
www.relationships-scotland.org.uk
Formed by the merger of Relate Scotland and
Family Mediation Scotland.

Resolution
Tel: 01689 820272
www.resolution.org.uk

Scottish Marriage Care
Tel: 0141 222 2166
www.scottishmarriagecare.org

Scottish Women's Aid
Helpline: 0800 027 1234
www.scottishwomensaid.org.uk

Women's Aid
Tel: 0808 2000 247
www.womensaid.org.uk

Women's Domestic Violence Helpline
Tel: 0161 636 7525
www.wdvh.org.uk

Glossary

Ancillary relief General term for the financial or property adjustment orders that the court can be asked to make 'ancillary' to a petition for divorce or judicial separation.

Annuity Money investment designed to produce regular fixed amounts of income, either for a fixed period or until death.

Application Document giving broad details of the order sought. All applications within divorce proceedings begin by filing a notice of application.

Care and attention A term used to describe an uplift (increase) in a solicitor's legal bill, which some solicitors apply if a case has been complex or has had to be dealt with especially quickly.

In chambers When the district judge or judge considers an application in private rather than in open court; the proceedings tend to be less formal than normal court hearings.

Charge (on property) Security entitling the holder of the charge to be paid out of the proceeds of sale when the house (or other property) is eventually sold.

Chattels An old-fashioned legal term used for personal effects, usually of a house, like furniture, paintings, jewellery and ornaments.

Community Legal Service (CLS) The body that oversees the granting of public funding for legal cases. Formerly the Legal Aid Board.

Conditional order A decree nisi in a cp dissolution.

Conflict of interest(s) Where a solicitor cannot act for a potential client because they would be unable to discharge their duty to the client, owing to a pre-existing professional relationship to another client or a duty owed to another.

Costs Solicitors' fees incurred.

Counsel The barrister who represents you at a hearing.

Decree absolute The document that shows you are divorced and able to remarry.

Decree nisi The court's certificate that you are entitled to a divorce.

Disbursements Amounts paid for court fees, barristers, etc.

Disclosure Full information about all matters relevant to any financial application; each spouse has a duty to give full and frank disclosure which, if they fail to abide by, may render a later court order invalid.

Discovery Procedure by which each party supplies to the other a list of documents relevant to an application and permits the other to inspect them.

Dissolution order A final decree in a cp dissolution.

District judge Judicial officer appointed by the Lord Chancellor; responsible for dealing with most applications to a divorce court.

Divorce court Any county court designated by the Lord Chancellor as a court where divorce proceedings can be heard; the Principal Registry in London serves as a divorce court. Divorce county courts not designated as Family Hearing Centres (FHCs) can deal only with the administrative process of divorces; any contested applications will be referred to an FHC.

Domicile Legal concept, not necessarily related to residence: domicile of origin is normally determined by the place where a person was born and is retained, unless a new domicile – a domicile of choice – is adopted by a conscious decision to take up permanent residence in, and actually move to, another country.

Equity (of a property) The net value of house or flat after mortgage debts are discharged and expenses of sale met

Exhibit Document referred to in, sworn with, and attached to an affidavit; usually identified by initials and number.

Ex parte An old term for an application made directly to the court without prior notification to the party or parties.

Family Hearing Centre A county court with the power to deal with the administrative process of divorce and any contested applications under the Children Act, or for financial relief.

Filing Leaving documents – petition and accompanying documents, affidavits, notices of application, for example – with the court office for sealing, and subsequent service.

Hearsay evidence A fact reported to a witness, as opposed to being known by the witness; second-hand knowledge; hearsay evidence can be accepted by a court in family proceedings.

Injunction Court order telling someone what he or she must do or must refrain from doing; the penalty for disobedience can be imprisonment.

Interim maintenance order A request that can be made for financial assistance prior to settlement.

Intestacy Dying without a valid will.

Maintenance Application Form and Maintenance Enquiry Form Standard forms sent out by the Child Support Agency to parents with care and absent parents respectively, asking them about their means and circumstances.

Matrimonial home rights Rights of occupation of a family home (or a home intended to be occupied as a family home) which last until decree absolute.

Martin or Mesher order Type of financial order where one spouse's/cp's interest in the matrimonial home is turned into a charge over the property that cannot trigger a sale until certain events happen, such as remarriage or death.

Mediation Alternative form of dispute resolution over issues arising from separation or divorce. Comprehensive (or 'all issues') mediation covers problems over both children and finances; other mediation (or conciliation: the terms are sometimes used interchangeably) services may deal with child-related disputes alone.

Minutes of order Draft terms of agreement placed before the court with a request that a consent order be made in those terms.

Mortgagee The building society, bank or other corporate lender, or individual lending money on the security of a house or flat.

Mortgagor The person who borrows money on mortgage, usually to enable him or her to buy a house or flat.

Nominal order An order for a nominal amount of maintenance (for example, 5p a year) made if, at the time an order for maintenance was made, payment could not be made or was not needed. This is done so that, if circumstances change, there is an order on the court's file that can be reviewed and increased.

Non-molestation order Order to prohibit one person from assaulting, harassing or interfering with another.

Notice of application Form on which applications to the court are made and containing details of what is applied for.

Occupation order Order excluding one spouse from the matrimonial home (or from part of it). Previously known as an ouster.

Penal notice A warning endorsed on a court order, notifying the recipient that he or she is liable to committal to prison for breach of the order.

Pending suit While the divorce is still continuing (i.e. before decree absolute).

Pleadings Formal statements or documents containing a summary of the issues in a case.

Pre-application protocol The directions that help the exchange of information between parties to resolve matters amicably prior to an ancillary relief application.

Public funding A term for 'legal aid': state financial help with the cost of legal proceedings.

Questionnaire List of questions delivered by one spouse to the other requiring further information and/or documentation about finances.

Recovered or preserved Gained or retained (money or property) in the course of legal proceedings.

Relevant child Child of the family under 16 years of age at the date of the decree nisi, or between 16 and 18 years and receiving instruction at an educational establishment, or undergoing training for a trade, profession or vocation (or up to any age, if disabled and dependent).

Reply Document filed by the petitioner in response to an answer and/or a cross-petition from the respondent, containing the petitioner's defence.

Reserved costs When decision on amount of costs to be awarded is deferred until later hearing.

Resolution Formerly the Solicitors' Family Law Association – the body that lays down good practice for family lawyers.

Sealing by the court The court's stamping of a document when it is filed at the court office or of an order or decree when it is issued.

Secured provision When some income-producing asset of the payer is put under the control of trustees and, if necessary, the income diverted to the payee to provide maintenance.

SERPS The earnings part of state retirement pension, based on National Insurance contributions paid by an employee on earnings between the lower and upper earnings limits. Since April 2002 this has become the State Second Pension, S2P.

Service The method by which the petition, notices of application, orders and decrees are supplied to the parties concerned.

Statement of open proposal A proposal made to your spouse/cp (that will be disclosed to the court) reflecting your preferred settlement.

Statutory charge The amount payable by a publicly funded person out of any property or cash that was recovered or preserved in the proceedings, where contributions to the Legal Services Commission are not sufficient to meet the legal costs of the case.

Summons Demand issued by a court for a person against whom a claim or complaint has been made to appear at the court.

Undefended divorce Where the dissolution of the marriage and how it is to be achieved are not disputed (even if there is dispute about matters such as the children or finances).

Sworn document A document containing personal details that you swear on oath in the presence of an independent solicitor to prove its accuracy.

Undertaking Promise to the court to do or not do something that is outside the court's powers to order, but is incorporated within a court order so that it is enforceable.

Unfunded scheme A pension scheme where the employee has a right or expectation to a pension benefit secured only by an undertaking from the employer.

Without prejudice Phrase used to prevent communications in the negotiation process being made known to the court at the final hearing if those negotiations fail to produce agreement. However, offers and responses to them can be disclosed to the court in evidence over costs.

Index

Which? Books

Which? Books provide impartial, expert advice on everyday matters from finance to law, property to major life events. We also publish the country's most trusted restaurant guide, *The Good Food Guide*. To find out more about Which? Books, log on to www.which.co.uk or call 01992 822800.

Other books in this series

Finance Your Retirement

Jonquil Lowe
ISBN: 978 1 84490 057 2
Price: £10.99

Finance Your Retirement is the essential step-by-step guide to a secure retirement, providing advice on saving for your pension, whether to opt for an annuity, how to access your money if you retire abroad and the basics of inheritance tax. There are helpful tips for maximising your budget using state benefits and investments such as unit trusts and OEICs, plus guidance on how to make your property work for you.

Buy, Sell and Move House

Kate Faulkner
ISBN: 978 1 84490 108 1
Price: £10.99

Navigating the property market is difficult, whether you are a first-time buyer or trying to climb the property ladder. *Buy, Sell & Move House* makes the process as smooth as possible, explaining how to avoid being gazumped, gazundered or getting stuck in a chain. This new edition of the bestselling guide takes you through each stage of the buying and selling process, providing realistic guidance on how to get the best from your agent and solicitor, what to check for when viewing a property and how to arrange the most suitable mortgage for your budget.

"Which? tackles the issues that really matter to consumers and gives you the advice and active support you need to buy the right products."